Chivukula and Musum's  of common sense policies that working Americans. Wage only fellow citizens who have large o stakes in our nation's productive assets. Our national leaders need to read and implement their road map to a fair and enriching economy for all Americans."

    J. Michael Keeling, CAE
    President - The ESOP Association
    Washington, DC

"*THE 3rd WAY* makes the case for action to spread wealth and ownership in a style we all can grasp. May it help mobilize people nationwide across the political spectrum on the best way to rebuild middle class America: greater capital ownership by regular citizens."

    Richard B. Freeman, PhD
    Herbert Ascherman Chair in Economics at Harvard University
    Senior Fellow, National Bureau of Economic Research (NBER)
    Senior Fellow, London School Centre for Economic Performance
    Co-Director, Labor and Worklife Program at Harvard Law School
    Fellow of the American Academy of Arts and Science

"*THE 3rd WAY* by Chivukula and Musum trace the American experience from the economic freedom that improved lives for two centuries to the more recent decline marked by record inequality of wealth and persistent unemployment–most dramatically at 40% for urban minority males. The authors then identify the way for new generations to again improve lives: Worker ownership that couples democracy and capitalism and in the process captures the best of capitalism and socialism."

    Ray Carey
    Chairman and CEO - ADT (Ret.)
    Author, *Democratic Capitalism: The Way to a World of Peace and Plenty*

"Mr. Chivukula, who is a well-known politician in the US, demonstrates in this book that he and his co-author, Veny Musum combine political acumen with thoughtful meditation on economic democracy. They deserve our congratulations."

    Jagdish Bhagwati, PhD
    University Professor of Economics, Law and International Affairs
    Columbia University

"Chivukula and Musum, co-authors of *THE 3rd WAY*, present a compelling political and economic basis for more inclusive capital ownership that would reverse the long-term trend of income inequality and would expand the middle class. Building off decades of research, they propose federal and state policies that are within reach of our current political system, and outline the dire consequences if policies are not embraced to encourage broader based employee ownership. This is an excellent compilation of research data and significant policy implications presented in straight-forward manner."

Mary Ann Beyster
President - Foundation for Enterprise Development
Fostering Innovation, Entrepreneurship and Ownership
Executive Producer, *We the Owners*

"*THE 3rd WAY* reminds us of a hopeful fact; values can, on occasion, trump ideologies. New Jersey provides us with a Republican Committeeman (Veny W. Musum) and a Democratic Assemblyman (Upendra Chivukula) who agree that America urgently needs a more inclusive and democratic form of capitalism. What these authors have discovered they have common is what matters. Their insights signal a new direction for American politics and economics."

Dr. Christopher Mackin
Founder - Ownership Associates
Professor, Labor and Worklife Program at Harvard Law School
Adjunct Lecturer, Rutgers School of Management and Labor Relations

"The authors of *THE 3rd WAY* have done of marvelous job of explaining why neither conventional capitalism nor conventional socialism is capable of solving the two most pressing problems of the day – the rising inequality of income and of wealth and the disappearance of the American middle class. Unlike most books that only serve to identify the problem, *THE 3rd WAY* prescribes specific legislative and governmental actions that can be taken to alleviate them. This is a must read for all politicians and citizens who have been asking what they can do to help restore economic democracy to America."

John Menke
President and CEO - Menke & Associates, Inc.
The Nation's Premiere ESOP Advisors

"America became a free, independent and self-governing people because it was created by men and women who first owned property. Not on loan from the King or Lord, but real ownership. From that developed the demand to control their government. Our freedom comes from ownership, not the ballot box. The means of production are no longer simply land and animals: an ownership society must also now include shares of companies. This way embodies growth, independence, self-reliance, dignity and real equality before the law and man."

Grover Norquist
Founder and President - Americans for Tax Reform

"THE 3rd WAY's emphasis on employee ownership as a way forward is a refreshing departure from the usual policy proposals on dealing with inequality that either have not worked, or have little chance of becoming law."
Cory Rosen, PhD
Founder - National Center for Employee Ownership

THE 3rd WAY is an excellent treatment of a thesis by the two distinguished authors who have made a serious contribution. The work is based on much research and merits praise for its innovative as well as provocative thoughts based on a storehouse of knowledge. The two authors are involved in real-world politics and the readers of the volume should compel their elected leaders for real world legislative actions to follow.

Manoranjan Dutta, PhD
Professor Emeritus of Economics at Rutgers, the State University of New Jersey; Fulbright Senior Specialist 2002-2007; Fulbright Research Scholar, 1958-1960; Ford Foundation Dissertation Fellow Founding Editor; Journal of Asian Economics, 1990-2008
Author of 19 books

"Upendra Chivukula has once again demonstrated, through his co-authorship with Veny Musum, why he has been such an effective legislator in the New Jersey General Assembly. His unique understanding of the U.S. economy and the path toward sustaining this country's middle class lifestyle is dependent upon business growth and ownership opportunities for workers. Entrepreneurship and business

development is where this country's future wealth building lies. This book will prove to be a focal point for those seeking to set the tone and create a new conversation in terms of where the U.S. economy is headed."

Sheila Y. Oliver (D)
Speaker - NJ General Assembly

"Turning the idea of spreading employee ownership into reality has long been a passion of mine – as indeed it was for President Reagan, whom I served as a special assistant. This idea resolves the great ideological conflict of our era by achieving socialist ideals through capitalist means. It is vitally important that we increase worker participation and control in our processes of wealth creation. It is equally important that we preserve our ingenious, freedom-expanding reliance on private property rights. This book is a most welcome entrant into the debate, its authors offering a credible pathway to a system that prizes employee ownership. It deserves the most widespread consideration and discussion."

Dana Rohrabacher
United States Congressman, (R) California
President Ronald Reagan's Speechwriter

"In this book, Chivukula and Musum offer a proposal to spread wealth through new forms of capital ownership for middle-class and poor Ameri-cans. *THE 3rd WAY* is a modern-day, updated version of a simple plan that the early twentieth century, black leader and visionary, Marcus Garvey, offered to his black followers through his organization, The Universal Negro Improvement Association (UNIA). However, unlike Garvey and the UNIA, the plan that Chivukula and Musum propose in *THE 3rd WAY* is offered to the vast majority of Americans, grounded in sound economic principles, presented in a non-technical fashion, and should be read by mass and scholarly audiences interested in the growing problem of wealth and income inequality throughout the world."

Marvin P. Dawkins, PhD
Professor of Sociology and (Former) Director of the Caribbean, African and Afro-American Studies Program - University of Miami

"***THE 3rd WAY*** is a communications breakthrough! The authors have "got" the essentials of Louis Kelso's message. And they have imparted that message so simply and accurately that others can understand it, too–and more important–translate it into political action and wise government policies."

Patricia Kelso

President of The Kelso Institute

Wife of the late Louis O. Kelso - Father of the ESOP movement

Co-author of many of Louis Kelso's most important books, congressional submissions, columns and speeches.

ECONOMIC REFORM or SOCIAL REVOLUTION
the solution to income inequality...

THE 3rd WAY

Building "Inclusive Capitalism"
through Employee Ownership

* HOW WEALTH IS CREATED *

Upendra Chivukula
Veny W. Musum

Copyright © 2016 Authored by Upendra Chivukula and Veny W. Musum
All rights reserved.
ISBN: 1494254603
ISBN 13: 9781494254605
Library of Congress Control Number: 2013921725
THE 3rd WAY Publishers

Upendra Chivukula: I dedicate this book to my mother because of the lessons learned from her, a strong, creative, and enterprising woman who made me who I am today. My main inspiration has been her fighting spirit that lifted our family from poverty to a comfortable life. Her role as a compassionate landlady made me understand that while earning money, one can help others by sharing wealth. I believe it is up to all of us to make a positive difference in other people's lives.

I also dedicate this book to my father, an accountant, who taught me the value of money and the need to spend it wisely since early childhood. He molded my character with his wisdom, which he shared through his conversations with me. His favorite quote, "Deserve and then desire," still resonates with me.

I also want to express my deepest regards and sincere appreciation to the enterprising men and women who run successful companies that provide employment for people to raise their families with dignity and with the hope for a better future.

Veny W. Musum: For my namesake and late grandfather, beloved husband of Maria Blasi, Venerando Musumeci, who came to this country penniless at six years of age from Sicily, Italy. He barely received any formal education for he had to go to work to feed the family. He was self-educated, a voracious reader, and an immense admirer of the great men and wisdom of the ages. He taught me by example. With relentless hard work he lifted himself and the generations that followed him out of poverty through the successful business he built from nothing with his indomitable will and own hands.

For my late father, John Blasi Musum, who taught me about life in every way.

For my late mother, Jane Marie Musum, whose love and sweetness will stay with me forever…

CONTENTS

Acknowledgments   xiv
Foreword   xvii
Preface   xxiii

Part I: Looming Turmoil!   1

Chapter 1: What's At Stake?   3

"I'm Mad As Hell And I'm Not Going To Take It Anymore"   3
[yet, hope springs eternal…]
Water Always Wins!   11
[the will of the people will always prevail in the end]
A Very Important Excerpt   12
[cogent and on target]
You Must Understand This!   14
[indispensable knowledge]
Some Political Shorthand   18
[the basics on ideology]
Concentration Of Wealth   21
[why it happens…and how shocking the disparity has become!]
How The Economy Really Works—Really   34
[how capitalists become so fabulously rich…and why you should join them]
A Solution Benefitting Both Sides   37
[something NEW!]
Capitalism Works, But Is Not Fair   41
[in your heart, you know it's true]
Socialism Is Fair In Theory, But Does Not Work   46
[go too far, and go off a cliff]

MLK Jr. — 58
[what history has taught us]

Economic Versus Political Freedom — 60
[African Americans got a political first step and the economic shaft]

An Explosion Of Political Empowerment — 62
[the time has come for worldwide economic empowerment]

Political Democracy Alone Is Not A Panacea — 67
[systems must be put in place to check popular avarice]

Chapter 2: What Needs To Be Done? — 74

The Best Ideas — 74
[a bipartisan way forward]

The Growth Code — 76
[one half of the equation]

How Much Is Too Much? — 80
[there's a sweet spot to government spending]

Not Just A New Deal—A Better Deal — 86
[reinventing the great society]

A Way Out For The Poor — 94
[change the system/change the result]

A New Form Of Capital Ownership — 97
[the best way to help the poor and middle class]

The World Will Beat A Path To Us — 100
[capital flows to the most favorable environment]

It's A Global Movement — 105
[examples of success abound worldwide]

How To Get Rich! — 108
[what do they know and do that the poor and middle class do not]

Greed Is Good — 112
[but, let everyone participate in wealth and job creation]

Chapter 3: What Is The Academic Rationale? 116

Hegel Had It Right 116
[right premise/wrong interpretation]
Owning The Means Of Production 119
[did the Communists screw up a good idea?]
Maslow 121
[ignore him at your peril]
Mao's Big Mistake 123
[millions died trying to reshape human nature]
The Exceptionalism Of The Few Meets The Self-Interest Of Us All 125
[human nature meets reality, and what to do about it]
Cooperation Versus Confrontation 127
[end the zero-sum game]
Common Sense 142
[should be common…]
Everyone Wins—Even Uncle Sam 144
[no significant net loss of tax revenue to the government]
The Foundation Of Binary Economics 145
[the economic underpinnings of this new way]
Concordian Economics 150
[further intellectual support for the ownership concept]
Stabilizing Employment 152
[employee ownership works on many levels!]

Part II: What Is An ESOP? What Other Steps Need To Be In Place? 159

Chapter 4: How The ESOP Really Works 161

Introduction To ESOPs 161
Historical Background 162

What Is An ESOP?	**165**
[the legal framework]	
ESOP Incentives	**167**
[legislative history]	
Managing Risk	**170**
[even the most risk-averse workers prefer shared capitalism]	
Open-Book Management	**173**
[some of what it takes to be a successful company in this new age]	
Corporate Corruption	**178**
[we have a problem…]	
Checks And Balances	**182**
[it works in politics/it can work in economics too]	
What Our Founders Knew	**186**
[heed the wisdom of the great thinkers in history]	
USA—We're No. 1	**188**
[our corporate tax system is a burdensome mess]	
Party's Over!	**192**
[cut corporate deductions, and establish a fair, effective tax rate]	
Chapter 5: How The Third Way Fosters Major Solutions For Society	**203**
An End To Alienation!	**203**
[are we all just insignificant cogs in a wheel?]	
Action Steps	**211**
[each of us can be a one-person army!]	
Notes	214
Bibliography	227
Index	240

ACKNOWLEDGMENTS

Upendra Chivukula

First, I would like to thank Veny Musum, who befriended me with sincerity and dedication to make a difference in the world.

I must thank Dr. Joseph Blasi from Rutgers and Susan Skiba, a Rutgers graduate student, for their tireless editorial support, which greatly enhanced the quality of this book.

I would like to extend my gratitude to swamis (spiritual teachers) who believe in my work and provide me with spiritual guidance.

I would like to thank my staff members Sheridan Balmeo and Gita Bajaj, who have helped me believe in myself in reaching greater heights in my career.

I would also like to thank Rutgers Professor of Economics, Manoranjan Dutta for his wise council in the development of this book.

I would like to thank all of my supporters who have supported me for more than seventeen years in elected office.

I would like to express my gratitude to my family, especially my grandchildren, who give me the energy to continue my work to leave behind a better world for them.

And of course, I would like to thank my wife and life partner for thirty-eight years. She has shared the best and the worst with support and love.

Last, but not least, a special thanks to Gavin, my dog and tireless companion, who helps me reflect during our many walks.

ACKNOWLEDGMENTS

Veny W. Musum

There are so many people deserving to be recognized for all the support and encouragement they have given me. First let me thank my co-author, Upendra Chivukula, who believed enough in me to first encourage me to take on this challenge.

I want to thank the three giants of academia, Dr. Richard Freeman from Harvard, Dr. Douglas Kruse from Rutgers, and especially Dr. Joseph Blasi, also from Rutgers, who without his extensive help and counsel, this book would not have been possible.

I want to thank my beloved sister Jayne Burns for her exceptional cover design, her son Harrison Burns for his help with interior graphic design and Anthony Rosania for a good portion of the original cover concept.

It is difficult to express what my other sister, Anita Walls and her wonderful husband Jimmy have meant to me. When my mother passed away at a relatively young age Anita became the de facto matriarch of the family – the one that held us all together. You mean the world to me sister.

I am grateful to Dean James Hayton at the Rutgers School of Management and Labor Relations for always making me feel completely welcome and a part of the university.

I want to show my appreciation to my fellow Bernards Township Committeemen Brian Workman and Republican municipal committee chair, Leslie Workman—the original idea for the book was first envisioned right at their kitchen table.

I wish to also thank my Republican county chair, Al Gaburo, for his invaluable support in this important endeavor.

I must express my heartfelt appreciation to Rutgers graduate student Susan Skiba for all the extensive editorial and footnoting help she provided.

It is important I recognize James L. Berry an expert realtor, appraiser and property manager whom I had the good fortune to find. He has become more than a professional I do business with, he is a trusted friend. Much of knowledge on the acquisition of properly as an excellent means of acquiring income producing capital came from James at Candid Appraisals in Naples, Florida. He is unquestionably the best of the best.

Our public relations firm Media Connect in NYC, especially David Hahn, Senior Partner/Managing Director and Brian Feinblum, SVP/Chief Marketing Officer have been terrific.

Everyone at our publisher Amazon – Create Space has been a pleasure to work with throughout every step of the publishing process.

I must add a special thank you to the exceptional folks at Premiere IT Systems. Their first class team lead by Parag Chhibber was instrumental in building our outstanding authors platform, the book's index, website and social media campaign.

We are indebted to my good and valued friend Larry Cirignano for accepting the position as Senior Political Advisor. Larry is a seasoned lobbyist in Washington DC and has been involved in numerous State, Federal and Presidential Campaigns. He will assist and advise us on taking the critically important concepts in this book and helping to make them a legislative reality.

Let me also thank my best friends, Dennis Cotter, Tom Schachtel, Joseph Salamone, Ven Konuru, Marco Rua, Steve D'Angelo, and Dennis Tierney, whose friendship in good times and bad have been a constant source of happiness and comfort to me.

Lastly, no words could ever express how much my beautiful wife, Patty, means to me. This book and everything I do has her blessed love behind it. She is the light of my life, and her tenderness and love I am eternally grateful for.

FOREWORD

If you want to see the one fresh economic growth idea that has finally jelled in American society and that cuts across party lines with the potential to create a large middle-class majority, then read on. This book presents one major idea: the American and indeed the world economy will do better and *privately* make more wealth available to more citizens if we encourage broad-based employee stock ownership in small businesses and large corporations.

It's authored by a long-standing activist Republican, Veny Musum, who, as a Republican Committeeman and businessman in New Jersey, represents an excellent example of a well-read passionate citizen intellectual. He is joined by a respected leader and activist Democrat, New Jersey Assemblyman Upendra Chivukula, the well-liked, brainy, policy-oriented Deputy Speaker of the New Jersey Assembly, a political officeholder capable of across-the-aisle dialogue and policy discussion when it's designed to benefit the middle class. Walk with them and be surprised.

Both political parties are observing that an economic Hurricane Sandy has slammed into the American middle class in the last few decades. Unlike our parents' immediate post–World War II generation, the middle class on average is *not* doing better each year. This book's solution is to broaden the ownership of private capital without redistribution from the rich to the poor, by creating many more capitalists who can supplement their wage income with some capital ownership and capital income. The authors' bipartisan way to accomplish these goals is for government to get out of the way of broadening property ownership.

The middle class is being hollowed out. Under eight years of President Bill Clinton, the wealthiest 1% of families received

45 cents of every dollar of total income growth in the economy. Under eight years of President George W. Bush, the wealthiest 1% of families received a disproportionate 65 cents of every dollar of income gains. Under Obama, the wealthiest 1% received 93 cents of every dollar, up from 45 cents when Clinton was President. So, despite the party in control, the problem is getting worse.

Wake up, America, the problem is a structural problem—namely, American capitalism does not have enough wealth-making capitalists. This book asserts that many of the profits of capitalism are made by those who own new, efficient technologies and gain income from them. They suggest private-sector ideas to expand the number of citizens who own corporate equity by imitating many existing corporations that have and work well with broad-based employee stock ownership. If more citizens owned a piece of the economy, namely, shares in the businesses where they work, they would have income and wealth alongside their wages that would often improve their economic situation and take the middle class in the right direction.

The fundamental analysis the authors are making holds water and makes scientific sense. The evidence is crystal clear that median wages adjusted for inflation have been going down for some decades. The families and individuals whose wealth is increasing are achieving the American Dream because they have some ownership of capital. They own portions of businesses, they have ownership interests in real assets, they own shares in companies they founded or where they work or manage—they are capitalists in the true sense of the term: they own capital and get income from it in addition to their working salary. The families and individuals whose wealth is increasing are achieving the American Dream and also benefitting from capital income, meaning that their capital ownership is increasing in value, and they draw dividends from their shares in businesses and corporations or have interest income on investments that adds up to something meaningful. America is a capitalist dream machine without enough capitalists.

FOREWORD

The key proposal of this book is to restructure tax incentives to expand the opportunity of citizens to own a piece of the rock. The authors offer a straightforward solution and agenda for restructuring the tax system, thus expanding the number of taxpayers while decreasing the rate of taxes. Their solution is to provide tax incentives to increase the chance for middle-class citizens to have ownership opportunities in the small businesses and the large stock market companies where they work through a variety of methods of moderate risk. Their message: cut taxes *and* expand private citizen ownership of the economy. They favor removing the barriers to greater support of Employee Stock Ownership Plans (ESOP) that would allow workers to gain shares in the companies where they work by having worker trusts in successful companies borrow the money to buy the stock without using worker savings. Over the last few decades, thousands of companies covering millions of workers (both small, closely held businesses and large, publicly traded businesses) have successfully used employee stock ownership plans.

The authors review federal legislation encouraging ESOPs at the federal level and call for a quite substantial expansion at the federal and state levels. They show how other tax incentives drown out those that are meant to broaden capital ownership and capital income. The key aspect of an ESOP is that it allows an average middle-class worker or manager to acquire stock in the company where they work without using their wages or savings and without pledging their assets as collateral. The capital ownership would be a second income for the citizen and his or her family, and the capital income on the shares, if they appreciate in value or provide dividends, would provide citizens just the kind of additional income that determines who is or is not wealthy in America.

Because their policy depends on the ESOP that grants stock to workers and not on workers sinking their wages and savings into buying company stock with their own cash, the authors' proposed policy avoids some of the extreme risk seen in horror cases. For example, in Enron nonunion workers were manipulated to use retirement savings and wages to buy company stock for cash in their 401(k) plan, and at United Airlines union and nonunion workers traded extensive wage and benefit concessions for stock ownership, essentially, buying every share of stock themselves but lacking important safeguards that we warned against. Yes, there are some very risky, bad forms of employee ownership, such as sinking all of your savings into your 401(k) plan or taking all of your investments and putting them in one stock. This book steers clear of the bad ideas.

The authors propose tax incentives for closely held companies and large stock market corporations to set up and fund employee stock ownership plans. They want the tax incentives expanded in Enterprise Zones to reset American policy on poverty to be oriented toward capital ownership rather than just transfer payments. They want to give strong incentives for banks and insurance companies and other financial institutions to loan funds to ESOPs that want to purchase corporate stock. This was widely done during the first Bush and the beginning of the Clinton administrations, and experience demonstrated that Wall Street firms were willing to actually market employee stock ownership as an idea when they had an incentive to do so (see Blasi and Kruse, 1991). They favor seed funding for fifty state centers that will help educate local business owners, managers, lawyers, accountants, consultants, and citizen and worker groups on the concepts.

This is the first time a thoughtful Democrat and a thoughtful Republican have presented a philosophical perspective on how to break through the political logjam affecting our economic policy discussions, particularly on restructuring the tax system, addressing the hollowing out of the middle class, and asserting where the proper activist role of government begins and ends. The authors do a very nice job of walking the reader through why you should care about this issue, what thinkers on the Left and Right have said about the issues, where current political ideas from both parties are failing the middle class, and how economic democracy is the quintessential American idea. That is what you do not want to miss because the stream of ideas is something truly unique, novel, and potentially game-changing. Elitists may not like their folksy style. Well, sit back and try it anyway—the book is written for the average man and woman on the street so they can appreciate all elements of the argument if and when political leaders decide to debate it.

The Founders of the American republic envisioned a society where broadened land ownership allowed citizens to support themselves through capital ownership and maintain their political independence from being manipulated by smoke-and-mirror routines of political parties as a result of their economic independence. They implemented multiple land reforms to spread the idea of the "yeoman farmer." President Abraham Lincoln correctly pushed this idea with the Homestead Act, which ultimately, although not perfectly, began a new series of laws to drastically create independent citizen-owned farms and increase economic independence, and which finally and correctly benefited previously excluded African Americans and women, both of whom had been excluded from civil society's economic benefits. We have documented the history of economic democracy as an American idea and how the Founders and political and corporate leaders and citizens and thinkers developed the idea in American history. Chivukula and Musum, in our opinion, are standing on solid ground in the American historical tradition (Kruse, Freeman, and Blasi, 2010).

It may be too soon to make precise macroeconomic predictions about every aspect of expanding economic democracy in America, but one can certainly state two reasonable claims: first, on average, empirical research suggests that broad-based employee ownership of this type would represent a respectable and effective economic system; and second, if the problem of the middle class is lack of capital ownership and capital income, then broad-based employee ownership must be considered as one of the critical policy responses.

One last question before you start reading: Are the authors standing on solid *political ground?* Luckily, to answer this question, we can turn your attention to some stunning political polling on these ideas and how American citizens view them. In 1975 the respected national political pollster, Peter D. Hart Associates, did a very detailed national poll to see what the American population thinks of the idea and the policy. They looked at how all stripes of Americans (by political party, by age, by gender, by region of the country) viewed these ideas. In a way, it is good that the poll was not done in the current polarized political atmosphere, but the results are stunning. The idea of employee share ownership and economic democracy was the only national economic policy that Americans across the political spectrum believed would do more good than harm. There was substantial bipartisan support, with strong support from independents, Republicans, and Democrats. A major majority of Americans were willing to support a presidential candidate who espoused such a policy. The research suggests an overwhelming number of citizens believed the idea would be good for both them, the firms involved, and the economic performance of the whole economy (Kruse and Blasi, 1999).

Joseph R. Blasi,
J. Robert Beyster Distinguished Professor of Employee Stock Ownership, Rutgers University School of Management and Labor Relations
Douglas L. Kruse,
Professor of Human Resource Management and of Labor Studies and Employment Relations, Director of the PhD Program, J. Robert Beyster Faculty Fellow, Rutgers University School of Management and Labor Relations

PREFACE

Pangaea: *"a single supercontinent forming about 300 million years ago" and beginning to split apart and rift around 200 million years ago, before the component continents were separated into their current configurations.*
Plate tectonics: *a scientific theory describing the large-scale motions of Earth's continental drift.*[1]

THE 3rd WAY is a very big idea. The Third Way was first popularized by lawyer and political thinker Norman Kurland of the Center for Economic and Social Justice (see www.CESJ.org). The world is changing! Much like plate tectonics, the earth is indeed shifting under our feet this very moment. It's high time we realize that, like in geology, the massive forces in nature are also at work in the human spirit. People's *human nature* will inexorably move them toward systems better designed to meet their needs. Indeed a political/economic/social movement of epic proportion is already underway. That movement is *employee ownership and economic democracy*.

> **HEADLINE:**
>
> The first ESOP (employee stock ownership plan) came into being in 1956. During the fifty-plus years since then, ESOPs have become popular enough that **there are now more employee owners (nearly 15 million of them) than union members in the private sector.**[2]
>
> Did you know that before just reading it? It's a fact. And folks, that was just the opening shot in an ongoing peaceful revolution you probably never heard about! With this book, we are going to blow this important movement wide open. Can you feel the earth beneath your feet begin to rumble?

For the most part, politicians don't lead, they follow. Once "We the People" in great numbers are made aware of the economic democracy and the employee ownership concept, a hue and cry for it will come from every village and hamlet in this nation and indeed across the globe! Then each of the two parties will literally scramble to plant its flag and claim the movement as its own out of political expediency. The movement will soon reach critical mass, and there will be no turning back—the world's political/economic/social systems will never be the same.

This book champions the exciting and emerging concept of "economic democracy" and the average citizen's ability to finally take control of his or her own destiny. Citizens are extraordinarily disenchanted with the fruitless, unending back-and-forth between conservatives and liberals, between Republicans and Democrats. Before you are the ideas that offer the only truly bipartisan solution.

Instinctively we all sense in our gut there just *has* to be something better than what we have now. Instability, estrangement, and downright misery are conspicuous at all levels of society. Virtually everyone seems to be feeling it! Everywhere you hear the discouraged cries from people in all walks of life. From people in small companies with modest jobs to executives in major corporations you hear their complaints ranging from anxiety to despair.

Remember, this is from people lucky enough to *have* a job! What can be done about the ever growing unemployed both in our small town to our big cities? Most of all, what can be done that would finally have some real substance and effectiveness in our most distressed urban areas? What *real* hope and *real* change can we deliver to these unfortunate soles?

Both the problem and the solution must involve a powerful dynamic that must successfully addresses all the political, economic, and social elements to get the enormous challenge solved.

The world and our nation are at a pivotal crossroad in history. The smoldering unease is obvious in far too many of our citizens today. We see this unease and downright anger displayed both on our TV screens and in our interpersonal relationships with all those close to us. The profound desperation is all around us. There just *has* to be a better way. Read on.

The solution represents a tectonic shift in the relationship between the two colossal economic forces of capitalism and socialism—which drive the social and political life of everyone in the United States and across the globe. Both economic systems have serious intrinsic flaws we have all come to recognize. Our book is a powerful mass-market fresh insight into the real solution to the ever-increasing anxiety and alienation permeating our entire social fabric. It is about the specific means and rationale for building an ownership society via ESOPs and the other half-dozen highly successful yet not well enough known methods for achieving such goals.

British Prime Minister Tony Blair, whose central theme was a "third way," *won unprecedented overwhelming consecutive victories* in 1997,

2001, and 2005. Though different from what we propose, Blair's version of the term "third way" refers to various political positions that try to reconcile and synthesize right-wing and left-wing policies.[3] However, the concept clearly demonstrates that **the worldwide electorate has an overwhelming hunger for some way to productively resolve the differences between the two dominant political forces.**

Tony Blair claimed the socialism he advocated was different from the traditional conception of socialism.[4] Blair's effort at bridging the divide between the two dominant political forces was certainly commendable. Nevertheless, despite the initial overwhelming appeal of his "third way," it is highly debatable whether, by the end of his term, he fully fulfilled the lofty expectations.

What we advocate in *THE 3rd WAY* (our version of this "third way") is a much more substantive policy proposal. Moreover, the positive results of economic democracy and employee ownership have been consistently *proven* to work wherever tried.

The most important and effective step we need to take immediately is to create a corporate tax system incentive in exchange for a transformation in the measure of employees' equity in their place of work. This is fundamental. And it will fundamentally correct the economic system we operate under for the better. The US corporate tax rate is currently the highest in the world. As leaders in both parties have expressed, to be more competitive in the global market, we need to cut corporate taxation. Yes, but *only* if it is offset with an *equivalent* move toward employee ownership. Only then can we obtain the greatest good for the greatest number. Only then can we unleash the *full* power of our nation's people!

Though the contents are vastly different, this book is designed and written for the masses just as Mao's *Little Red Book* was—one of the most printed books in history.

The palpable, serious, daily social unrest on both sides of our society, from the Tea Party to Occupy Wall Street, and the entire silent but gravely disenchanted majority in between, desperately

PREFACE

needs a third voice of reason. We contend this new way forward is not simply a new ideology; it is the *only* effective long-term means of keeping the dream of widespread prosperity and social harmony.

Though the book is specifically written for everyone, its intellectual "centers of gravity" are such people and leading institutions as Professors Joseph Blasi and Douglas L. Kruse (Rutgers University, School of Management and Labor Relations) and Richard B. Freeman (professor of Economics, Harvard University; Faculty Fellow). They are intimately and actively behind this book because of their decades-long research on this topic.

Today far too many of our citizens barely make it from week to week living lives of worry and struggle in what is championed as the richest nation on earth. If things are bad for them now, what on earth will they do when they reach retirement age? Is the American Dream now just fool's gold and a romanticized recollection of a bygone era? Why the heck is this happening and what can be done about it?

The answer, like most lessons can be learned from history if we have both the inclination to take the time to study it and have the wisdom to understand the lessons she is teaching us. It was Abraham Lincoln who in The Homestead Act, enacted during the Civil War in 1862, provided that any adult citizen, or intended citizen, who had never borne arms against the U.S. government could claim 160 acres of surveyed government land. Claimants were required to "improve" the plot by building a dwelling and cultivating the land. After 5 years on the land, the original filer was entitled to the property, free and clear. This decisive move by one of our most brilliant Presidents gave much needed opportunity to propertyless people of that age.

In the same way in this information age Americans and those seeking prosperity across the globe must create mechanisms for their people to gain some degree of an *ownership* share in the ever expanding *technological* advancement we witness all around us every day. Today technology drives capital. You must be part of it, or you will be left behind.

Today Americans must be granted a new wiser plan, a "just third way" opened up by the brilliant Louis Kelso decades before. It's a new, alternative version of government involvement and a business dynamic that surpasses both unfocused capitalism and all forms of socialism. With it we will create a more participatory, unified, and empowering "Second American Revolution" leading to the kind of both fair and prosperous society we all long for.

In 1776, we hoped to be an *economic democracy* for those with initial citizenship, which was thankfully expanded to exclude no one. We then took the first steps into *political democracy*. Had technology not advanced, Jeffersonian democracy would have, for the most part, produced a fair and equitable society. At that time, if measured by market forces, 95 percent of the inputs into production (goods and services) were produced by labor and 5 percent by capital, which was mostly land. Land was low in value. It was plentiful. And it took an inordinate amount of labor to be productive.

Make no mistake: the advancement of technology is indeed a much-welcomed, wonderful thing. Today's smart cell phones have more computing power than what put a man on the moon! *The problem is our political systems have not kept pace with the technology.*

In 1776 *everyone* with citizenship had potential economic power because *labor* was the main source and everyone was born with it. Therefore, economic power was *democratically diffused.*

Then, as you see from the chart below, as *technological change advanced,* capital workers grew at an exponential rate. The inputs of capital workers and labor workers have roughly *changed places*! Capital workers now produce at least 90 percent of the input to the economy, with only 10 percent coming from labor.

PREFACE

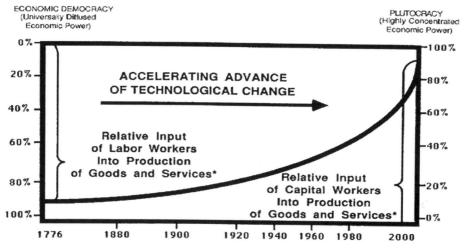

Figure 1. Changing participation of labor workers and capital workers (Graph by Louis O. Kelso and Patricia Hetter Kelso)

Adam Smith said, "There is only one way to earn income—produce something." If that is true, we are de facto in a real mess.

In today's highly industrialized world, *wealth* has a close connection to both technology and capital formation. Technological power marches on, yet labor can only work so hard for so long. Tragically, for the most part, **we have decoupled labor from capital**. The masses of labor *own no capital* and therefore *can't possibly keep up*. Herein lies the root cause of the pervasive, precipitous decline in the standard of living for both the middle and lower classes. The blessings of technological advancement caused their ability to keep pace with income via just their labor *to be slashed over time*.

This is *why*, in this day and age, the poor stay poor and the rich get richer.

The end result is that our society has evolved into a *plutocracy* (from Ancient Greek, *ploutos* meaning "wealth" and *kratos* meaning "power, dominion, and rule"). It's the rule by the wealthy, or the powerful supported by wealth.

In addition, of course, all the methods of finance now in law, which were written by those in power, support the perpetuation of the current system. Only an educated populace via the power of democracy (in lieu of violent revolution, which we do not endorse) can ultimately make the necessary changes and corrections to the system they live under to provide for a more equitable playing field.

Why the concentration of wealth happens must be fundamentally understood. Moreover, an equitable means for dealing with it without killing the golden goose of prosperity must be ascertained.

When you consistently have 5 percent of the people owning the capital that provides 90 percent of the input into production, *you have a recipe for revolution.* And we have reached the limits of redistribution. We have run out of money to paper over the problem! The nearly $20 trillion national debt is now at an unsustainable level. **We must modernize the underlying system to ramp up an employee-ownership economy and allow the vast majority of the populace to participate in the capitalist system—not from another failed state redistribution scheme, but via their place of employment.**

Of all the concepts presented in this book, the most critically preeminent is the pressing relationship between labor and technology. It is the singular concept deserving its paramount emphasis. We must understand this decisive relationship and how we must deal with it effectively in the modern age.

PREFACE

While a person has natural limits to the labor he or she can produce, technology continues relentlessly and to an infinite degree to stride on—ever expanding its capabilities. Technology and, more importantly, its fundamental connection to capital and by extension capitalism must be reconciled. Who *owns* the capital is the point. Unless we reconcile a bold new system to *re-couple* labor and capital and address this intensifying inequity in the modern world, we are on an inescapable collision course toward a calamity of epic scale.

It is imperative that our elected officials, the media, and most importantly the general public realize what must be done. Never forget, this was written by both a Democrat and a Republican.

The ever-widening gap between technology and labor is a cold reality. The central question for our age is how we resolve the two as it relates to public policy. We cannot rely on politicians only to drive this change; it must be an organic, newly educated movement from the populace! The decisions we make have massive social, economic, and political implications. We must get this right. And the time to act is now.

Dire consequences await all of us if we do not act appropriately and expeditiously! This book presents the understanding of a bold new paradigm before you. The employee ownership and economic democracy movement is already successfully underway. We must nurture and build on it in geometric proportions.

Capitalism works, but is not fair.

Socialism is fair in theory, but does not work.

Here is the solution:

THE 3rd WAY

Part I:
Looming Turmoil!

Chapter 1:

WHAT'S AT STAKE?

"I'm Mad As Hell And I'm Not Going To Take It Anymore"
[yet, hope springs eternal…]

Socialism has been discredited. Plutocracy is in the process of being discredited. Democratic capitalism has yet to be tried.
—Louis O. Kelso, political economist,
lawyer, author, and merchant banker[5]

Like massive tectonic plates, the two most fundamental forces in economics, labor and capital are inexorably pulling away from each other with catastrophic consequences. We are employing an 18th century economic model that is utterly failing to address our 21st century technological capital/labor reality.

Labor's power, the sweat of one's brow, is essentially fixed while capital's power, driven by technological advancement, strides relentlessly upward. All those working for wage only income are in a crisis. Disconnected and excluded from this unprecedented capital expansion, they are every day marching inescapably toward a further deteriorating and desperate situation!

There just *has* to be a better system. The level of unrest, alienation, and downright despair is palpable at all levels of society. It's everywhere. It has spread from those working at the local convenience store to people working for Fortune 500 companies.

And these are people *with* jobs! What about the countless unemployed both in our seemingly idyllic suburbs and in the steaming caldron of our worst urban areas apparently trapped by their economic circumstances? What true hope do we have for them? What successful, tangible, proven real plan can we offer?

The political, economic, and social fabric are all involved and intertwined in both the problem and the solution.

In America and indeed across the globe, the simmering discontent in our souls and the dismay in our hearts and on the faces of far too many are apparent. To be sure, we have seen the episodic manifestation of such discontent and dismay in acts big and small, from speaking to our relatives and friends, to unsettling events on our TV screens. The existential longing is self-evident. There just *has* to be a better way. And there is.

"Now is the winter of our discontent" was coined by Shakespeare and put into print in *Richard III* in 1594. This famous phrase has lived on in the lexicon of our consciousness for centuries. It means that perhaps the time of unhappiness is coming to an end. Be that the case if the principles outlined in this thesis are heeded!

> *Capitalism inevitably and by virtue of the very logic of its civilization creates, educates and subsidizes a vested interest in social unrest.*
> —Joseph A. Schumpeter,
> economist and political scientist[6]

Surely we are in a time of great upheaval, with much more to follow if serious, substantive action is not taken. We already have people in the streets, both the Tea Party on the Right and Occupy Wall Street on the Left. Thankfully, major levels of serious violence have not broken out—yet.

> *The financial wealth of the top 1 percent of households [in the United States] exceeds the combined wealth of the bottom 95 percent.*
> —Ralph Nader, political activist,
> author, lecturer, and attorney[7]

The only way to avoid the unrest and catastrophe we are barreling toward is to come up with a truly new paradigm that will both spur robust economic growth and do it in a way that is fair and equitable to the entire populace. This paradigm is *not* what we are hearing ad nauseam from both the Far Right and the Far Left. Rather, it is *a third way*. It is a unique way that uses the engine of the private economy to properly share the blessings of prosperity with *all* the employees *who do the work* that is crucial to the creation of such wealth. Economic democracy is the only rational way forward.

What is economic democracy? Economic democracy exists when the units of economic organizations are owned and controlled by the masses of people who work in them. These are people who have a genuine long-term interest in the organization and the communities in which they operate, rather than just top management and remote shareholders whose overriding interest is short-term financial gain. Economic democracy is a socioeconomic philosophy that proposes to shift power from only corporate shareholders to a larger group of stakeholders that includes workers, customers, suppliers, and the broader public. There are many different ways for employees to gain a share in a business.

Unfortunately, inherent inequality, unfairness, and ineffective and/or inefficient fatal flaws are the touchstones of the current dominant economic systems. The fact is inequality and, more importantly, the unfairness of opportunity form the linchpin to the ever-simmering unrest throughout the world. It is long overdue that we deal with it in a common sense, substantive way free from ideology.

THE 3RD WAY

> *Capitalism is the legitimate racket of the ruling class.*
> —Al Capone, famous American gangster in the 1920s and '30s

> *The historical experience of socialist countries has sadly demonstrated that collectivism does not do away with alienation but rather increases it, adding to it a lack of basic necessities and economic inefficiency.*
> —Pope John Paul II[8]

Rather than another failed government "stimulus" or "make-work project," the economic democracy movement offers a simple, common sense program designed to expand ownership of the means of production to every member of the company (public or private) who participates in generating that company's profits. The father of this movement is the late Louis O. Kelso (December 4, 1913–February 17, 1991), a political economist in the classical tradition of Adam Smith, Karl Marx, and John Maynard Keynes. The umbrella title for the economic democracy program is called an *employee ownership* (EO) plan.

EOs can take several forms:

- **Employee Stock Ownership Plan (ESOP):** A defined-contribution plan that provides a company's workers with an ownership interest in the company. Shares are given to employees and are held in the ESOP trust until the employee retires or leaves the company. Employees do not purchase shares with their savings; rather the company pays for the shares out of profits.

- **401(k) plan**: A type of retirement savings account in the United States that takes its name from subsection 401(k) of the IRS Code. The company matches employee contributions to a retirement savings plan in the company and also gives workers the opportunity to buy stock with pretax wage deductions.

- **KSOP**: A qualified retirement plan that combines an employee's stock ownership plan (ESOP) with a 401(k). Under this type of retirement plan, the company matches employee contributions with stock rather than cash. KSOPs benefit companies by reducing expenses that would arise from separately operating an ESOP and a 401(k) plan. The KSOP instantly creates a market with sufficient liquidity needed for shareholders wishing to sell their stake. KSOPs also provide added motivation to employees to ensure the profitability of the company, because the added profitability directly enhances their retirement plans.[9]

- **Employee stock purchasing plan** (ESPP): A tax-efficient means to encourage workers to buy company stock, often at a discount, in order to secure loyalty and create a common bond between labor and management. The amount of the discount depends on the specific plan but can be as much as 15 percent lower than the market price.

- **Stock options:** A call option on the common stock of a company granted by the company to an employee as part of the employee's remuneration package. The objective is to give employees an incentive to behave in ways that will boost the company's stock price. If the company's stock market price rises above the call price, the employee can exercise the option, pay the call price, and be issued ordinary shares in the company; the employee experiences a direct financial benefit from the difference between the market and call prices. If the market price falls below the stock call price at the time the option needs to be exercised, the employee is not obligated to call on the option, in which case the option will lapse.[10]

- **Cooperative**: An autonomous association of persons who voluntarily cooperate for their mutual economic benefit. Cooperatives include organizations and businesses that are owned and managed by the people who work there (a worker cooperative).

- **Profit sharing:** Various incentive plans introduced by businesses that provide direct or indirect payments to employees based on the company's profitability, in addition to employees' regular salary and bonuses.[11]

- **Gain sharing**: A program that returns cost savings and output incentives to the employees, usually as a lump-sum bonus. It offers workers payments based on the performance of work units rather than of the whole enterprise. It is a productivity measure, as opposed to profit-sharing, which is a profitability measure.

- **Direct ownership**: Workers buy stock directly on the stock market.

- **Citizens trust**: A new concept not connected to employment that allows every citizen to enjoy the benefits of ownership. This is done by allowing them to borrow money to purchase economic assets that will later provide them income.

- **Consumer Stock Ownership Plan (CSOP):** Louis Kelso innovates the (CSOP) in 1958 to enable farmers in California's central valley to become owners of Valley

Nitrogen Producers, the fertilizer processing plant of which they are the principal customers.

Another derivation would be **The Alaska Permanent Fund,** a constitutionally established permanent fund managed by a state-owned corporation established in Alaska in 1976.

Shortly after the oil from Alaska's North Slope began flowing to market the Permanent Fund was created. It was designed to be an investment where at least 25% of the oil money would be put into a dedicated fund for future generations, who would no longer have oil as a resource. The Alaska Permanent Fund sets aside a certain share of oil revenues to continue benefiting current and all future generations of Alaskans.

We differentiate between systems involving *financial ownership*, where the workers' rewards depend on share prices, and group or company *profit-sharing or bonus systems* that reward workers on the basis of group or company performance.[12]

The financial ownership rubric includes employee stock ownership plans (ESOPs), majority or direct ownership, defined-contribution retirement plan money invested in one's own firm, cooperatives, stock purchase plans, and employee stock options.[13]

The profit-sharing rubric includes gain sharing, profit sharing, bonuses linked to performance and/or cost savings, and so on.

Elements of both are found in the relatively new instrument called the KSOP.

The bottom line is the best course for the future of work for many must be development of the natural human evolution of employee ownership. All forms of employee ownership are indeed a celebration of the concept of private property. With EO, you unleash all the inherent personal and massive societal benefits through intrinsic personal motivation.

> ### The Capitalist Manifesto
> Louis O. Kelso and Mortimer J. Adler
>
> Of itself, the income tax does not tend in the slightest degree to broaden the diffusion of the ownership of capital. It relieves existing capitalists of a large portion of the wealth their capital produces, but it does not make new capitalists. But where deductions against such heavy income taxation are permitted for contributions to plans resembling our present profit-sharing—particularly stock-bonus—plans, the income tax can be made to have a significant effect in bringing about the transition to a completely capitalistic economy. This can be done within existing tax rates.
>
> To recognize the importance of these devices, it is necessary to distinguish between *profit-sharing* or pension plans, which are merely designed to supplement income to be spent by households on consumption, and *equity-sharing* plans designed to make new capitalists. Only the latter can be significant in broadening the capital-owning group within the economy.
>
> "Equity-sharing plans should not be built around the concept of retirement, as that is currently understood in our "full employment" economy. The objective should be to build permanent, diversified capital estates—estates that will enable the new capitalists to shift their participation in production from the employment of their labor to the employment of their capital."[14]

*I can't help but believe that in the future we'll see in the United States and throughout the Western world an increasing trend toward the next logical step—**employee ownership**.*

—President Ronald Reagan, fortieth president of the United States, in his speech on Project Economic Justice[15]

Instead of being a cog in a machine, workers who have decision making power over their jobs come to work with a sense of satisfaction that relatively few employees have in our economy today!
—Senator Bernard Sanders, self-described democratic socialist from Vermont, in his address to attendees of the 2012 Las Vegas Conference and Trade Show by ESOP Association[16]

Water Always Wins!
[the will of the people will always prevail in the end]

Energy and persistence conquer all things.
—Benjamin Franklin, US founding father, author, politician, scientist, and diplomat[17]

In studying one of the great figures of the twentieth century, Gandhi, we can learn extraordinary historic lessons from India. The British had *all* the power, *all* the money, *all* the political and economic and military control, and yet the people of India prevailed in the end! A similar situation occurred in America's Revolution, and we all know how that turned out.

The quest for liberty and self-actualization is like the relentless drip of water on a rock. Despite the strength of the resistance, the human drive to be one's own master will *always* win in the end. One has only to gaze at America's Grand Canyon to see what both time and water can cut and bring forth. It is and shall be the same for politics.

On the Right we see the emergence of the Tea Party. It is an organic outgrowth of a large segment of society recognizing the *failed* use of government power to bring about the required levels of prosperity to match the extraordinarily unprecedented levels of government spending.

On the Left we see the Occupy Wall Street movement rising up with an equal level of frustration. The movement, though unfocused, is nothing but public outcry for equitable participation in the economic process.

Neither side plans to take it quietly much longer!

A Very Important Excerpt
[cogent and on target]

The basic moral problem that faces man as he moves into the age of automation, the age of accelerating conquest of nature, is whether he is really fit to live in an industrial society; whether his institutions will adjust rapidly enough...whether freed from the necessity to devote his brain and brawn to the production of goods and services, he can address himself to the work of civilization itself.
—Louis O. Kelso, political economist,
lawyer, author, and merchant banker[18]

Louis Kelso's Economic Vision for the 21st Century
By Norman G. Kurland and Dawn K. Brohawn

In the 20th century, many lived lives of quiet desperation, struggling from paycheck-to-paycheck, or from hand-to-mouth, with no ownership stake in society's wealth-producing assets. Most 20th century Americans were limited to a choice between the wage-systems of capitalism and the wage-systems of socialism. Many lost hope that they and their descendants would ever share in the American Dream.

> Just as Lincoln provided opportunities for propertyless people in 19th century America to gain a piece of the world's shrinking land frontier, 21st century Americans will gain their ownership share in the limitless technological growth frontier. In the 21st century, Americans will be given a new choice, a **"just third way"** opened up by Louis Kelso, an alternative model of development that transcends both Wall Street capitalism and all forms of socialism. Choosing this road will lead America back to its revolutionary roots to a more participatory, unified and empowering "Second American Revolution" and a more just, free and efficient market economy. America will then again serve as "the last best hope of mankind."[19]

Kelso long believed he had not originated a new economic theory but only discovered a vital fact that the classical economists had somehow overlooked. This fact was the key to understanding why the private-property, free-market economy was notoriously unstable, pursuing a roller-coaster course of exhilarating highs and terrifying descents into economic and financial collapse.

This missing fact, which Kelso had uncovered during years of intensive reading, research, and thought, drastically modifies the classical paradigm that has dominated formal economics since Adam Smith. It concerns the effect of technological change on the distributive dynamics of a private-property, free-market economy. Technological change, Kelso concluded, makes tools, machines, structures, and processes ever more productive while leaving human productivity largely unchanged. The result is that primary distribution through the free-market economy (whose distributive principle is "to each according to his production") delivers progressively more market-sourced income to capital owners and progressively less to workers who make their contributions through labor.

You Must Understand This!
[indispensable knowledge]

Labor is prior to, and independent of, capital. Capital is only the fruit of labor, and could never have existed if labor had not first existed. Labor is the superior of capital, and deserves much the higher consideration.
—Abraham Lincoln,
sixteenth president of the United States[20]

In order to *ever* understand how the economy works, you must first understand its most basic principle. To ever understand how capitalism works, you must first understand capital. And to ever understand how even socialism or communism works, you must indeed also first understand capital.

Capital (economics)
From *Wikipedia*, the free encyclopedia

In a fundamental sense, capital consists of any produced thing that can enhance a person's power to perform economically useful work—a stone or an arrow is capital for a caveman who can use it as a hunting instrument, and roads are capital for inhabitants of a city. Capital is an input in the production function. Homes and personal autos are not capital but are instead durable goods because they are not used in a production effort.

Further classifications of capital that have been used in various theoretical or applied uses include:

- *Financial capital*, which represents obligations, and is liquidated as money for trade, and owned by legal entities. It is in the form of capital assets, traded in financial markets. Its market value is not based on the historical accumulation of money invested but on the perception by the market of its expected revenues and of the risk entailed.

WHAT'S AT STAKE?

> - *Public capital*, which encompasses the aggregate body of government-owned assets that are used to promote private industry productivity, including highways, railways, airports, water treatment facilities, telecommunications, electric grids, energy utilities, municipal buildings, public hospitals and schools, police, fire protection, courts and still others.
> - *Natural capital*, which is inherent in ecologies and protected by communities to support life, e.g., a river that provides farms with water.[21]

Look at how our nation (and much of the rest of the world) has devolved from an **economic democracy** with universally diffused economic power into a virtual **plutocracy** with highly concentrated economic power. The linchpin for understanding why this has happened is rooted in both a firm grasp of the nature of capitalism *and,* perhaps more importantly, the critical role of the accelerating advancement of technological change.

The production of goods and services once dominated by the relative input of labor workers has been completely transposed by the relative input of capital workers into the newly produced goods and services. Without society implementing substantial steps to bridge this sea change in our economic life, a formula for gross inequality and disenchantment leading to real unrest is virtually inevitable.

Another critical contribution made by Louis O. Kelso and Patricia H. Kelso is the chart below. Though apparently simple in design, its concepts are extraordinarily powerful.

What this chart shows is that *labor* is being increasingly decoupled from *capital.* This is a most serious issue! Perhaps ironically, the date 1776, in addition to marking America's independence, also happens to be when many historians mark the beginning of the industrial revolution.

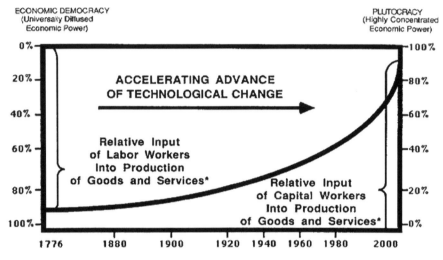

Figure 2. Changing participation of labor workers and capital workers (Graph by Louis O. Kelso and Patricia Hetter Kelso)

As a nation leading the way for all of humanity we embarked on the initial steps into *political democracy*. Had technology been frozen in time, Jeffersonian democracy would have, essentially, produced a just and equitable society. Back in 1776, if measured by market forces, 95 percent of the inputs into production (goods and services) were produced by labor and 5 percent by capital, which was mostly land. Land was relatively inexpensive for the common man to acquire. Yet it took an excessive amount of labor to be productive.

WHAT'S AT STAKE?

To be clear, the welcomed, unrelenting progress in technology is without a doubt a blessing for mankind and our general improvement in the average person's standard of living. For example, today's smart cell phones have more computing power than what put a man on the moon! *The real dilemma is our political systems have simply not kept pace with technology.*

In 1776 economic power was *equitably diffused.* At that time *all* citizens had potential economic power because *labor* was the primary source and everyone was born with a relatively even ability to work and thus acquire wealth. Today the game has completely changed.

As you see from the chart, capital now produces at least 90 percent of the input to the economy, with only 10 percent coming from labor. As *technological change advanced,* the input from capital grew at an exponential rate and the contribution to the overall economy from capital verses labor has essentially *switched places*!

Herein lies the root cause of the pervasive, precipitous decline in the standard of living for both the middle and lower classes. The blessings of technological progress caused their ability to keep pace with income via just their labor *to be slashed over time.* This is *why,* in this information age, now more than ever, the poor stay poor and the rich get richer.

The end result is that our society has evolved into a *plutocracy* (from Ancient Greek, *ploutos* meaning "wealth" and *kratos* meaning "power, dominion, and rule"). It's the rule by the wealthy, or the powerful supported by wealth.

So, if it's true as Adam Smith once said, "There is only one way to earn income—produce something." then we are no doubt in an undeniable mess destined to only get worse and worse. The time is coming (sooner than one might think) that the social fabric represented as an elastic band will snap and all hell will break loose. The challenge will surely not be solved with more sloganeering and eloquent but empty speeches. We are all sick

THE 3RD WAY

to death of these! What we need are *real leaders* with the wisdom to take *real steps,* and steer a bold yet sensible new course away from the turmoil just ahead. We the people will no doubt rally in droves to such a leader.

> *The trouble with today's techniques of finance is that they're designed to make the rich richer. None are designed to make the poor richer. That's why the poor are poor. Because they're not rich.*
> —Louis O. Kelso, political economist,
> lawyer, author, and merchant banker[22]

Some Political Shorthand
[the basics on ideology]

> *A claim for equality of material position can be met only by a government.*
> —Friedrich Hayek, an Austrian, later turned British,
> economist and philosopher best known for his
> defense of classical liberalism[23]

We feel it's important to include at least a modicum of political theory as a backdrop to a fuller understanding of the context in which any political movement operates. Our political theory is economic democracy and the employee ownership and empowerment that go along with it. We are here to report its wonderful possibilities. This movement can thrive in almost any ideology along the political spectrum—except at the extremes of the "political power paradigm" seen at each of the very ends of the spectrum.

What's ideology, you may ask? That's a very important question with an answer that's essential to know. Let's get *Webster's Dictionary*'s definition:

ide·ol·o·gy
1 : visionary theorizing
2 **a**: a systematic body of concepts especially about human life or culture
b: a manner or the content of thinking characteristic of an individual, group, or culture
c: the integrated assertions, theories, and aims that constitute a sociopolitical program[24]

Perhaps one of the finest, easiest-to-understand methods of grasping what can be the overwhelming subject of politics can be found in the "Political Power Paradigm" illustration below (see fig. 3).

Putting aside the social-issue aspects of political thought (gun control, abortion, drug legalization, etc.), the graphic is best used to understand the *economic* component of political ideology. Remember, the serious business of politics is worth every citizen's time because in many ways it directly affects almost every aspect of your daily life. People who do not take the time to understand what is really going on with the political dimension of their lives, frankly, are fools.

Something like this should be taught in every one of our schools. Tragically, most people have little or no gravitas in their understanding of this most important subject. This chart should be a great help.

This chart outlines a basic scale to help you understand the relative strength between the two fundamental competing forces: the power of the government (or state) versus the power of the individual.

THE 3RD WAY

POLITICAL POWER PARADIGM

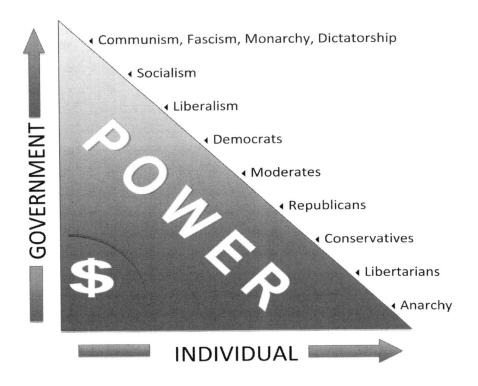

Figure 3. The political power paradigm (Source: Veny W. Musum, © 2013)

We are not here to make any judgment about which of these broadly outlined systems is best. The main point of sharing this essential nugget of knowledge is to assure everyone that the employee ownership and economic democracy movement is that *very rare case that can thrive in any of the ideologies along the political spectrum* (other than the most extreme ones—communism, fascism, monarchy, dictatorship on one end, anarchy on the other end).

What encouraging news!

WHAT'S AT STAKE?

> **Optimal Inequality for Economic Growth, Stability, and Shared Prosperity:**
> **The Economics behind the Wall Street Occupiers Protest?**
> By Richard B. Freeman
>
> Can the US reduce inequality toward its optimal level and reverse the movement toward economic feudalism? I believe that the concerted efforts of concerned citizens can do this; and the activities of the occupiers are a sign of change in society. The increased opposition of conservatives (some in the "tea party" movement) to "crony capitalism" is a sign that the campaign to rein in the excesses of inequality in the economy and polity cut across ideological lines.[25]

Concentration Of Wealth
[why it happens...and how shocking the disparity has become!]

We may have democracy, or we may have wealth concentrated in the hands of a few, but we can't have both.
—Justice Louis Brandeis,
US Supreme Court justice, 1916–1939[26]

The illustration below demonstrates the enormous levels of wealth concentrated by the very richest in the world today. One may wonder how such staggering sums of money can be rolled up and concentrated in so few hands. The answer is simple—capitalism is a very powerful wealth-producing concept. It works.

THE 3RD WAY

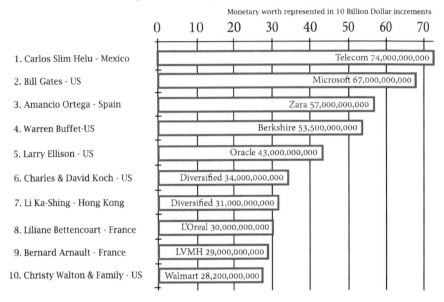

Figure 4. *Forbes* "The World's Billionaires 2013" Kroll, Luisa. (2013, March), Vol. 191, Issue 4. Pp. 85-90.

Another way to express the disparity of income is to realize the world's highest-paid billionaire for 2013 is worth $74,000,000,000. In contrast, the average median income for that same year was $32,104. That billionaire's sum of wealth was more than the combined income of 2,305, 008 median-income earners.

To use a visualization ratio of dollars to grains of sand, a gallon can hold roughly 36.96 million grains of sand. This billionaire would have his gallon filled with nearly 37 **million grains** of sand, while the median-income earners would get just 16 **grains** of sand per worker.

Even the current Federal Reserve chair Janet Yellen said on May 7, 2014 the "worrisome" trend of "growing inequality" can "determine the ability of different groups to participate equally in the democracy." She went on to say, "...there's no question that we've had a trend toward growing inequality and I personally find it very worrisome trend that deserves the attention of policy-makers."[27]

Could just raising the minimum wage solve the problem? In fact, this is one area where the two co-authors of this book disagree. Yet, we do agree on the importance of raising the capital wage for all workers. Since 1938 the federal minimum wage has been raised a total of 29 times.[28] Yet, the problem of income inequality has only gotten progressively worse. Regardless of where one stands on the minimum wage issue, one thing is clear; it has not solved the problem of inequality.

The view of Upendra Chivukula is that the minimum wage and regular increases of the minimum wage allows entry level workers to at least be able to afford a more sustainable beginning level wage as they enter the workforce. He is in favor of a livable entry wage that can really support a family. A famous study actually conducted in New Jersey by economists Alan Krueger of Princeton University and David Card of the University of California at Berkeley, concluded that the April 1992 increase in the New Jersey minimum wage led to no loss of employment in the fast-food industry. Co-author Chivukula believes that the moral value of setting minimum labor standards will encourage all employers to treat entry-level workers more fairly.[29]

On the other hand, co-author Veny Musum has the view that even if the minimum wage did work, that it affects such a small segment of the population; it does too little to move the overall income inequality needle for the vast majority of workers.

He holds that many would argue it has many aspects to it that are even counterproductive. For example, youth unemployment particularly for minorities now hovers at a disastrous fifty percent. Most importantly, he contends you are kicking out the first rung of the ladder for many of our youth that desperately need an entry-level *start* in the workplace.

According to a paper written in 2000 by Fuller and Geide-Stevenson, 73.5% of American economists agreed that a minimum wage *increases* unemployment among unskilled and young workers, while 26.5% disagreed with this statement.[30]

Co-author Musum's view is it is supply and demand axiomatic - when you raise the price on something, you get less demand for it.

In spite of this disagreement, we indicate in other parts of this book, labor unions should negotiate for capital shares even more aggressively than just wages. That will, in the long term, best serve their members and the business organizations they are associated with. J. Michael Keeling, President of The ESOP Association said it best, "Wage only income continues falling farther and farther behind fellow citizens who have large ownership stakes in our nation's productive assets." In the long run wages on labor can never keep pace with the technological, geometric growth and power of capitalism. Continually chasing your tail after only wages fails to address the systemic, underlying root cause of the problem – ownership of capital. We both believe that capital income has an important role to play in advancing the overall idea of the "livable wage" and a fair share among working people.

Today one may presume with the existence of massive amounts of 401(K) stock owned by ordinary Americans it might refute the claim of exclusive capital ownership to just the rich. Unfortunately, research by NYU Economist Edward Wolff suggests not. Using 2010 data, he estimates that **80.8 percent of stocks in mutual funds and 91.5 percent of business equity are held by the top 10 percent of American society.** So despite the marketing claims that Wall Street is owned by all of us, the evidence indicates otherwise. The public markets of Wall Street remain the preserve of exclusive capitalism.[31]

The chart below (see fig. 5) shows that in the period from colonial days to modern times, the ownership of labor power and the ownership of capital in fact *don't change*. There was a little bump up after the Homestead Acts, which was a deliberate policy to get

WHAT'S AT STAKE?

capital into the hands of people who weren't born with it, in what was still an agrarian age. Otherwise, as the chart shows, nonresidential capital has been owned by the top 5 percent. This is the real force that regularly brings about catastrophic cycles of unrest that blow the lid off society and that we worry about.

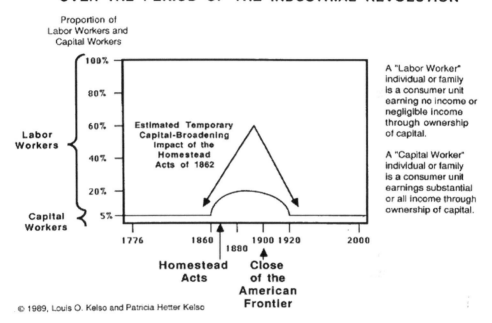

Figure 5. Concentration of the ownership of capital over the period of the industrial revolution[32]

In 1862 Congress passed and President Lincoln signed the Homestead Act into law. Lincoln's House Speaker, Galusha A. Grow (R-PA), often called "The Father of the Republican Party" steered the act through Congress as promoting social and political equality, saying, "I want the government to protect the rights of man." Grow's words highlight the belief that among the basic human rights was the right to own property and that right should extent to all persons.

The Homestead Act gave ownership of 160 acres of underdeveloped federal land west of the Mississippi River to families for a small fee and five years of residency.[33]

Of special note is, when Republican Speaker Galusha Grow finally retired from the House of Representatives in 1902; he gave one last speech on "Labor and Capital." Having seen both the successes and limitations of the Homestead Act, he proposed that because there were growing limitations on capital in the form of land, **the future will be in assisting property ownership <u>via shares of corporations</u>. Profit and equity sharing could be used to provide access to property rights to workers in the new industrialized economy.**[34]

Today we recognize that labor's share of national income includes the value of nonwage income, such as stock options, stocks, and bonuses. However, this nonwage income is now heavily concentrated among the very wealthy. The level of inequality has become severe, and this is not good.

It is simply unsustainable to continually have 5 percent of the population own the capital that provides 90 percent of the productive input. Understand the vast majority of wealth will flow from this production to those 5 percent holding the capital! Even more troubling is, based on historical trends; the problem left uncorrected is only going to get much worse over time. And we just don't have the money to pacify the problem much longer! With a nearly $20 trillion unsustainable national debt we have reached the limits of redistribution. The only way out of this desperate situation is a bold, modernized system allowing a majority of our citizens to participate in the wealth building capitalist system via their place of employment. To say if nothing substantially is done we are on straight line collision course toward serious unrest and even revolution is *not* hyperbole.

By giving workers across the economic spectrum a share of profits and company stock, shared capitalism could perhaps help mitigate the rising inequality in income and wealth that has characterized the United States since the 1970s and 1980s. The reason is that *capital* income has risen more than *wage* income, with labor's actual wage share of income and growth falling in the 2000s. So, those with a share of business profits or appreciation in the value of equities or real estate have done better than wage earners. As reported in *Shared Capitalism at Work*:

> Cheerleaders for the "ownership society" tout the growing share of US households owning stock—up from 31.7 percent in 1989 to 51.9 percent in 2001. What is less often advertised is that stock ownership remains highly concentrated. The bottom 90 percent of households owns only 23 percent of all stock and just 12 percent of all directly held stock (which confers direct control or voting rights on stockholders). Only 27 percent of households in the bottom 90 percent of the wealth distribution own (directly or indirectly) more than $10,000 of stock. If ownership is measured by households' ownership stake in the corporate sector of the US economy, a large majority of American households have little or no meaningful claim to membership in the ownership society.
>
> This concentration of stock ownership implies a corresponding concentration of income from capital, which contributes to growing income inequality since dividends and capital gains have been a growing share of market-based income in the past thirty years, and capital income disproportionately goes to high-income households. Employee stock ownership may help reduce this growing inequality by contributing to broad-based wealth building and income growth across the economic spectrum.[35]

So we see it is not enough to claim we are developing into an ownership society based mainly on the growing percentage of households owning stock. When we delve deeper into the real numbers, we see the increase in stock ownership is being concentrated in the hands of those at the top. Rather than a reason for optimism, the current growth of stock ownership is an indication of just how disproportionately wealth is being spread across society.

Figure 6. How the top .001% live (Source: CNBC Originals, *Untold Wealth: The Rise of the Super Rich*)

The concentration of wealth in the United States is frankly becoming alarming. The richest 1 percent of Americans control more wealth than 90 percent of the population combined! Yet, as we go higher and higher in the wealth pyramid the disparity becomes *even more alarming*:

- Within the top 0.1 percent, 48 percent of income goes to the upper 0.01 percent.

- However, within the upper 0.01 percent, **49 percent of that income goes to the upper 0.001 percent.** Most of the wealth is going to the top one-thousandth of 1 percent of the population![36]

Figure 7 below graphically shows that the income disproportion between the groups is just shocking. As you can see, the chart only depicts up to the top 0.01 percent. **The ratio of the upper 0.001 percent is literally off the chart!** Moreover, this disparity is getting increasingly worse over time.

Part of the increase in upper-bracket earnings took the form of a massive growth in CEO pay. Estimates by *Business Week* and the Institute of Policy Studies show a CEO-to-worker pay ratio of 42:1 in 1980, of 107:1 in 1990, and of 325:1 in 2010. Much of this high CEO pay took the form of stock options, restricted shares, and bonuses. When share prices rise, the owners of options and shares benefit, even if price rises reflect factors outside their control. When share prices fall, boards dominated by executives often issue new options at the abnormally low market prices, which then pay off handsomely when the market recovers. Some firms did this immediately after 9/11, turning a national disaster into a way of lining their own pockets.[37]

THE 3RD WAY

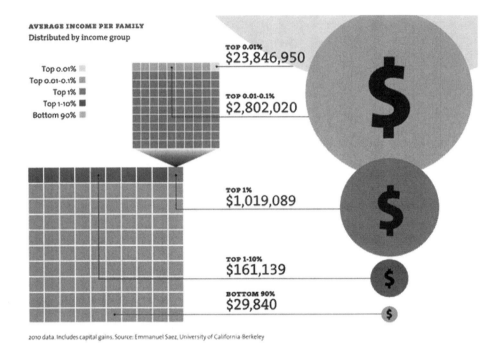

Figure 7. Average income per family, distributed by income group (Source: Emmanuel Saez, University of California, 2010)

As figure 8 shows, compensation for CEOs at the top is much more related to stock and stock options (both equity and capital instruments) than to salary alone. Do they know something the rest of us need to learn?

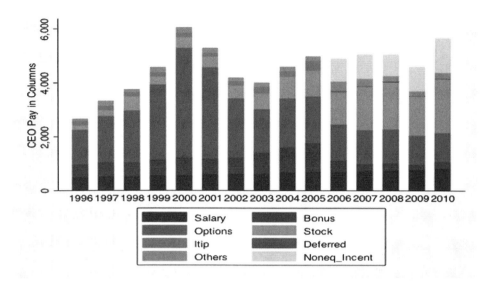

Figure 8. Pay at top related to incentive pay via capital income (Source: Giuliano Bianchi, *Essays on CEO Compensation: New Evidence on the Managerial-Power vs. Optimal Contracting Debate* [Universita di Bologna, 2013], 10)

Finally, an Experiment on Productivity and Human Nature

> **Optimal Inequality for Economic Growth, Stability, and Shared Prosperity: The Economics behind the Wall Street Occupiers Protest?**
> By Richard B. Freeman
>
> In a laboratory experiment, Alex Gelber and I (Freeman and Gelber, 2010) organized subjects into groups of six and asked each person to solve a packet of mazes. We rewarded them for the number of mazes they completed under three incentive systems: a low inequality system in which everyone in the group

received the same amount of money regardless of what theyproduced; a high inequality system that gave a large prize to the person who solved the most mazes and nothing to anyone else; and an intermediate incentive system that gave increasing rewards to persons who ranked higher in the maze competition. Figure 2 shows that this design produced an inverse-U relation between inequality and output. The group with no incentives had the lowest output, the group in which only the top person earned a prize had a modestly higher output while the group with the middling level of inequality solved the highest number of mazes.

Figure 2: Reported number of mazes solved in maze experiment at given incentives

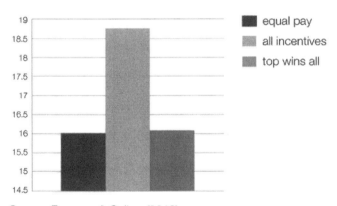

Source: Freeman & Gelber (2010)

Outside the laboratory, evidence suggests firms that incentivize the bulk of workers do better than firms that give incentives primarily to a few high-paid executives. Presumably as a result, companies in the US and elsewhere have increasingly adopted profit-sharing and gain-sharing modes of pay, employee stock ownership schemes, and all-employee stock options.[38]

WHAT'S AT STAKE?

What We Know:

- In a participatory workplace, the evidence is: higher output/higher productivity.

- There is little or no evidence that huge executive compensation results in better company performance.

- There is also lots of evidence that inequality breeds rent-seeking (economic benefit through political manipulation), crony capitalism, and crime—a.k.a. Wall Street, finance, banks too big to fail, etc.

All this obviously points to the fact that we must rapidly and boldly design an incentive system to significantly promote the much-desired involvement of the bottom 90 percent of households in the significant benefits of ownership. Otherwise we will continue to see the growing inequality, which is both unfair and a clear recipe for serious social unrest.

All these items unmistakably point to three very salient points:
1. The widening gap between the rich and the middle class and poor is becoming more and more shocking.
2. The most probable way to acquire and grow wealth is through the acquisition of equity—that is, ownership.
3. For the growing wage disparity to be abated, workers need a way to participate in the acquisition of these same equity assets.

THE 3RD WAY

How The Economy Really Works—Really
[how capitalists become so fabulously rich...and why you should join them]

> *Advocates of capitalism are very apt to appeal to the sacred principles of liberty, which are embodied in one maxim: The fortunate must not be restrained in the exercise of tyranny over the unfortunate.*
> —Bertrand Russell, philosopher, logician, mathematician, historian, and social critic[39]

In Our Industrial Society, Who Produces What?

Now, let's look at the grim statistics, and we'll see why our present setup doesn't work without massive government interference and massive redistribution of earnings. Here's a simple parable to essentially explain the whole system.

Let's go back ten thousand years to the simplest form of labor and capital. Let's take a caveman using a flint knife to make shoes. Here, the caveman's *labor* is working with one primitive piece of *capital* (the flint knife) to *create wealth* in the form of useful produce (in this case, shoes), which he turns out at a rate of ten pairs per day. In this operation, we might say the man's *labor* was contributing perhaps 90 percent while the *capital* (flint knife) was contributing perhaps 10 percent. If the man owned both his own labor and the capital tool, he would be entitled to all of what he and the tool produced. But if he had rented the tool from some other owner, the tool owner ought to be entitled to about 10 percent of the wealth produced (that is, 10 percent of the shoes). In that scenario, for every day's production of ten pairs of shoes, the laborer ought to get 90 percent or nine pairs and the tool-owner ought to get 10 percent or one pair for the use of the tool. Fair enough?

Now let's move our caveman down through history to, say, a century ago, about the time the industrial revolution was beginning

WHAT'S AT STAKE?

to pick up speed. Now we find our man working with a machine capable of making eighteen pairs of shoes a day. However, the man's labor is no more productive than it ever was; the increased production is due entirely to the machine. And if someone else owns the machine, that owner is entitled to the extra shoes the machine produces. Following this logic, the laborer should get nine pairs of shoes for his day's work; the machine owner should get the remaining nine pairs. Thus, in this instance, labor contributes and gets paid 50 percent of the total; capital contributes and gets paid 50 percent of the total.

As a final step, let's bring our caveman up to modern times, in the midst of the automation explosion. Now he works with a machine that produces ninety pairs of shoes a day. However, as before, his labor is no more productive than it ever was; again, the increased production is due entirely to the improved machine. And as before, if someone else owns the machine, that owner is entitled to the extra shoes the machine produces. Following this logic, the laborer should still get nine pairs of shoes for his daily work, and the machine owner should get the other eighty-one—or nine times as many as the laborer![40]

Capital Now Produces Nine Times as Much as Labor

Here in a nutshell is what's wrong with our present economic system. We have two factors of production, *capital* and *labor*, and they each contribute to the production of goods and services. But during the past few decades, America (and indeed the rest of the world) has become more and more industrialized. The *capital* (tools) factor has grown in relation to the *labor* factor (muscles and brains) so that today *capital* produces at least 90 percent of all we eat, wear, and use. *Labor* produces less than 10 percent.

If each factor of production were paid in proportion to its contribution to total production, then *capital* would wind up getting nine times as much as *labor.* This would be fine and dandy if everybody owned a reasonable share of capital so they could share in the wealth it produced. But alas, this is not the case. Ownership of productive capital is so incredibly *concentrated* that almost nobody owns any of it.

You Don't Own Any Part of the Thing That Produces Most of the Wealth

Briefly stated, that's your problem, Mr. Wage Earner. You're trapped in a system wherein 90 percent of what's produced is now produced by a factor other than your labor—a factor you neither own nor control! Meanwhile, your labor, which is all you do own and all you can trade for a living, is becoming less and less valuable in the production process. No wonder you're having a rough time!

No Wonder Our Present System Works Only through Government Intervention

So, what does the government now have to do to keep this crazy system working? Plenty!

First, there's the whole apparatus of powerful labor unions that wants industry to pay out to labor a share of the wealth that is out of proportion to what labor contributes to total production. Unions should be focused on securing *real capital* for its members instead of only wages.

Second, there's the whole apparatus of taxes under which the government confiscates and then redistributes about two-thirds of all the wealth that capital earns.

Third, there's the whole apparatus of government subsidies and price supports to help keep inefficient producers in business and thus keep their employees working.

Finally, there's the whole government "make work" policy set forth in the Employment Act of 1946, which committed the economy to provide a job for everybody who wanted to work, whether their labor was needed or not. This includes big public-works projects, trillion-dollar "stimulus programs," and the current military "overkill" levels of spending.

Add it all up, and you have an economic system that works only by endless expedients and stimulants—and one that will eventually slip into complete state control and ultimate collapse or feudalism if for no other reason than it is wholly lacking in simple *logic*.

A Solution Benefitting Both Sides
[something NEW!]

> *"The inherent vice of capitalism is the unequal sharing of blessings; the inherent virtue of socialism is the equal sharing of miseries."*
> —Winston Churchill, British prime minister, statesman, orator, historian, and Nobel Prize–winning author[41]

Clearly both capitalism and socialism have their own inherent shortcomings. Rarely, if ever, is there an issue of this magnitude that can attract a strong, positive response from all quarters. In researching this book, the concepts put forward here have received surprising and unprecedented support from everyone we shared the idea with—Republicans, Democrats, independents, union leaders, businesspeople, workers, entrepreneurs, the rich, the poor, the middle class.

The big solution is to *greatly enhance* the mechanisms of employee stock ownership programs (ESOPs) currently in place and dramatically expand the people who can participate. ESOPs are a relatively simple means of allowing workers to directly take part in the wealth of companies they themselves have worked to create.

The beauty of ESOPs is they are a win-win solution for all parties. The corporation wins because, as we will expand on later, the data shows both growth and profitability are generally the result of instituting ESOP programs. The work force wins because workers can directly participate in both the growth and ownership of the

THE 3RD WAY

riches they were indispensable in building. Even the government wins because the more companies are successful, the greater is the prosperity to move the nation forward. Furthermore, the more workers who participate, the less need there is for social services.

Why then has this marvelous idea not seen dramatically wider exposure thus far? There are two primary reasons:
1. The incentives to get companies involved in ESOP programs need to be markedly enhanced at the local, state, and federal level to attract many more of them.
2. Not many businesspeople or workers, or politicians for that matter, are even *aware* of these programs and their remarkable success! Certainly the media has not yet picked up on the power of ESOPs to make both political and social change for the better a reality!

In the purely political arena, for the first time, a major issue has the potential to reach a commonsense consensus from both sides of the aisle, which can be illustrated by the graphic below:

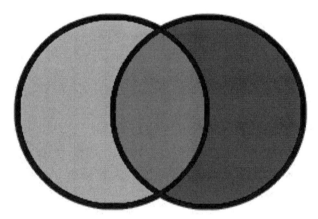

Republicans — EO's — Democrats

Figure 9. An Illustration of the overlapping support from both Republicans and Democrats for the Employee Ownership (EO) issue

Of significant note is the man most responsible for first bringing the ESOP concept to light: Democratic Senator Russell B. Long of Louisiana. A specialist on tax law, he began serving as an influential member of the tax-writing Senate Finance Committee in 1953 and was its chair from 1966 until Republicans assumed control of the Senate in 1981. As a senator, Long was a strong champion of tax breaks for businesses. At one point he said, "I have become convinced you're going to have to have capital if you're going to have capitalism." Long's contributions to US tax laws include his landmark work on ESOPs; he took Louis Kelso's work on theories of capital ownership and formed it into law.[42]

The New York Times

Russell B. Long, 84, Senator Who Influenced Tax Laws
By John H. Cushman Jr.
Published: May 11, 2003

A Democrat, he [Long] exercised great influence as chairman of the Committee on Finance. The *Wall Street Journal* once called him the fourth branch of government.

Mr. Long was a pioneer in establishing employee stock option plans, and he sometimes said that making them commonplace was one of his most important accomplishments.[43]

A current model for moving the ESOP movement forward can be found in legislation by a former speech writer to President Ronald Reagan, Congressman Dana Rohrabacher (R-CA). President

THE 3RD WAY

Reagan was perhaps the most vociferous supporter of the ESOP movement ever to be president.

> **THE WHITE HOUSE**
> WASHINGTON
>
> I am delighted to extend my warm greetings to all those gathered for the Fifth National Conference of the ESOP Association of America.
>
> From the time of our Founding Fathers, our nation has recognized the desirability of the broad private ownership of economic resources. Individual property ownership is a key element in the maintenance of a free society and is essential to human progress.
>
> More than a hundred years ago Abraham Lincoln signed the Homestead Act to encourage individual ownership and development of the nation's land resources. This legislation was instrumental in bringing generations of our people into the mainstream of American life.
>
> In today's modern economy, the Employee Stock Ownership Plan concept affords the opportunity to broaden the base of capital ownership and gives a fair chance to all Americans to participate in the proprietorship of their country. We cannot overestimate the value of simultaneously expanding the available pool of capital and permitting many of our citizens to be part of the enterprise of America for the first time.
>
> It is my hope that the steady growth of ESOPs that we have witnessed in the past ten years will be greatly increased by the passage of the 1981 Economic Recovery Tax Act. ESOPs can play a unique role in furthering the vitality and growth of our economy by increasing the productivity of American workers and making our industry more competitive.
>
> You have my best wishes for an enjoyable conference and your continued progress in the future.
>
> *Ronald Reagan*

Figure 10. Letter to ESOP Association from President Regan (Source: ESOP Association of America)

So, as one can see, from its birth to its early developmental stages, the ESOP movement has received strong support from both enormously powerful Democrats and Republicans.

Nevertheless, the primary purpose of this publication is to stir the fire of demand for this kind of dramatic, positive *real change* from every circle of the masses of society. We must not continue to wait for politicians, however well meaning, to drive this change. It needs to be organic, rising up from the populace! We shall command, if necessary, our elected leaders from both sides of the aisle to actively work quickly to bring a major solution that works and is fair to the people.

Capitalism Works, But Is Not Fair
[in your heart, you know it's true]

Capitalism has destroyed our belief in any effective power but that of self interest backed by force.
—George Bernard Shaw, Irish playwright and co-founder of London School of Economics[44]

Figure 11. (Illustration by Stephen Gilpin)

Do we really need to list examples here? Has anyone reading this not seen, heard of, or personally experienced a situation where a wrong was evident in the business world that just screamed out, "Unfair!"? How many times have we seen the stories where a business folds and its CEO and top brass move on with multimillion-dollar "golden parachutes"? We also too often see examples of "lockouts," where a temporary work stoppage or denial of employment occurs during a labor dispute initiated by the management of a company.

Then there are the innumerable everyday examples where workers, both blue and white collar, are wronged. They work their hearts out for years, even decades, and either get passed over for proper compensation or worse yet are let go for a variety of reasons—many times unjustified. Here are just some examples of discrimination:

- Race or color
- Ethnicity or national origin
- Sex or gender
- Pregnancy
- Religion or creed
- Political affiliation
- Marital status
- Citizenship
- Disability or medical condition
- Age
- Sexual orientation
- Gender identity
- Language abilities

Most of the time the reason can be as simple as a corporate "clique" that gives preferential treatment to one set of employees at the expense of others. To avoid legal action against the employer, management is *very* careful to make sure this type of discrimination is *silent* in form. African Americans have experienced this type of discrimination forever, it seems. And for certain (though it has lessened somewhat), it continues to this day. Called "silent racism," it has consistently hurt blacks, but they often have a difficult time proving it.

Then there are the other ways worker get hurt via:

- Downsizing

- Corporate restructuring

- Replacement by lower-wage workers

All this is met with the usual retort to the harmed employee that "life is not fair."

Of course, there are antidiscrimination and labor-rights laws in place to give some small measure of protection. However, let's be real: a single employee going up against a well-funded, well-organized corporate machine has the odds stacked against him or her in so many ways. First of all, *the burden is on the employee to prove the employer was wrong.* Then, the employer often has the distinct advantage, in money, time, legal counsel, and experience, to successfully fend off an individual worker or even a group of workers.

Scores of people in all kinds of US industries are getting laid off and can't afford their mortgage payments—a factor in the housing-industry collapse. The banking industry also collapses because the mortgages are financed through the banks, which have taken too much risk. The problem compounds.

Furthermore, concurrent failures in trade policy, easily noted in our import/export relationship with China, are disturbing. Chinese suppliers, though experiencing a lull at the moment, have been booming for decades, while American suppliers struggle. Manipulation of currency, unequal labor practices, and unfair trade policy put the United States at a distinct disadvantage. Trade imbalances of nearly $30 billion per month have ominous implications. Consistent total US trade deficits of over $40 billion a month are an additional very dire sign.

Adam Smith, widely considered the father of modern economics, proposed the idea of comparative advantage in his book *The Wealth of Nations*, and it was developed into the law of comparative advantage in the 1817 book *On Principles of Political Economy and Taxation* by David Ricardo.[45] The law of comparative advantage explains why it is profitable for two parties to trade, even if one of the trading partners is more efficient in every type of economic production. This principle supports the economic case for free trade—although, in the case of China, it must be fair trade and without currency manipulation.

Pure capitalism without a plainly *fair* trade relationship is a disaster. It has a profoundly negative effect on the balance of trade. The more goods and services that are imported means less that are purchased from local manufacturers. In turn meaning that fewer goods are produced in the local economy, therefore fewer jobs are needed.

Couple this with our highest in the world corporate tax rate of over 35% and you see a real drag on business and a systemic problem for the US economy and maintaining our standard of living.

So, key elements to keeping an economy vibrant and growing are free and fair trade and keeping corporate tax rates in check.

It's becoming obvious to both sides of the isle that cutting corporate taxation to reasonable levels would no doubt contribute greatly to helping our overall noncompetitive situation. So let's do it—but *only* if accompanied by those dollars being rightly shared with new employee owners.

As we have asserted, capitalism *does* work to produce economic growth. The data supporting capitalism's successes are impressive. The world's GDP per capita shows exponential growth since the beginning of the industrial revolution. **The real question then is: Is capitalism being *applied* in a modern format designed to facilitate the greatest good?**

Many theorists and policymakers in predominantly capitalist nations have emphasized capitalism's ability to promote economic growth, as measured by gross domestic product (GDP), productive capacity, or standard of living.[46] This argument was central, for example, to Adam Smith's advocacy of letting a free market control production and price and allocate resources.

From the years 1000–1820, the world economy grew sixfold, 50 percent per person. After capitalism started to spread more widely, in the years 1820–1998, the world economy grew fiftyfold (i.e., ninefold per person).[47] In most capitalist economic regions, such as Europe, the United States, Canada, Australia, and New Zealand, the economy grew by nineteen times per person, even though these countries already had a higher starting level.

Proponents of capitalism argue that increasing GDP per capita is empirically shown to bring about improved standards of living, such as better availability of food, housing, clothing, and health care.

Proponents also believe a capitalist economy offers far more opportunities for individuals to raise their income through new professions or business ventures than other economic forms offer. To their thinking, this potential is much greater than in either traditional feudal or tribal societies or socialist societies.

To be clear, our argument is not with capitalism as an economic system. Our serious concern is its application in a modern world where economic equity is long overdue and essential if we are to progress as a society.

Again, the best way to move this process forward, we contend, is to look to the inordinately high level of corporate taxation and the morass of loopholes designed to manipulate and ameliorate such damaging high levels of taxation. Clearly this needs to be reformed. Reform it yes, but *only* if accompanied by those dollars being rightly shared with new employee owners.

Socialism Is Fair In Theory, But Does Not Work [go too far, and go off a cliff]

> *Socialism values equality more than liberty.*
> —Dennis Prager, American syndicated radio talk show host, syndicated columnist[48]

This is an easy one. Examples abound where countries have gone over the deep end via evolution or revolution to a form of government that at first seemed fair and that would offer the greatest good to the greatest number. Eventually, reality set in!

Political systems lacking economic democracy that have tried to fix inequality have not worked. Despite its different shades of gray, the basic idea we are talking about is at its core virtually the same. Whether it's called Marxism, socialism, communism, statism, liberalism, black liberation theology, fascism, radical theocracy, monarchism, or dictatorship, it consists of centralization and concentration of power in the state and at the expense of the individual and individual liberty.

First let's understand in its *fullest* form what we are dealing with here. A communist state is one with a form of government characterized by single-party rule or dominant-party rule by a communist party and a professed allegiance to a Marxist-Leninist ideology as the guiding principle. Before, this meant public ownership of all or most means of production by the communist party-run state to further the interests of the working class. Today, a communist state, as in China and Vietnam, for instance, can exist alongside a mixed economy. According to Marxist-Leninists, the state is a tool in the hands of the ruling class, which in a socialist society is the working class; so a socialist state is, according to Leninists, a state of the working class.[49]

In practice, communist states do not refer to themselves as communist states because they do not consider themselves currently a communist society. Instead, they constitutionally identify themselves as socialist states or workers' states. The primary goal of these states, which also explains their official name, is to guide their respective countries in the process of building socialism, ultimately leading to communism.

The following convincing list of current and former communist/socialist states should make it clear to anyone that the underlying ideology is a truly failed concept:

Cuba

As of 2002, some 1.2 million persons of Cuban background (about 10 percent of the current population of Cuba) reside in the United States. Many of them left the "Socialist Paradise" island in utter desperation for the United States, often by sea in small boats and fragile rafts. They would do virtually anything to get out!

Dictator and "maximum leader" Fidel Castro and his communist/socialist ideology have been a shining example of its utter failure. Even his sister, Juanita Castro, and his two daughters, Alina and Pupo Castro, have fled this socialist experiment.

THE 3RD WAY

Castro's rule was severely tested in the aftermath of the Soviet collapse (known in Cuba as the Special Period), with such effects as food shortages.[50]

The Cuban government has been accused of numerous human rights abuses, including torture, arbitrary imprisonment, unfair trials, and extrajudicial executions. The Human Rights Watch organization alleges the government represses nearly all forms of political dissent and that Cubans are systematically denied basic rights to free expression, association, assembly, privacy, movement, and due process of law.[51]

Cuba had the second-highest number of imprisoned journalists of any nation in 2008 (the People's Republic of China had the highest). As a result of ownership restrictions, computer ownership rates in Cuba are among the worlds lowest. The right to use the Internet is granted only to select locations, and they may be monitored. Connecting to the Internet illegally can lead to a five-year prison sentence.

The Cuban state adheres to socialist principles. Most of the means of production are owned and run by the government, and most of the labor force is employed by the state. Currently, some individual production and trading are allowed, along with some foreign investment.

For some time, Cuba has been experiencing a housing shortage because of the state's failure to keep pace with increasing demand. The government instituted food-rationing policies in 1962, which were exacerbated after the collapse of the Soviet Union and the tightening of the US embargo. Cuba now imports up to 80 percent of food used for rations.

Former Soviet Union

The Soviet Union was a single-party state ruled by the Communist Party from its foundation until 1990. The Soviet state was structured under a highly centralized government and economy.

The Soviet Union and its Eastern European satellite states, known as the Eastern Bloc, engaged in the Cold War, a prolonged global ideological and political struggle against the United States and its Western allies, which it ultimately abandoned in the face of economic troubles and both domestic and foreign political unrest. In the late 1980s, the last Soviet leader, Mikhail Gorbachev, tried to reform the state with his policies of *perestroika and glasnost*, but the Soviet Union collapsed and was formally dissolved in December 1991.

From its creation, the Soviet Union's government was based on the one-party rule of the Communist Party (Bolsheviks). The stated purpose of the one-party state was to ensure that capitalist exploitation would not return to the Soviet Union and that the principles of democratic centralism would be most effective in representing the people's will in a practical manner.

On April 3, 1922, Stalin was named general secretary of the Communist Party of the Soviet Union. Lenin had appointed Stalin the head of the Workers' and Peasants' Inspectorate, which gave Stalin considerable power.

In 1928, Stalin introduced the First Five-Year Plan for building a socialist economy. While encompassing the internationalism expressed by Lenin throughout the revolution, it also aimed to build socialism. In industry, the state assumed control over all existing enterprises and undertook an intensive program of industrialization. In agriculture, rather than adhering to the "lead by example" policy advocated by Lenin, forced collectivization of farms was implemented all over the country.

Famines ensued, causing millions of deaths; surviving kulaks (independent farmers) were persecuted, and many sent to gulags to do forced labor. Social upheaval continued in the mid-1930s. Stalin's Great Purge resulted in the execution or detainment of many "Old

Bolsheviks" who had participated in the October Revolution with Lenin. According to declassified Soviet archives, in 1937 and 1938, the NKVD (the Soviet police agency) arrested more than one and a half million people, and 681,692 were shot—an average of 1,000 executions a day. The deaths during the 1930s as a whole were estimated to be in the range of 10 million to 11 million.

Eventually, the socially devastated and economically bankrupt and failed former Soviet Union was officially dissolved on December 26, 1991.[52]

China

The People's Republic of China is still a single-party state governed by the Communist Party of China.

The Chinese, social activists, and some members of the Communist Party of China have all identified the need for social and political reform. While economic and social controls have been greatly relaxed in China since the 1970s, political freedom is still tightly restricted.

Censorship of political speech and information, most notably on the Internet, is openly and routinely used in China to silence criticism of the government and the ruling Communist Party. In 2005, Reporters Without Borders ranked China as 159th out of 167 states in its annual World Press Freedom Index, indicating a very low level of perceived press freedom. The government has suppressed demonstrations by organizations that it considers a potential threat to "social stability," as was the case with the Tiananmen Square protests of 1989.

A number of foreign governments and NGOs routinely criticize China, alleging widespread civil rights violations, including systematic use of lengthy detention without trial; forced confessions; torture; mistreatment of prisoners; and restrictions of freedom of speech, assembly, association, religion, the press, and labor. China executes more people than any other country, accounting for 72 percent of the world's total executions in 2009.⁵³

Since the introduction of market-based economic reforms in 1978, China has become the world's fastest-growing major economy. As of 2012, it is the world's second-largest economy after the United States, by both nominal GDP and purchasing power parity (PPP), and it is also the world's largest exporter and second-largest importer of goods.

As the social, cultural, and political consequences of economic growth and reform become increasingly manifest, tensions between conservatives and reformists in the Communist Party are sharpening. Zhou Tianyong, the vice director of research of the Central Party School, argues that gradual political reform as well as repression of those pushing for overly rapid change over the next thirty years will be essential if China is to avoid an overly turbulent transition to a democratic, middle-class society.

As for China and whatever label you want to currently put on its political system, the government is neither purely communist nor capitalist. Rather, it is a form of oligarchy with a relatively small group at the top calling most of the shots. As we all saw in the Tiananmen Square protests and subsequent massacre of 1989, and despite what we might see currently on the surface, real unrest is bubbling below. Their moment of reckoning will inevitably come.

North Korea

North Korea refused to participate in a 1948 United Nations–supervised election held in the south, which led to the creation of separate Korean governments for the two occupation zones. North and South Korea each claimed sovereignty over the whole Korean peninsula, which led to the Korean War of 1950. The Armistice Agreement of 1953 ended the fighting, but the two countries are officially still at war against each other—a peace treaty was never signed.

North Korea is a single-party state under a united front led by the Korean Workers' Party (KWP). After the collapse of the Soviet Union and a series of natural disasters, a famine occurred, causing the death of between 900,000 and 2 million people.

Many outside organizations describe North Korea as a totalitarian, Stalinist dictatorship with an elaborate cult of personality around the Kim family and one of the lowest-ranking human rights records of any country. The North Korean government denies this.[54]

In the 1990s North Korea faced significant economic disruptions, including a series of natural disasters, economic mismanagement, and serious resource shortages after the collapse of the Eastern Bloc. These resulted in a shortfall of staple grain output of more than one million tons below what the country needed to meet internationally accepted minimum dietary requirements. The North Korean famine, known as "Arduous March," resulted in the deaths of between 300,000 and 800,000 North Koreans per year during the three-year famine, which peaked in 1997. The deaths were most likely caused by famine-related illnesses such as pneumonia, tuberculosis, diarrhea, and starvation.[55]

If a picture is worth a thousand words, the one below of the entire Korean peninsula unmistakably illustrates the difference (in productivity) between capitalist South Korea and communist/socialist North Korea. The communist North is still literally in the "Dark Ages," lacking any semblance of a modern, prosperous society, while the capitalist South has been booming since the end of the Korean War.

It has been approximately sixty years since the Korean War (June 25, 1950–July 27, 1953) and the official separation of the two nations. What a difference!

WHAT'S AT STAKE?

The overt socialism of the previous four nations provides obvious examples of utterly failed systems. Yet, the subtle, creeping socialism of Europe and the increasing role of government in the United States and other countries are potentially as pernicious over time.

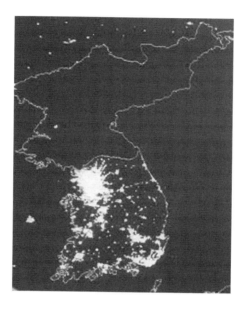

Figure 12. "North Korea by Night" (Public domain photograph from US Department of Defense)

Suppression of GDP and the aspirational dreams of individual citizens is the rule in those countries, while the victims lay wasted, drugged in the pabulum of empty promises and slogans. Brainwashed often by soaring but empty rhetoric, in the end they are left with nothing. Even in China, whose economy is booming, inequality is at record proportions. Creeping but ever-increasing power and assumption of wealth by the state is not part of the solution; it is indeed part of the problem—a big part.

THE 3RD WAY

The Pilgrims

Americans, especially politicians, educators, and the media, ignore the ultimate failure of such forms of government tyranny described above, and there's no better example of this attitude than regarding our nation's first experiment with socialism.[56]

The history you're about to read has been largely ignored, probably purposely, by the vast majority of our "government-run" educational institutions, which have a bias toward furthering their vision of a society of, by, and for the government.

Figure 13. "Puritans Going to Church," 1885 image by artist George Henry Boughton (Source: Library of Congress)

In 1620, a group of English Puritans left Great Britain and sailed across the Atlantic on the *Mayflower*. Not only were they breaking away from what they considered religious persecution, but they were leaving the Old World, which had been, in their viewpoint, materialistic, selfish, greedy, and unprincipled.

Their vision for the New World was to build a society constructed on a new foundation of communal sharing and social altruism. Their aim was based on communism, under which there would be no private property and all would work, and the harvest thereof would be shared in common.

The outcome of this experiment with "commune-ism" is documented in the diary of William Bradford, the governor and head of the colony. The results of this first "collective" were disastrous and led to famine and starvation, both physically and spiritually.

There is an ancient proverb that says: "Those who do not learn from history are doomed to repeat it."[57]

Karl Marx (1818–1883) was a contemporary and admirer of Charles Darwin (1809–1882). He even wanted to dedicate his first book, Das Kapital, Vol. 1 (1867), to Darwin, for in Darwin's book On the Origin of Species (1859), Marx believed he had found the natural science basis for his economic theories.

What most people do not remember, because it has been omitted from most American history textbooks, is that Christians in America had experimented with Marxism 250 years earlier and had proven it to not work! In 1620, the Pilgrims tried communism and after only one year, abandoned it as totally unworkable.

In 1609 the Pilgrims had fled the restrictive environment of the Church of England and moved to Holland to freely practice their religious convictions. On August 1, 1620, forty of them set sail on the *Mayflower* with sixty-two others souls, under the leadership of William Bradford. Before setting up the community of Plymouth, Massachusetts, they composed one of the great documents in human history, the Mayflower Compact. It guaranteed just and equal laws to govern all residents of the community, regardless of their religious convictions. The concepts contained in the compact were all based on biblical reasoning.

The Pilgrims received the funding to go to the New World from London merchants who wanted an economic profit from the venture. Under their contract with those merchants, whatever they produced was to be put into a common warehouse, with each one getting one equal share. All the land, buildings, and end products were communally owned.

Half of the Pilgrims died during the first winter, including Bradford's wife. As governor, Bradford realized that collectivism had been a costly and destructive mistake. He and others realized that socialism gave no incentive to the most creative and industrious among them to work any harder than anyone else. Collectivism had prevented the exercise of personal motivation.

Bradford wrote about the experience:
> The experience that was had in this common course and condition, tired sundry years…that by taking away property, and bringing community into a common wealth, would make them happy and flourishing—as if they were wiser than God…For this community [so far it was] was found to breed much confusion and discontent, and retard much employment that would have been to their benefit and comfort. For young men that were most able and fit for labor and service did repine that they should spend their time and strength to work for others men's wives and children without recompense…that was thought injustice.

The Pilgrims tried collectivism, socialism, and communism and found that it produced sloth and laziness and destroyed incentive. What did they do about it?

They trashed part of their contract with the London merchants, learned from the local Indians how to produce better crops and harvest more fish, assigned private property rights of land to all members, and gave members the right to profit from their industry. What happened next?

Bradford wrote about this institution of Christian capitalism:
> This had very good success for it made all hands industrious, so as much more corn was planted than otherwise would have been.

Their excess product caused them to originate the celebration we now know as Thanksgiving—not to thank the Indians for saving them, but to thank God for giving them a better way. They did want to share with the Indians out of their bounty to express their appreciation for their help, but their celebration was to thank God.

Figure 14. "The First Thanksgiving," Jean Leon Gerome Ferris, 1912 (Source: Library of Congress, public domain)

The Pilgrims paid off their London sponsors. Their success initiated the "Great Puritan Migration," which fostered the rapid colonization of America.

Inspired by the Pilgrims' success, Thomas Hooker would found the first and greatest constitutional colony, in Connecticut. Massachusetts also adopted its Body of Liberties, which included ninety-eight protections to individual rights, including no taxation without representation, due process of law, trial by a jury of peers, and prohibitions against cruel and unusual punishment.

This is the true story of Thanksgiving, and the lessons it teaches need to be learned by us all.

In theory, socialism is the absolute, perfect economic system. The problem is, in practice socialism completely falls apart, largely due to the lack of individual motivation. Why become a doctor when you can be a janitor and earn the same wage? Capitalism gives you a direct correlation between competence/effort and success. Note that every attempt at socialism has been an enormous failure. We need a system based on economic democracy as the solution to widespread inequality.

MLK Jr.
[what history has taught us]

Capitalism knows only one color: that color is green; all else is necessarily subservient to it, hence, race, gender and ethnicity cannot be considered within it.
—Thomas Sowell, American economist, social theorist, political philosopher, and author[58]

Dr. Martin Luther King Jr. triggered landmark *political* freedom for an entire race of people. Thank heaven for his great work. Nevertheless, it would be presumptuous to claim those same people, despite literally trillions poured into redistribution programs, have achieved even close to a satisfactory level of *economic* freedom during the same time frame. What is remarkable is that their well-grounded level of frustration is now clearly being matched by the rest of us! The real question is, how do we combine economic and political freedom?

History has taught us that people have struggled through centuries, first for political freedom and then for economic freedom.

WHAT'S AT STAKE?

India's independence was achieved when the people who fought for it used an approach of noncooperation with the ruling government. The mighty British Empire had to relinquish power to the poor because the determined people of India, under the great leadership of the Mahatma Gandhi, would accept the status quo no longer.

African Americans united under Dr. King's leadership to fight for basic civil rights in the 1960s. But civil rights did not guarantee economic freedom. Today, teenagers from minority communities have a very high rate of unemployment. In some cities, these rates of unemployment are beyond 50 percent. This is a powerful recipe for unrest and disaster on many levels!

> *The minimum wage is the black teenage unemployment act... the guaranteed way of holding the poor, the minorities and the disenfranchised out of the mainstream is if you price their original services too high.*
> —Arthur Laffer, American economist,
> member of Reagan's Economic Policy Advisory Board[59]

Let us be clear. We are not against the minimum wage, but we need to focus not *just* on wages; we need to also provide incentives for equity and ownership by labor. The never-ending fight for increasing minimum wage continues even today. There has to be a better way. That way can be through *equity rather than just wages*. Let these young people gain the vitally important sense of *ownership* in something!

Make no mistake: if the levels of smoldering discontent we are currently seeing are not dealt with effectively, we will indeed see upheaval and possibly severe economic dislocation and unrest in the streets at some point. The central purpose of this book is its call for a truly new, substantive solution leading to a gentle evolution toward a just and effective society, rather than one devolving into violent revolution.

There is a clear quest for economic power. Nevertheless, it must be delivered in a new way. Capitalism has been proven to work, but is not fair in its delivery. Similarly, socialism, while claiming to be fair, has proven to not work, over time and in so many different countries and societies. Clearly a new bipartisan way—*THE 3rd WAY*—is the ultimate way forward instead of a one-party doctrinaire approach.

That way is economic empowerment implemented through one's place of employment and *not* through government redistribution.

Economic Versus Political Freedom
[African Americans got a political first step and the economic shaft]

Civil government, insofar as it is instituted for the security of property, is in reality instituted for the defense of the rich against the poor, and for the defense of those who have property against those who have none.
—Adam Smith, Scottish philosopher
and pioneer of political economy
(from The Wealth of Nations, 1776)

High unemployment and its concomitant unrest in this country and indeed worldwide is becoming a serious chronic problem. And while the unemployment rate for adults remains far too high, the rate for teens is even more troubling. The white teen unemployment rate is dreadfully high at over 20 percent. However, the black teen unemployment is shocking at consistently over 40 percent. The massive social problems as a result of this chronic situation are expensive in both dollars and lives wasted and lost.

In the political arena, the lessons of history have shown us a way forward. We also need an equally enduring, parallel *economic* solution.

WHAT'S AT STAKE?

All of civilization has the grand tradition of Athenian democracy to thank for blazing a historic path of individual liberty that the rest of humankind would inexorably follow. The Athenians changed the world forever! Athens had one of the first known democracies, developed in the Greek city-state of Athens around 550 BC. Other Greek cities set up democracies, and even though most followed an Athenian model, none were as powerful, stable, or well-documented as that of Athens.[60]

For our purposes, it is important to understand where in history a key element of personal liberty was born. Perhaps we can find there an economic parallel to this incredibly powerful movement. It was initiated in a relatively small corner of the globe and grew exponentially. It blossomed because political democracy is a damn good idea. So, too, is the emerging idea of *economic* democracy!

Now we hope to catalyze the *next* major development in human history. For while the ancient Greeks blazed an enormously important path in the area of political freedom, we know humankind has not yet fully implemented a parallel system able to bring forth the massive economic freedom and empowerment one would hope for.

The great ancient Greek historian and Athenian general Thucydides made, for our book, a very prophetic statement: "We do not say that a man who takes no interest in politics is a man who minds his own business; we say that he has no business here at all." We might infer that if one has no interest in politics, one has no validity as a citizen. We take it one step further and proclaim that if one has no business, no economic ownership, one has no real power.

One of the greatest examples of the dichotomy between political and economic freedom is in the African American community. Certainly real progress has been made. However, we believe (and an overwhelming majority would agree) that the economic progress has not been nearly enough, and in many cases their situation of late is getting worse.

The Civil Rights Act of 1964 was a landmark piece of legislation in the United States that outlawed major forms of discrimination against both African Americans and women, including racial segregation. It ended unequal application of voter registration requirements and racial segregation in schools, at the workplace, and by facilities that served the general public ("public accommodations").[61]

Powers given to enforce the act were initially weak but were supplemented in later years. Congress asserted its authority to legislate under several different parts of the US Constitution, principally its power to regulate interstate commerce under Article I, Section 8; its duty to guarantee all citizens equal protection of the laws under the Fourteenth Amendment; and its duty to protect voting rights under the Fifteenth Amendment.

The Civil Rights Act was signed into law by President Lyndon B. Johnson, who would later sign the landmark Voting Rights Act into law. Through these landmark pieces of legislation, African Americans were given a *political ladder* to attain a good measure of political power. However, most unfortunately, there was no parallel piece of legislation that offered the same *economic ladder* to bring the majority of them and the rest of us in the working class up to a standard of prosperity that all should be able to enjoy.

An Explosion Of Political Empowerment
[the time has come for worldwide economic empowerment]

> *Democracy and socialism have nothing in common but one word, equality. But notice the difference: while democracy seeks equality in liberty, socialism seeks equality in restraint and servitude.*
> —Alexis de Tocqueville,
> French political thinker and historian[62]

In the twenty years or more in which I have been developing a theory of democracy as the only perfectly just form of government, I slowly came to realize that political democracy cannot flourish under all economic conditions. Democracy requires an economic system which supports the political ideals of liberty and equality for all. Men cannot exercise freedom in the political sphere when they are deprived of it in the economic sphere.
—Mortimer J. Adler, American philosopher, educator, and author[63]

In the graph below, we can clearly see over the last two centuries an unprecedented explosion of political empowerment to all of humanity, at least as demonstrated by the unmistakable spike in the number of nations embracing democracy over autocratic regimes. This relatively quiet revolution has reshaped the world we live in!

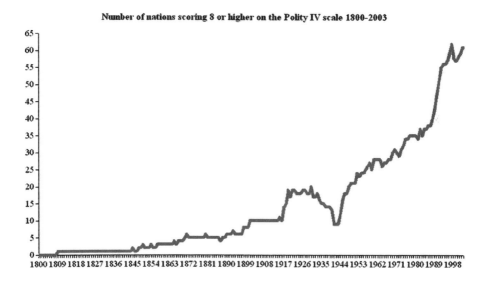

Figure 15. Number of nations scoring 8 or higher on the Polity IV scale 1800–2003 (Source: Polity IV Project, Center for Systemic Peace, August 28, 2006)

The next chart shows the latest visual by the Polity IV Project, which displays a complete insight into all three major current forms of government:

- **Democracy**.

- **Autocracy**, a system of government in which a supreme political power is concentrated in the hands of one person whose decisions are subject to neither external legal restraints nor regularized mechanisms of popular control.[64]

- **Anocracy**, a regime type where power is not vested in public institutions (as in a normal democracy) but spread among elite groups that are constantly competing with each other for power.[65] Examples of anocracies in Africa include the warlords of Somalia and the shared governments in Kenya and Zimbabwe. The Polity IV data set recognizes anocracy as a category, and it lies exactly in the middle between autocracies and democracies.

Clearly the unmistakable trend, demonstrated by the democratic line, is the explosion of political empowerment since the turn of the century. That trend is matched by the striking opposite trend, demonstrated by the autocratic line.

In an effort to paint a complete picture of world governance, anocracy has been added. Many both hope and feel the emergence of anocracy is a possible transitional stage from pure autocracy toward democracy, the most desired form of rule.

Remember, all these graphics depict the distinct trend toward *political* expansion of freedom and empowerment. Obviously the time is long overdue for the concomitant growth of *economic* empowerment, best embodied in the employee ownership/ESOP movement, to greatly expand.

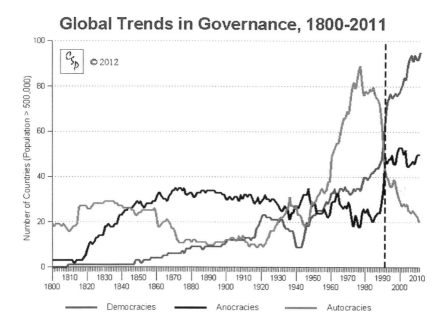

Figure 16. Polity IV Project: Global trends in governance, 1800-2011 (Source: Center for Systemic Peace Global Report, December 1, 2011)

The Polity IV Project continues the Polity research tradition of coding the authority characteristics of states in the world system for purposes of comparative, quantitative analysis. The Polity conceptual scheme is unique in that it examines *qualities* of democratic and autocratic authority in governing institutions. The Polity project has proven its value to researchers over the years, becoming the most widely used data resource for studying regime change and the effects of regime authority.

Democratization is the transition to a more democratic political regime. It may be the transition from an authoritarian regime to a full democracy, from an authoritarian political system to a semidemocracy, or from a semiauthoritarian political system to a democratic political system.[66]

The time has come for an equally important revolution. This time it must occur in the *economic* area. It can be done without pain. It must be done to keep both potentially serious unrest quelled and it represents a commonsense approach to true economic fairness.

As alluded to earlier, economic democracy is the liberating concept with the power to move the entire society forward. Economic democracy exists when the masses of people who work in businesses large and small gain a degree of justifiable ownership.

The residual benefits are the proven increases in productivity, as demonstrated by the data in the book *Shared Capitalism at Work*. This very important definitive analysis is based on the National Bureau of Economic Research (NBER) data set of over forty thousand employees in fourteen US companies with at least one type of shared capitalist program.

Shared Capitalism at Work: Employee Ownership, Profit and Gain Sharing, and Broad-Based Stock Options

By Douglas L. Kruse, Richard B. Freeman, and Joseph R. Blasi

The historical relationship between capital and labor has evolved in the past few decades. One particularly noteworthy development is the rise of shared capitalism, a system in which workers have become partial owners of their firms and thus, in effect, both employees and stockholders. Profit-sharing

> arrangements and gain-sharing bonuses, which tie compensation directly to a firm's performance, also reflect this new attitude toward labor.
>
> **Six "take-away" findings on shared capitalism**
>
> Shared capitalism is a significant part of the US economic model.
>
> Worker co-monitoring helps shared capitalist firms overcome any workers shirking.
>
> The risk of shared capitalist investments in one's employer is manageable.
>
> Shared capitalism improves the performance of firms.
>
> Shared capitalism improves worker well-being.
>
> Shared capitalism complements other labor policies and practices.
>
> This volume provides essential studies for understanding the increasingly important role of shared capitalism in the modern workplace.[67]

Ultimately, moving to the system advocated here in *THE 3rd WAY*, which greatly expands worldwide economic empowerment to the masses, is simply the right thing to do.

Political Democracy Alone Is Not A Panacea
[systems must be put in place to check popular avarice]

Pride, envy, avarice—these are the sparks that have set on fire the hearts of all men.
—Dante Alighieri, major Italian poet of the Middle Ages, called the "Father of the Italian language"[68]

An important word of caution here! It's critical that democratization have a transcendent system that will avoid devolution into populist dependence voted for by a majority of a nation's electorate. *THE 3ʳᵈ WAY* changes the fundamental way people view their interactions with both their government and place of employment. Because once people realize they have the power to vote themselves massive benefits that can't be supported in the long term, potential calamity is at hand.

There is no more perfect example than Greece. The nation of Greece, the *birthplace* of democracy, is effectively bankrupt. Widespread corruption, coupled with an unsustainable socialist system, has finally pushed the nation over the brink. No one forced these unwise measures on Greece. Its citizens did it to themselves!

Greece is the ideal example of where the role of government got very bloated while at the same time, the concept of broadened ownership of the means of production never occurred. So Greece is faced with two bad alternatives: increasing the size of government or eliminating social support that people have come to depend on. What we are proposing is broad-based ownership of businesses that leads to less dependence on government.

Greece is now begging for a bailout from the European Union (EU). Here's everything you need to know about what's wrong with Greece's bailout agreement: the government is using $571 million from its latest bailout payment to repay a group of foreign bondholders; thus the proverbial "borrowing from Peter to pay Paul."[69]

This is being done by the government of a nation that is bankrupt, has a 21 percent unemployment rate, and saw its economy in the first quarter of 2012 shrink by an alarming 6.5%. Currently, Greece is coping with shortages of food and medicine, and its electrical grid is only running because of government intervention.

How did this happen? After fourteen consecutive years of economic growth, Greece went into recession in 2008.[70] An indication of the trend of overlending in recent years is the ratio of loans to savings, which exceeded 100 percent during the first half of the year. By the end of 2009, the Greek economy faced the highest budget deficit and ratios of government debt to GDP in the EU.[71] The 2009 budget deficit stood at 15.4 percent of GDP. This and rising debt levels (127 percent of GDP in 2009) led to rising borrowing costs, resulting in a severe economic crisis.

Table 1. Greece average GDP growth by era[72]

Greece	
Average GDP growth by era	
1961–1970	8.44%
1971–1980	4.70%
1981–1990	0.70%
1991–2000	2.36%
2001–2007	4.11%
2008–2011	–3.45%

Greece was accused of trying to cover up the extent of its massive budget deficit in the wake of the global financial crisis. Now it is faced with drastic austerity measures.

As a result of the ongoing economic crisis, industrial production in the country went down by 8 percent between March 2010 and March 2011. Between 2008 and 2012, unemployment skyrocketed, from a generational low of 7.2 percent in the second and third quarters of 2008 to a high of 23.1 percent in May 2012, leaving over a million jobless. Meanwhile, youth unemployment peaked at 54.9 percent in May 2012.

A recent OECD Wages report found that, in absolute figures, the average gross income in Greece fell from 20,457 Euros in 2010 to 15,729 Euros in 2011. That's equivalent to a real decline of 25.3 percent, taking into account a 3 percent rate of inflation.

Again, to a great extent, they did this to themselves.

Alexander Tytler (1747–1813), a Scottish-born English lawyer and historian, was critical of democracies. He claimed a pure democracy is always temporary in nature; it simply cannot exist as a permanent form of government. He said a democracy will continue to exist up until the time voters discover they can vote themselves generous gifts from the public treasury. From that moment on, the majority always vote for the candidates who promise the most benefits from the public treasury. The result is that every democracy will finally collapse due to loose fiscal policy, and that is always followed by dictatorship.[73]

The average age of the world's greatest civilizations from the beginning of history has been about two hundred years. During those two hundred years, these nations always progressed through the following sequence:

- From bondage to spiritual faith

- From spiritual faith to great courage

- From courage to liberty

- From liberty to abundance

- From abundance to complacency

- From complacency to apathy

- From apathy to dependence

- From dependence back to bondage

This is the heart of the Greek crisis. Why? The Greek debacle would never have happened if Greek citizens owned the means of production in their economy and had greater personal wealth, rather than having to depend on redistribution and welfare. Now they are at war with the European Union over this welfare system but have no greater movement toward economic democracy. Despite catastrophic hardships, they have learned nothing—how tragic.

Again, simply installing *political* empowerment via democracy alone without parallel broad-based *economic* empowerment is fruitless. Because many economists across the globe have not yet fully understood the underlying problems, they have completely failed to solve them. This is so because *they are operating on fundamentally old, outdated assumptions.* As another utterly brilliant quote from Louis Kelso explains, here's why:

Why I Invented the ESOP LBO
By Louis O. Kelso, Chairman, and Patricia Hetter Kelso,
Vice President,
Kelso & Company, San Francisco

"Several years of hard intellectual detective work led me to conclude that the problem lay with the *assumptions* underlying the concept of the free market. One of them was wrong. And the original error was sown by none other than the father of modern economics, Adam Smith, himself.

It was simply not true, as Smith had assumed and economists after him still assume, that *only* human labor produces goods and services, i.e., real wealth. Nor is the corollary true, that, therefore, labor jobs and labor employment are the only ways people can produce and earn income. In the real economic world there are in fact *two* ways in which people can make productive input. One is through labor. The other is through CAPITAL (land, structures, tools, machines and processes) the creatures of scientific and technological advance.

Nor was it true, as Smith also assumed, and a US national economic policy, the Employment Act of 1946 also assumes, that productive power was as democratically and effectively distributed *after* the Industrial Revolution as it had been in the preindustrial eons before technology harnessed the energy of Nature, although (and this is at the heart of the problem), *it was in that preindustrial era that our ideas about free market economics and our principles of democracy were formed.*

We had been running the economy on a myth (the "rising productivity of labor") to protect ourselves from the fact that technological progress really substituted capital input for labor input. Regardless of whether new jobs came into being to replace those destroyed, as capital input increased, labor's input, relative to capital's, declined. Under the property rule of the free market, each participant receives the value of his or her contribution. Therefore, working people's *legitimate* income share was proportionally shrinking, while capital owners' was increasing. Technological advance was causing the productiveness of capital to rise. But working people owned no nonresidential capital.

The problem was that, although the logic of a market economy had not changed, the facts of production had changed.[74]

Ultimately, what is advocated here in *THE 3rd WAY* is essential to help guide government, academia, business, and *most* importantly, the electorate toward a much wiser economic system that substantively benefits all immediately and for the long term.

Chapter 2:

WHAT NEEDS TO BE DONE?

The Best Ideas
[a bipartisan way forward]

Always aim at complete harmony of thought and word and deed. Always aim at purifying your thoughts and everything will be well.
—Mahatma Gandhi, preeminent leader of Indian nationalism; inspired movements for nonviolence, civil rights, and freedom across the world[75]

Anyone who has direct experience with the political process knows that in most cases for legislation to become law, it requires a measure of bipartisanship. The principles outlined here in *THE 3rd WAY* represent perhaps one of the best opportunities to take advantage of that reality. What we propose is the middle path between the welfare state and just cutting taxes—a massive expansion of ESOPs.

For legislation to become law, it has to go through a committee in both the House of Representatives and Senate. It then must be passed on the floor in each branch of Congress. Then it has to go through the reconciliation process, where members of each house work out any differences in the bill's language. It then goes back to each body again. If it passes both the House and Senate again in its final form, it is sent on to the president. Only then, if the president signs the legislation does it become law.

So you can see there are many opportunities for a piece of legislation to be blocked during each step. If a particular piece of legislation is blocked by one side or the other, the possibility of passage is remote. A small group of organized opposition can make it almost impossible for desired legislation to gain passage. Our nation's founders wisely wanted it this way so any impulsive or reckless legislation would be slowed down and potentially stopped to avoid dire mistakes becoming the law of the land.

Of course, the Supreme Court can also strike down a law or any part of it if it is determined to be unconstitutional. This is a final check and balance on the system.

What makes the possibility for the concepts put forth in this book to achieve passage is the fact that need to advance employee ownership has bipartisan support from seemingly very disparate ideologies. For example, Senator Bernie Sanders, a socialist from Vermont, and Congressman Dana Rohrabacher, a conservative Republican from California and President Ronald Reagan's former speechwriter, both support the employee ownership and ESOP ideas.

What is needed for any legislative action to move forward at a more rapid pace, however, is a groundswell from the populace. The people are the real force behind any action! We believe once the vast majority of citizens learn about the enormous advantages of employee ownership, they will call on (even demand) their elected officials to take up this vitally important issue and move it forward.

In a democracy, no one can stop the will of the people once they are informed, united, and vocal in their desires!

The Growth Code
[one half of the equation]

> *Are we interested in treating the symptoms of poverty and economic stagnation through income redistribution and class warfare, or do we want to go at the root causes of poverty and economic stagnation by promoting pro-growth policies that promote prosperity?*
> —Congressman Paul Ryan,
> Republican Party nominee for vice president of the
> United States in 2012[76]

Championed by the Free Congress Foundation is a proposal called "The Growth Code." Its President and CEO, Jim Gilmore, who served as governor of Virginia from 1998 to 2002, is the driving force behind it. The Growth Code is a great idea, yet we contend it has just *one-half of the equation*. Without this book's proposal to grant tax breaks to business *by sharing the wealth with employees* via ESOPs, the Growth Code's good idea will never gain the *massive popular support to make it happen*. That is what our book is all about.

Much of what the Free Congress Foundation proposes has real merit. The following lays out their proposals:

> Over the course of nearly a half-century following World War II, America built and enjoyed the most prosperous economy in the history of world. Rising incomes, low unemployment and steady long-term growth were hallmarks of this extraordinary period. On a personal level, we all felt that America was a land of limitless opportunity—where some talent, a solid idea and a lot of hard work would pay off with a good and maybe even great quality of life.

WHAT NEEDS TO BE DONE?

Over the last few years, however, something has changed. Today many Americans live paralyzed in fear of losing their jobs and not being able to make ends meet. Experts now tell us to expect high unemployment and a slow-growth economy for years to come. Worse still, Americans are not optimistic that things will get better; a recent Gallup poll found that only 54 percent of Americans believe that today's youth will have a better life than their parents—the lowest number since 1983. They are justified in this belief—projections from the Free Congress Foundation indicate that a family of four under the new economic reality will earn nearly $100,000 less over a period of 15 years than they could have expected to earn a few years ago. [Please see the chart below.]

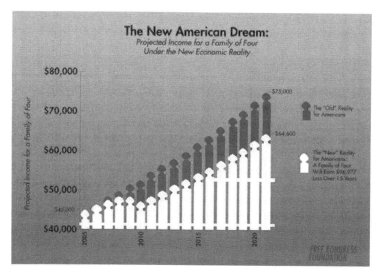

Clear and decisive pro-growth policies are the solution to our economic challenges—not new taxes or tax increases, not class warfare, not punishing the small businesses that serve as the economic backbone of our country, and not betraying promises made to America's seniors by changing Social Security or Medicare for those at or near retirement age. The Growth Code, at its core, argues that we do not need to accept a dim and stagnant economic future as our destiny. Our country can grow again and thrive again and revitalize the economic engine that was once the envy of the world and the thrust for the American dream.

The Growth Code

Made up of five steps, *The Growth Code* is simply, squarely and precisely focused on the tax code and restoring America to a sustainable economic growth trajectory:[77]

- A simple unified 15 percent rate on all business income, regardless of the type of entity;
- Tax rates of 10 percent, 15 percent, and 25 percent on individual income as currently defined under the IRC;
- Immediate expensing of capital equipment;
- Elimination of the abhorrent practice of double taxation;
- Any household living in poverty will receive a family tax credit of $4,300.

What will these steps mean to people, businesses and the economy? Under *The Growth Code*:

- Small businesses will no longer be taxed as individuals. Instead they will be taxed as entities and pay no more than 15 percent on their revenue in taxes. All businesses will pay the same rate.
- Tax brackets will be lowered and dramatically simplified for individuals across the board, including the middle class.

WHAT NEEDS TO BE DONE?

- Profits made abroad will no longer be taxed when brought home for reinvestment. This will bring an explosion of capital investment in America.
- Taxes on dividends, distributions and capital gains will be eliminated.
- Every American will pay taxes. Americans living in poverty will pay less.
- The mortgage deduction and charitable giving deduction will be protected.
- American companies will finally be able to compete on a level playing field against our biggest competitors, such as Japan, China and the largest economies in Europe.

Independent economic modeling studies by former Treasury Department officials have projected that enactment of *The Growth Code* will lead to:

- A dramatic drop in the unemployment rate from 9.1 percent to 4.7 percent;
- A 14.5 percent increase in GDP;
- A 14.8 percent increase in federal tax receipts;
- A 35.3 percent boost in capital investment.

Americans have always looked at our country as the "city upon a hill" from the time of the Puritans to John F. Kennedy to Ronald Reagan. *The Growth Code* is our way back to economic prosperity so we can all again see a brighter future where the American Dream is secure and thriving.[78]

The Growth Code is reasonable, but requires some expansion. Everyone with genuine good intentions for our nation and society is both seeking and proposing ideas to grow our economy.

Prosperity is the salve that cures many wounds! We like the idea many have put forward of unburdening business from the onerous taxation (the highest in the world right now) that chokes growth.

However, without businesses reengineered to *share the wealth* with their employees, this good idea will never gain the overwhelming support needed to make the complete concept a reality. Read on and continue to discover the *other half* of the equation missing—ESOPs and employee empowerment.

How Much Is Too Much?
[there's a sweet spot to government spending]

A wise and frugal Government, which shall restrain men from injuring one another, which shall leave them otherwise free to regulate their own pursuits of industry and improvement, and shall not take from the mouth of labor the bread it has earned. This is the sum of good government, and this is necessary to close the circle of our felicities.
—Thomas Jefferson, US founding father,
principal author of the Declaration of Independence,
and third president of the United States[79]

Here's the big payoff. We could replace a great deal of our social spending and bring the national deficits down if we moved toward a system based on economic democracy. The key is a diffusion of money and power by greatly expanding the employee ownership movement. Masses of people could be taken off government relief rolls *if* they had the essential capital and income-producing assets that ownership brings.

First, let's be clear: a social safety net is absolutely a real need as a concept of basic fairness in our society. Yet, a sound example of where a prudent level of government spending *should* be was pioneered by former House Majority Leader Dick Armey, called the "Armey-Curve." Below is an excerpt. We believe it deserves consideration.

Get Society Rich Quick: The Ideal Level of Government Spending

From: http://thinkbynumbers.org/economics/gdp/ideal-level-of-government[80]

It is commonly claimed that government spending is good for the economy, but the statistics show the opposite. Most recent studies find a negative correlation between total government size and economic growth. Why is economic growth important? Because wealthier societies are generally happier societies.

No matter how good things get for us, we always want more. Human beings want better:

- food
- housing
- entertainment
- transportation
- health services

A certain level of government spending is necessary to maintain an economy that can provide and improve these things. A well-functioning economy requires government to:

- enforce contracts
- protect a country from foreign invaders
- keep people from stealing from each other
- keep people from hurting each other

Government expenditure on these functions increases a country's productivity. [The "Armey-Curve" postulates there is indeed an optimal level of government spending and when it is exceeded, the growth and prosperity of a nation consistently plummet as government spending continues to rise.]

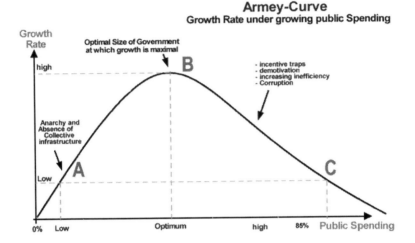

Graph Source: http://theuklibertarian.com/2010/07/12/paul-mckeever-on-why-libertarians-love-economic-arguments/

However, when government spending exceeds these mandates, it takes the country's human and material resource allocation decision-making power away from the massive collection of individual intelligences. This is a bad idea because individuals are just better at deciding how [to allocate] resources to satisfy their own desires since:

- They cumulatively have access to infinitely more detailed and specific information than any small group of politicians and bureaucrats do.
- Satisfying as many desires as possible (by maximizing productivity) is their sole incentive.

WHAT NEEDS TO BE DONE?

Politicians, on the other hand, do not allocate resources as productively (satisfy fewer human desires) because they:

- Only have access to general demographic data
- Are primarily incentivized to obtain campaign contributions to get reelected

The ability to obtain campaign contributions is primarily dependent on the candidate's ability to divert the nation's resources to corporations and special interest groups. Hence, resources are not specifically allocated to maximize their productivity, but are allocated in the pursuit of political goals.

This graph presents data on the relationship between size of government and economic growth for the twenty-three long-standing members of the Organization for Economic Cooperation and Development.

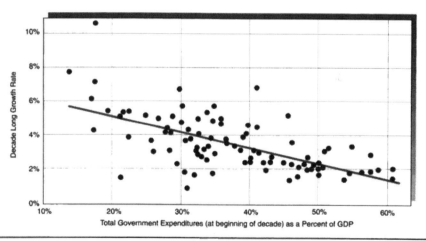

Sources: OECD, OECD Economic Outlook (various issues); and World Bank, World Development Indicators, CD-ROM, 2001.

Graph source: http://www.oecd.org/eco/economicoutlook.htm

The data show that a 10 percent increase in government expenditures as a share of GDP reduces the annual rate of growth by about 1 percent. The data also imply that the size of government in these countries is beyond the range that maximizes economic growth.

The graph contains four dots (observations) for each of the twenty-three countries (one for each of the four decades during the period 1960–1999). Each dot represents a country's total government spending as a share of GDP at the beginning of the decade and its accompanying growth of real GDP during that decade. As the plotted line in the exhibit shows, there is a clearly observable negative relationship between size of governments and long-term real GDP growth. Countries with higher levels of government spending grew less rapidly. The line drawn through the points suggests that a 10-percentage-point increase in government expenditures as a share of GDP leads to approximately a 1-percentage-point reduction in economic gro*wth*.

Source: http://www.oecd.org/eco/economicoutlook.htm

WHAT NEEDS TO BE DONE?

What the chart above shows is that governments with the highest government spending consistently had significantly lower growth rates.

In the next figure, the Rahn Curve chart shows that growth is maximized by governments that focus on core "public goods," such as the rule of law and protection of property rights. But when governments expand beyond a certain growth-maximizing level (the research says about 20 percent of GDP), the result is slower growth and less prosperity.

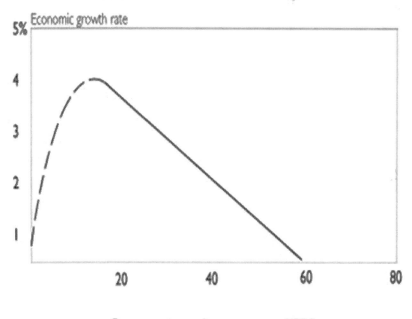

Figure 17. The Rahn Curve (Source: Tim Worstall, Adam Smith Institute, July 16, 2011)

The Rahn Curve is based on an economic theory developed by Richard Rahn, a senior fellow of the Libertarian-oriented Cato Institute, which proposes there is a level of government spending that maximizes economic growth.[81] The theory is used by classical liberals to argue for a decrease in overall government spending and taxation. The curve suggests the optimal level of government spending is 15–25 percent of GDP.

To continue to drain resources from the private sector in favor of some type of government stimulus and/or redistribution makes about as much common sense as bloodletting, which was an ancient concept advocating the withdrawal of quantities of blood from a patient to cure or prevent illness and disease. The theory was that if a person was weak and sick, removing some of his or her essential life-force would put him or her on the road to recovery. Today it is universally abhorred as a legitimate practice.

Though provocative, bloodletting is an interesting analogy for the kind of unwise government spending we are seeing today. How similarly foolish to think we can fix a "sick" economy by draining more and more productive private wealth and putting it in the hands of governments and their bureaucrats, who in reality produce nothing.

The real answer is to empower *people*, not *governments*.

Not Just A New Deal—A Better Deal
[reinventing the great society]

The New Deal is plainly an attempt to achieve a working socialism and avert a social collapse in America.
—H. G. Wells, English author in many genres, including science fiction, contemporary novels, history, politics, and social commentary[82]

WHAT NEEDS TO BE DONE?

WIIFM—Everyone's Favorite Radio Station: What's In It For Me? WIIFM for the Employee?

We have a plan for a better way of life for you, for your family, and ultimately for all America.[83] This is a plan to provide you and your family with a *second* income—not from wages earned by labor but from dividends earned by stock. You would *own* stock, in the same way you might own a farm or a rental-income property. The income from it would belong to you, and no one could take it away from you—ever. And after your death, it could be passed along tax-free to your spouse or your children or whomever else you so willed.

It would be a *livable* income, enough to reasonably provide for you and your family whether or not you were able to hang onto a wage-paying job.

In fact, on a smaller scale, it would be the same kind of "income from a capital estate" that has supported almost every well-to-do family in America and such recent families as the Roosevelts, Kennedys, and Bushes. If it's right and proper for our first families, it's right and proper for *you.*

The second income plan helps families at all income levels—starting at the bottom. If you're the head of a low-income family (say one of the millions of American households that's struggling along on less than $15,000 a year), here is how the plan would work for you:

1. Over a five-year period, you would be enabled via your employer to acquire about $100,000 worth of newly issued corporate stock in your employer, in chunks of about $20,000 a year, through a system of insured financing through which the stock would pay for itself with its own dividends in about seven years of your starting date.
2. After the stock had paid for itself, you would own it, free and clear, and you would be entitled to every dime of its

dividend earnings. Since most major corporations earn about 20 percent on their capital (before taxes), and since under this plan all net earnings would pass to the stockholder *untaxed*, your $100,000 worth of corporate stock would pay you an income of about $400 a week, or $20,000 a year—year in, year out.

Thus you would have *two* incomes from the two ways of being productive in our present-day industrial economy. Your *first income* would be from wages paid to you for your productive labor (assuming you're able to find and keep a job). Your *second income* would be from dividends paid to you as an owner of productive capital (represented by your stock).

The second income plan helps families at middle-income levels, too. The whole objective of the second income plan is to help families buy and own productive capital (stock) and to do so at *all* income levels. Thus, a part of the plan is aimed at encouraging corporations to set up many more *employee stock-ownership trusts.*

For instance, if you work for a corporation, this plan (through certain tax incentives) would encourage that corporation to finance insured loans for this specific purpose as part of its expansion by issuing new stock to its *employees*. As an employee of the corporation, you would have this special way of obtaining stock. The stock would be held in a tax-free trust; it would be bought by the trust with bank-borrowed money; it would paid for out of its own dividend earnings; and after it is paid for (say in five years), it would belong to the individual employees, who would receive its dividend income.

If you worked for such a corporation, you, too, would wind up having two incomes: one from wages, the other from dividends.

Some Q & A:

Q. What happens if you squander the income-producing stock you acquire?

A. You're out of luck. That's a note of caution. If you squandered your nest egg of stock, you just did something really stupid. You would then have to make your fortune as best you could on your own. Your mistake would stand as an example for others to avoid.

Q. What happens if, after you acquire your stock, you find someone else's stock is doing better?

A. Tough luck. You're in the same position as a settler under the Homestead Act. Not all farms so acquired were equally productive, but that didn't mean that the Homestead Act wasn't basically a good idea. Moreover, the very fact that the corporations had qualified for insured loans on their stock would be some assurance they were sound.

Q. Why can industry pay out as much as 20 percent on its capital (or stock)? We thought most stocks paid dividends around 5 percent?

A. True—most stocks at present do pay about 5 percent in dividends. But that is after taxes, after earnings withheld for future expansion, and after ever-increasing redistribution of the income produced by capital to the nonowners of capital. Actual corporate earnings of most large and successful enterprise are around 20 percent. Under present practice, federal and state corporate income taxes take more than half of it. Then the corporation itself withholds half or more of what's left. This leaves about 5 percent for the stockholders. Under *THE 3ʳᵈ WAY's* second income plan, *the full 20 percent could be paid out.*

Nevertheless, perhaps workers and management may on occasion decide to have less than the full 20% paid out to employee shareholders so some amount of profits could be retained for working capital and for growth and expansion. Congress could also develop a tax on excess retained earnings in order to encourage corporations to pay out a larger portion of earnings to shareholders.

THE 3RD WAY

WIIFM for the Employer? Tax Policy

We strongly suggest that the existing legislated tax incentives for ESOPs be greatly enhanced, thus making them extremely appealing to the business and the investor class! This win-win approach will ensure *THE 3ʳᵈ WAY* becomes a significant, permanent movement.

Premise: The big incentive should be available to all US businesses, whether public stock market or privately held corporations.

Direct incentive for employer: Either 50 percent, or 100 percent tax credit (for distressed areas) of the value of employer stock contributed to employees' compensation. A contribution is made either directly or indirectly, such as to a trust or an ESOP, for eventual distribution to employees. For example, if the employer contributed stock valued at $1 million, the employer would get a $1 million tax credit on its tax return if it is a C corporation, or shareholders holding shares outside the stock compensation scheme would be able to claim pro rata their share ownership part of the $1 million tax credit. (If it was a 50 percent credit, the amount would be $500,000.) (Note, from 1975 to 1984, there was a 1 percent tax credit for the value of shares contributed to an ESOP.)

It is recommended that this proposal have the necessary anti-discrimination rules now common for ESOPs as a part of ERISA, the Employee Retirement Income Act of 1974, to ensure that not just the highly paid or executives would get the stock. Prior legislation that unfortunately did not attain passage (such as HR 786) included those type of provisions, such as one stating that the top-paid employee can get no more stock from the compensation plan than the lowest-paid employee can.

Optional: Limit the credit only to contributions to an ESOP. Since ESOPs operate under all sorts of rules preventing discrimination in favor of highest paid, there would be no discrimination.

Our present corporate taxing system has the highest taxes in the world. Of course, the current thinking is to make the rich pay their fair share and that corporate taxes are just another means to that end. However, this approach does not come without a tremendous cost to society. It is axiomatic: what is taxed, you get less of. Why, then, would we arbitrarily want to suppress the creation of wealth? Answer: because the perception, as well as the reality, is that wealth is being concentrated in fewer and fewer hands.

The enhanced ESOP program advocated above would change all that for the better.

> **The 2012 Libertarian candidate for president, Gary Johnson, also made a very interesting and compelling statement on the subject of US corporate taxation as a real way to create jobs:**
>
> Q: Why are you running for president?
>
> A: I'm the only candidate that is talking about a balanced budget in the year 2013 and eliminating a corporate income tax as the real way to create jobs.
>
> Q: Why's that?
>
> A: Everyone else is parsing it in terms of lowering the corporate income tax. Eliminate it. It's not that big of a generator of income, and it's a double tax. Get rid of it and you would have an explosion of hiring. As a corporation, why wouldn't you base your business in the United States (and the jobs that went along with that) with no corporate tax? The advantage to not taxing corporations would be an advantage to all of us. That income would get distributed to shareholders, at which point it would get taxed.[84]

There is a stark reality that needs to be addressed from the outset. For business owners and holders of capital to share their equity through ESOPs, we must recognize it will take an aggressive, *simple-to-understand* offer of **100 percent tax credits in urban and rural enterprise zones and 50 percent tax credits in all other areas** to get the kind of massive conversion to the system needed to change the social order for the better.

In the United States, urban enterprise zones [UEZs] and rural enterprise zones [REZs] are intended to encourage development in blighted neighborhoods through tax and regulatory relief to entrepreneurs and investors who launch businesses in the area.[85]

WIIFM for the Employer? Lending Policy

Premise: Incentivize banks to make these kinds of "employee friendly" loans to corporations that want to set up ESOPS.

Interest exclusion of 50 percent: This provision in the original ESOP legislation allowed a bank or other financial institution to exclude 50 percent of the interest income on qualifying ESOP loans from the lender's taxable income. The purpose of this provision was to greatly encourage banks and other lenders to make ESOP loans to facilitate the transfer of ownership from the current generation of owners to the successor generation.

Major financial institutions and numerous banks in the United States reacted to this tax incentive by setting up ESOP teams that actively met with large stock market companies and also closely held companies to offer them the technical assistance to set up large employee ownership programs. The tax incentive performed beautifully with the banks because they received the additional deductions for their corporate taxes. But it also helped expand ESOP plans because many banks decided to pass some of these savings on to companies financing ESOPs with attractive *lower* interest rates. Imagine the major Wall Street banks were promoting broad based employee ownership and the government foolishly ended this policy. Brilliant!

This provision had a five-year sunset clause, but during those five years, it had a measurable impact in stimulating increased bank lending for ESOP transactions. Most unfortunately, this provision in the tax code was allowed to be phased out by the Bush and then Clinton administrations.

And now the current president and politicians on both sides of the isle constantly bemoan wage inequality, the shrinking middle class and the poor trapped in poverty. Yet the facts are it was our political classes who *removed* the critical incentives to greatly expand employee ownership and concurrent wealth creation. Tragically the current crop in Washington do not seem to have the knowledge and/or vision to know what needs to happen to spur real, sustainable wealth for all. For some time they have *done nothing of real substance to structurally improve the economic lives of their citizens*. Rather in their "wisdom" we know now they actually did the contrary!

We are "keeping it real" here in this book. So let's be frank. Letting this provision sunset under both the Bush and Clinton administrations (despite many of the other good things they accomplished) was really, really stupid. It's what cut the legs out from under the exponential growth of the ESOP program spreading into many of the "big name" Fortune 500 companies that were joining the movement at full capacity. We should get that lending policy provision back—and we can, if we summon the political will, *driven now by a much more informed public.*

Gladly every business owner (in a public or private corporation) we have spoken to has expressed support for the positive changes we advocate here. They uniformly remark, after hearing the above proposed changes in the corporate tax system and lending policy, they would much prefer giving stock to the workers in their companies than sending all those dollars off to the government. Moreover, with a reinstitution of the highly successful lending policy we have already seen work before; we would see an unrestrained explosion of welcome new employee ownership and a dramatic diffusion of significant wealth and real economic democracy.

Finally, another goal on the technical side of our proposal should be eventually founding "centers of learning" in all fifty states. These would serve to educate and assist businesspeople, academics, politicians, and especially lawyers and accountants specifically skilled in both the establishment and operation of ESOPs and all the various forms of employee ownership. No doubt this component of the movement's growth will be seized upon in other parts of the globe. We know these institutions are already well under way in many other advanced parts of the world. It is only going to get bigger and bigger in every respect. Let's not be left behind.

There is good news at this point. The adoption of ESOPs based on nearly a dozen pieces of prior federal legislation (outlined later in this book) has been proven to work thusfar. Yet, for it to have truly immense impact, the newest programs ***need to be as bold as what we have just outlined.***

A Way Out For The Poor
[change the system/change the result]

I am a Republican, a black, dyed in the wool Republican, and I never intend to belong to any other party than the party of freedom and progress.
—Frederick Douglass, American social reformer, orator, writer, and statesman. After escaping from slavery, he became a leader of the abolitionist movement, gaining note for his dazzling oratory and incisive antislavery writing.[86]

WHAT NEEDS TO BE DONE?

Wherever there is great property there is great inequality. The affluence of the rich supposes the indigence of the many.
—Adam Smith, Scottish philosopher
and pioneer of political economy[87]

Perhaps the most exciting feature of *THE 3rd WAY* is its potential to dramatically reshape the most neglected, even blighted inner-city areas of this country. Its ambition is matched by its transformative ability.

Moreover, implementation of the systems advocated in this text would for the first time in a significant way decouple the bonds of inequality without resorting to another failed government-run redistribution scheme. For the first time, the prosperity of the rich could be accessed fairly in a way designed to *boost productivity* rather than hinder it.

For *THE 3rd WAY* to be truly and fully successful, we must also make sure we address the issue of the poor via enterprise zones and an *enhanced* **100 percent tax credit for these special areas**. Surely this is a bold step. Offering very impressive tax incentives to businesses willing to both invest and share the fruits of their equity with their employees (who most likely reside primarily in those blighted and surrounding areas) would accomplish it. Yet for dramatic results, extraordinarily bold, commonsense steps as proposed here are required.

The current welfare-state system actually rewards much of what we don't want—dependency, laziness, gangs, and drug dealing. What poor people *need* is a way to break into the entrepreneurial class! What is desperately desired is a new, innovative, reasonable approach that yields real results.

Think of the savings in social-welfare costs, not to mention the costs of incarcerating all those who have chosen an unwise path! Yet, let's be frank, what promising paths were available to most of them?

THE 3RD WAY

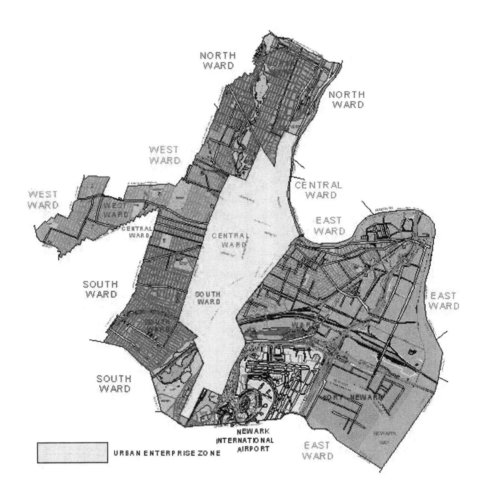

Figure 18. New Jersey's largest city, Newark, and its urban enterprise zone

Yes, there are some fine organizations doing great work to educate our youth on personal finance, including:

- Jump$tart (www.jumpstart.org), which is dedicated to improving the financial literacy of our youth and strives to prepare youth for lifelong successful financial decision making.

- Junior Achievement (www.ja.org), which empowers young people to own their economic success by fostering work-readiness, entrepreneurship, and financial literacy skills to inspire students to dream big and reach their potential.

However, coupling these efforts with an enterprise zone/employee ownership movement would be an incredibly powerful antipoverty program indeed!

Certainly, some have "made it out" of crushing poverty to make a success of their lives. One of the authors' grandfathers, Venerando Musumeci, was such a man. He came to this country from Sicily in 1906 as a six-year-old. He was so poor, he had to put tin in his shoes whose soles had worn through. Needing to support the family, he had to leave grammar school after attending for just a couple of years. So, his level of education was quite limited. However, through incredibly hard work and determination, he built Musum Company & Sons, a thriving barber- and beauty-supply business that at one time was one of the largest in the state of New Jersey.

But the odds, especially in today's highly corporatized, information-age world, are most assuredly stacked against today's youth and poor. Where do they go to gain a sense of belonging and empowerment? Gangs, unfortunately.

A new way must be found to match the realities of today. Working hard is just not enough in most cases. Endless crackdowns on gangs and crime are just not enough. A new, simple, commonsense system facilitating upward mobility in both wealth and capital must be found.

A New Form Of Capital Ownership
[the best way to help the poor and middle class]

The system that enables the most people to earn the most success is free enterprise, by matching up people's skills, interests, and abilities. In

contrast, redistribution simply spreads money around. Even worse, it attenuates the ability to earn success by perverting economic incentives.
—Arthur C. Brooks, American social scientist[88]

Louis Kelso's opposition to the "antipoverty" policies that have been commonly used to reduce economic hardship places some serious constraints on any solutions he might propose for advancing economic justice.[89] In fact, he concisely states the problem confronting him:

> In an industrial economy such as ours, is it possible to order things so that (1) all families are in a position to earn what amounts to a decent standard of living, (2) by an organization of the economy which preserves and respects the rights of private property in capital instruments as well as in labor power, and which (3) distributes the wealth produced among those who contribute to its production in accordance with the principle of distributive justice stated above?[90]

Not surprisingly, Kelso answers the above question with a resounding yes, giving the core of his solution in the form of three principles of economic justice. In summary they are:

1. **The Principle of Distribution**: Each participant in the production of wealth should receive a share proportionate to the market value(s) of the labor and capital they contribute to the enterprise.
2. **The Principle of Participation**: Each household must have the opportunity to earn a decent standard of living through effective participation in the production of wealth, whether by property in labor, capital, or both.
3. **The Principle of Limitation**: No one may exclude others from effective participation in the production of wealth through excessive concentration of ownership, whether in capital, labor, or both.

So how does the ESOP fit into all of this? As envisioned by Kelso, the ESOP involves three different targets he identified as obstacles to achieving democratized capital ownership: the corporation, the government, and the credit system.

1. **The modern corporation**, by retaining some or all of its earnings for future expansion, both weakens the rights of capital owners to receive all wealth produced by their property and also aggravates the concentration of wealth by placing the value of newly created capital directly into the hands of existing shareholders.
2. **Government policy**, in the absence of ESOPs, tends to encourage earnings retention by corporations (as a way to shelter personal income). It also discourages significant transfers of capital holdings to workers by levying taxes on such transfers and not offering enough of a corporate tax incentive to promote a widespread movement.
3. **The credit system** makes capital acquisition nearly impossible by requiring collateral in most cases, which restricts borrowing for acquisition of capital to the few who already own significant capital estates.

Specifically, there needs to be incentives for those with money, such as banks, to prioritize lending to those creating and operating employee-owned corporations. A commonsense message needs to be sent to transform our nation's current financing practices to be for all the people, not just for the already rich.

In combination, the elimination of these barriers through ESOPs has helped millions of workers become capital owners, and this well-established success is inspiring many people to take a new look at Kelso's proposals as a means of spreading capital ownership to even more people.

THE 3RD WAY

The World Will Beat A Path To Us
[capital flows to the most favorable environment]

> *The tax on capital gains directly affects investment decisions…*
> —John F. Kennedy, thirty-fifth president of the United States[91]

The case for an overhaul of America's corporate tax code is becoming more and more obvious with each passing day. We are now at a point where both sides of the aisle are reaching consensus, and the time for corrective action is at hand.

We all can agree about the need for action. The rub remains: What substantive measures will be enacted in *exchange* for the easing of corporate taxation so that genuine positive transformation can take place? The overwhelming idea making the most sense is to use the pivotal issue of EOs and ESOPs as an integral part of *comprehensive* corporate tax reform.

We need *direct* benefits to the working class in exchange for the kind of corporate tax reform we all seek. Below are excerpts from two powerful articles (one from each side of the political spectrum) that cogently making the case for corporate tax reform.

The Need for Pro-Growth Corporate Tax Reform
Prepared for the US Chamber of Commerce,
Douglas Holtz-Eakin, August 2011

A wide variety of policymakers have recognized the need for reform of the corporation income tax, including the Obama Administration,[1] the leadership of the Senate Finance Committee[2] and the House Ways and Means Committee,[3] the Simpson-Bowles Commission[4] and "Gang of Six."[5] The US corporate tax rate is one of the highest in the world, and it

WHAT NEEDS TO BE DONE?

is becoming increasingly evident that workers, as opposed to consumers or shareholders, bear most of the burden of a high corporate tax.[6] In addition, the code is too riddled with special exemptions and targeted benefits, and reform would raise the long-run growth potential of the US economy.

Fundamental changes in the corporate tax code are clearly overdue. The last major corporate tax reform took place 25 years ago.

[1] President Barack Obama: 2011 State of the Union Address, 25 January 2011.

[2] Applebaum, Binyamin: "Corporate Tax Reform Proves Hard to Change." *New York Times*, 27 January 2011.

[3] Cohn, Michael: "House Holds Hearing to Compare Tax Reform." *Accounting Today*, 25 May 2011.

[4] "The Moment of Truth: Report of the National Commission on Fiscal Responsibility and Reform," December 2010.

[5] See "A Bipartisan Plan to Reduce Our Nation's Deficits: Executive Summary," July 2011.

William C. Randolph: "International Burdens of the Corporate Income Tax." CBO publication 2006-09, August 2006. [92]

The international economy is changing, but US tax policy is not. With America having the highest corporate tax rates in the industrialized world, the need for action is urgent.

In 2013 alone, at least 484 US firms, with a value of more than $43.6 billion, have been acquired by foreign interests.[93] One factor is that foreign interests can offer a higher price because of a smaller tax liability after acquiring the new firm.

When the United States last cut its corporate tax rate in 1986, 218 of the world's 500 largest corporations measured by revenue were in the United States. Today, that number is 137.

Other nations are taking actions to welcome foreign capital into their economies. A 2012 analysis by PricewaterhouseCoopers conducted for the World Bank showed 133 corporate tax reductions since 2006. The cuts reflect a world that is recognizing the need to adjust tax rates to attract new investment and provide incentives for multinational corporations to repatriate overseas profits. The United States is not among these countries.

The additional layer of taxes under a worldwide system has at least two undesirable consequences. First is a "lockout" effect: companies face a disincentive to repatriate their international profits because doing so would trigger a higher tax on that income. For US companies, this amounts to an accumulated $2 trillion in deferred international income—money that is kept overseas as a means of avoiding additional US tax. Second is the "move-out" effect: companies with significant foreign operations relocate to countries with lower tax rates and territorial tax structures.

The political class almost universally agrees there needs to be a restructuring and modernization of the corporate tax structure. Unfortunately, the power of the people needs to sternly direct politicians to the concept that it must be done *only* if it results in the acquisition of ownership and real capital by the common person.

The Progressive Case for Corporate Tax Reform
By Bruce Stokes
Senior Transatlantic Fellow for Economics, German Marshall Fund
January 26, 2012

In his January 2012 State of the Union address, President Barack Obama called for cutting taxes for companies that produce in the United States, especially high-tech manufacturers. He proposed eliminating deductions for firms that move jobs abroad. And he suggested a minimum tax on all multinational corporations.

The suggestions echoed, but were less sweeping, than Obama's proposal in his January, 2011 State of the Union that Congress should, "Get rid of the loopholes. Level the playing field. And use the savings to lower the corporate tax rate for the first time in 25 years—without adding to our deficit."

Both appeals were shrewd political maneuvers designed to appeal both to progressives, who have long complained about corporate manipulation of the tax code, and to conservatives who have long fretted that high US corporate tax rates undermine the competitiveness of American companies in the global market.

And the president is not alone. GOP presidential candidate Mitt Romney advocates cutting the corporate tax rate, as does his Republican opponent Newt Gingrich.

Progressives need to make corporate tax reform (not simply corporation bashing) a cornerstone of their economic agenda in the 2012 election campaign. It is good economics, good politics, and the right thing to do.

Who Bears the Corporate Tax Burden?

Corporate taxation has long been the subject of contentious debate. Progressives have argued that since the corporate tax is largely borne by the owners of capital, who tend to have higher incomes than other taxpayers, high rates of corporate taxation are inherently fairer than income taxation and should figure more prominently in the American tax code. Conservatives have contended that the corporate tax burden is simply passed on to consumers in the form of higher prices and paid for by workers through lower wages, making corporate taxation regressive. Businesses also assert that cutting corporate taxes would attract large investment flows into the United States, which would create jobs or expand the taxable income base, raising revenues.

The current US corporate tax rate of 39 percent is the highest among major economies. This factoid alone has framed the debate over corporate taxation, convincing people on both the left and the right that America needs a lower corporate tax rate that puts it some place in the middle of the international pack.

Broadening the Base

The US tax base, the universe of taxable corporate profits, was just 13 percent of the economy in 2007. The [European-based Organization for Economic Cooperation and Development] OECD average, not including the United States, was 22 percent. So, while the effective US corporate tax is 6 percentage points higher than the OECD average, the US tax base is 9 percentage points of GDP smaller than the average in comparable countries. There is great room to broaden the corporate tax base while cutting rates, raising additional deficit-cutting revenue.

> The United States needs to create jobs and increase revenues to lower public indebtedness. Corporate tax reform can be a means to pursue both these goals. Lowering corporate taxes can be part of the solution—if done right, with an eye to competitiveness, revenue neutrality or enhancement, and fairness.[94]

It is true in a global sense that capital will flow to places in the world largely based on nations with the most hospitable taxing climate. This sets *THE 3rd WAY* revolution as an important international model for both intrinsic fairness and economic growth, both in the United States and worldwide.

It's A Global Movement
[examples of success abound worldwide]

Personal liberty is the purpose of government, to protect liberty—not to run your personal life, not to run the economy, and not to pretend that we can tell the world how they ought to live.
—Ron Paul, former congressman from Texas, three-time candidate for the presidency of the United States; best known for his libertarian viewpoints[95]

> ## Yes, There Is an Alternative to Capitalism: Mondragon Shows the Way
> By Richard Wolff
>
> In May 2012, I had occasion to visit the city of Arrasate-Mondragon, in the Basque region of Spain. It is the headquarters of the Mondragon Corporation (MC), a stunningly successful alternative to the capitalist organization of production.

MC is composed of many cooperative enterprises grouped into four areas: industry, finance, retail and knowledge. In each enterprise, the co-op members (averaging 80–85 percent of all workers per enterprise) collectively own and direct the enterprise. Through an annual general assembly the workers choose and employ a managing director and retain the power to make all the basic decisions of the enterprise (what, how and where to produce and what to do with the profits).

As each enterprise is a constituent of the MC as a whole, its members must confer and decide with all other enterprise members what general rules will govern MC and all its constituent enterprises. In short, MC worker-members collectively choose, hire and fire the directors, whereas in capitalist enterprises the reverse occurs. One of the co-operatively and democratically adopted rules governing the MC limits top-paid worker/members to earning 6.5 times the lowest-paid workers. Nothing more dramatically demonstrates the differences distinguishing this from the capitalist alternative organization of enterprises. (In US corporations, CEOs can expect to be paid 400 times an average worker's salary—a rate that has increased 20-fold since 1965.)

Given that MC has 85,000 members (from its 2010 annual report), its pay equity rules can and do contribute to a larger society with far greater income and wealth equality than is typical in societies that have chosen capitalist organizations of enterprises. Over 43 percent of MC members are women, whose equal powers with male members likewise influence gender relations in society different from capitalist enterprises.

MC displays a commitment to job security I have rarely encountered in capitalist enterprises: it operates across, as well as within, particular cooperative enterprises. MC members created a system to move workers from enterprises needing fewer to those needing more workers—in a remarkably open, transparent, rule-governed way and with associated travel and other subsidies to minimize hardship. This security-focused system has transformed the lives of workers, their families, and communities, also in unique ways.

The MC rule that all enterprises are to source their inputs from the best and least-costly producers (whether or not those are also MC enterprises) has kept MC at the cutting edge of new technologies. Likewise, the decision to use a portion of each member enterprise's net revenue as a fund for research and development has funded impressive new product development. R&D within MC now employs 800 people with a budget over $75m. In 2010, 21.4 percent of sales of MC industries were new products and services that did not exist five years earlier.

In addition, MC established and has expanded Mondragon University; it enrolled over 3,400 students in its 2009–2010 academic year, and its degree programs conform to the requirements of the European framework of higher education. Total student enrollment in all its educational centers in 2010 was 9,282.

The largest corporation in the Basque region, MC is also one of Spain's top ten biggest corporations (in terms of sales or employment). Far better than merely surviving since its founding in 1956, MC has grown dramatically. Along the way, it added a co-operative bank, Caja Laboral (holding almost $25bn in deposits in 2010). And MC has expanded internationally, now operating over 77 businesses outside Spain.

THE 3RD WAY

> MC has proven itself able to grow and prosper as an alternative to (and competitor of) capitalist organizations of enterprise.
>
> During my visit, in random encounters with workers who answered my questions about their jobs, powers, and benefits as cooperative members, I found a familiarity with and sense of responsibility for the enterprise as a whole that I associate only with top managers and directors in capitalist enterprises. The easy conversation (including disagreement), for instance, between assembly-line workers and top managers inside the Fagor washing-machine factory we inspected was similarly remarkable.
>
> Our MC host on the 5visit reminded us twice that theirs is a co-operative business with all sorts of problems: "We are not some paradise, but rather a family of co-operative enterprises struggling to build a different kind of life around a different way of working."[96]

How To Get Rich!
[what do they know and do that the poor and middle class do not]

> *Intelligence solves problems and produces money. Money without financial intelligence is money soon gone.*
> —Robert Kiyosaki, American investor, self-help author, motivational speaker, and financial commentator[97]

One of the more current figures enlightening average people about effective ways of increasing personal affluence who first got wide exposure on a PBS special is Robert Kiyosaki. For many in his audience, this was the first time they heard substantive information on how many in the investor class attained their wealth.

WHAT NEEDS TO BE DONE?

Robert Kiyosaki is an American investor, businessman, self-help author, motivational speaker, game inventor, financial literacy activist, and occasional financial commentator.[98] Kiyosaki is perhaps best known for his *Rich Dad Poor Dad* series of motivational books and other material published under the Rich Dad brand. He has written more than fifteen books, which have combined sales of over 26 million copies. Three of his books, *Rich Dad Poor Dad*, *Rich Dad's Cashflow Quadrant*, and *Rich Dad's Guide to Investing,* have been number one on the top ten best-seller lists. Kiyosaki has been a staunch proponent of entrepreneurship, business education, and investing, and that comprehensive financial literacy concepts should be taught in schools around the world.

The entitlement mentality is epidemic, creating people who expect their countries, employers, or families to take care of them. Donald Trump and Robert Kiyosaki, both successful businessmen, believe you cannot solve money problems with money. You can only solve money problems with financial education. Kiyosaki lays out the fundamental principles in his landmark book, *Rich Dad Poor Dad*.

As discussed in that book, Kiyosaki developed his unique economic perspective through exposure to a pair of disparate influences: his own highly educated but fiscally unsophisticated father, and the multimillionaire eighth-grade dropout father of his closest friend. The lifelong monetary problems experienced by his biological "poor dad" (whose income was never quite sufficient to meet family needs) pounded home the counterpoint communicated by his "rich dad" ("the poor and the middle class work for money," but "the rich have money work for them").

His books compellingly advocate for the type of financial literacy that's never taught in schools. He nails the principle that income-generating assets from businesses and investments always provide healthier results than even the best of traditional jobs. One needs to understand how those assets might be acquired.

THE 3RD WAY

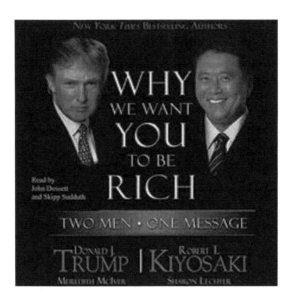

Figure 19. (Source: Rich Press, 2007)

Together with industry notables like Donald Trump, Kiyosaki drives home the concept that each of us resides in at least one of the four quadrants of the Cashflow Quadrant™. Where we are is determined by where our main source of income comes from. Many of us rely on paychecks and are therefore employees, while others are self-employed.

Employees and self-employed individuals reside on the left side of the Cashflow Quadrant. The right side of the Cashflow Quadrant is for individuals who receive their cash from businesses or investments they own. Employee ownership is a truly splendid way for the masses to bridge this most important gap.

For our purposes, it is critical for the average individual to first grasp and then internalize these principles. Of course, one cannot say Kiyosaki's methods are the *only* ways to acquire wealth.

WHAT NEEDS TO BE DONE?

However, any person of means who is honest with you will confide that his concepts must be considered.

Figure 20. Rich Dad's Cashflow Quadrant (Source: Robert Kiyosaki and Sharon L. Lechter, *Rich Dad's Guide to Financial Freedom*, 2001)

The main take-away from an understanding of what Donald Trump and Robert Kiyosaki teach is that a major key to wealth creation and retention is the acquisition of capital. One needs to *own* something of income-generating value as a major element in acquiring wealth.

One of the common denominators has to be the importance of *ownership*, whether in a business or in investments.

Greed Is Good
[but, let everyone participate in wealth and job creation]

Socialism proposes no adequate substitute for the motive of enlightened selfishness that today is at the basis of all human labor and effort, enterprise and new activity.
—William Howard Taft, twenty-seventh president of the United States and later chief justice of the US Supreme Court[99]

Our concept is not about failed redistribution schemes of the past. It's about broadening wealth! It's about innovative, more intelligent public policy that works *with* human nature and best harnesses its power. It explores a fresh mind-set: the idea of getting everyone to think and act like owners – because they are. Together the team builds capital wealth beyond what their company would provide in cash compensation alone.

> **HEADLINE:**
> Did you know that **most of Silicon Valley is working under some form of employee ownership program?**[100] It's a fact. Silicon Valley is one of the most important, productive, job-producing sectors of our nation, or any nation for that matter. Coincidence? Or could it be that when labor and management work in concert for common goals with common incentives and shared equity, great things are more likely to happen.
>
> Can you feel the earth beneath your feet beginning to rumble again?

The ancillary benefits of such a fresh perspective by all parties are innumerable. One important example is the important issue

WHAT NEEDS TO BE DONE?

of unemployment. Let's render it down to the most basic principles: *unsuccessful businesses do not add to their work forces!*

If a business is not experiencing growth, the issue of adding to its employee base is a nonstarter. Many factors contribute to this undeniable principle. Number one is identifying a need and providing goods and services to fill that need. Nevertheless, for growth to continue to occur, we suggest, an underlying fundamental cycle of growth is also essential to drive a company's and (by extension) a nation's employment picture.

A successful business has the real potential to accelerate its demand for labor. The United States and indeed many parts of the world are struggling with chronic levels of serious unemployment levels. A great place to start to rectify this malady is the following cycle: grow jobs, grow productivity, grow business, grow wealth.

We suggest, and it has been backed by data, that the employee ownership concept consistently contributes positively to every one of these factors. A highly motivated, equity- empowered labor force can absolutely serve to make a positive difference in the overall prospects of any business. This is just common sense.

Figure 21. Business growth cycle

Never overlook the healthy underlying "culture" of a business regarding its potential for success. That healthy culture de facto serves to establish the correct environment for further employment opportunities. We *must* take strong legislative action to foster such an environment.

It is true a new economic model based on a corporate-tax reduction linked to an enhanced ESOP system will profoundly improve every quintile of the populace, even at the lowest rungs. Imagine the socially transformative effect when the average person is given the opportunity to participate in the power that equity and capital formation can provide.

Now imagine the almost unimaginable socially transformative effect when members of the underclass, even former gang members, first hold a stock certificate in their hands! Imagine how they and others will *think* and *act* differently.

Acknowledging the wisdom of moving to this blended method helps us establish the basis for this *proper evolution* to a better system.

> *What kind of society isn't structured on greed? The problem of social organization is how to set up an arrangement under which greed will do the least harm; capitalism is that kind of system.*
> —Milton Friedman, American Nobel Prize–winning economist, statistician, and author[101]

A comment on Dr. Friedman's quote is in order, for a system based on greed doing the "least harm" is still repugnant. Instead, THE 3rd WAY adopts the audacious premise that capitalism structured in a *new* and more perfect way has the potential to do a great deal of tangible *good* for all people—employees, employers, and society as a whole.

I prefer this quote from Louis Kelso:
> Abraham Lincoln said the purpose of government is to do for the people what they cannot do for themselves. I believe

that man is so structured that he cannot control his own greed. If he had been able to do that we probably would never have emerged from the protozoic slime. I mean it's just the nature of the beast to think of himself first—if not exclusively. But nature had an economic plan for world society. Nature thought that economic autonomy—i.e., making every human capable of participation in production and earning the income he needs for himself and his dependents—was a good idea. It is an idea that agrees with the inner man. But the arrangement of "one person, one labor power" is about as far as nature can go. After that, it is up to government, labor, and management to devise the institutions that enable us, in the advanced industrial age we live in, to earn our income by engaging in production in ways that are consistent with modern economic reality.[102]

Chapter 3:

WHAT IS THE ACADEMIC RATIONALE?

Hegel Had It Right
[right premise/wrong interpretation]

Governments have never learned anything from history, or acted on principles deducted from it.
—Georg Wilhelm Friedrich Hegel, German philosopher whose work on "idealism" revolutionized European philosophy and was an important precursor to Continental philosophy and Marxism[103]

In Europe, Prime Minister Tony Blair was *swept* into office in Great Britain riding the concept of a "third way." He clearly had the right political strategy, yet we know it involved the wrong ideological premise. *THE 3rd WAY* should not be just "socialism light." Rather, it needs to be a complete paradigm shift to a new conclusion for humankind. All these ideas about massive, fundamental change emanate from the great German philosopher Georg Wilhelm Friedrich Hegel.

Indeed, Hegel's dialectic was one of the primary principles Karl Marx cited as a basis for his "Communist Manifesto." Marx became interested in the philosophical ideas of the Young Hegelians, followers of Hegel's work, and began to work out his theory of dialectical materialism. Dialectical materialism is a strand of Marxism synthesizing Hegel's dialectics that proposes that every economic order grows to a state of maximum efficiency, while simultaneously developing internal contradictions and weaknesses that contribute to its systemic decay.

Hegel's dialectic emphasizes the process of historical change arising from contradiction and class struggle based in a particular social context. History, Hegel contends, progresses by learning from its mistakes.

Marx's theories about society, economics, and politics (collectively known as Marxism) hold that all societies progress through the dialectic of class struggle: a conflict between an ownership class that controls production and a lower class that produces the labor for goods.[104] Heavily critical of the current socioeconomic form of society, capitalism, Marx called it the "dictatorship of the bourgeoisie," believing it to be run by the wealthy classes purely for their own benefit, and he predicted that, like previous socioeconomic systems, it would inevitably produce internal tensions that would lead to its self-destruction and replacement by a new system, socialism. He argued that under socialism, society would be governed by the working class in what he called the "dictatorship of the proletariat," the "workers' state," or "workers' democracy." He believed that socialism would, in its turn, eventually be replaced by a stateless, classless society called communism.

Essentially Marx believed society would inexorably evolve to these inevitable stages:
1. Feudalism
2. Capitalism
3. Socialism
4. Communism

But here are the tectonic economic shifts that today make the most sense for moving toward true human progress:
1. Wealth and power based on land ownership—feudalism
2. Industrial revolution—capitalism
3. Information age—an ownership society

We employ the art of arriving at the truth by the exchange of logical arguments. But now we arrive at a profound new conclusion based on Hegel's famed dialectic. But first a definition of *dialectic*:

> **Dialectic**: A process by which one element, the thesis, is contradicted by an opposing element, the antithesis. This contradiction is resolved by a synthesis of the thesis and antithesis. The synthesis then becomes the new thesis and the sequence repeats. This is the process by which Marx believes history proceeds, a dialectic of class antagonism. The proletariat victory will be an end to the dialectic and thus an end to history.[105]

Milton Friedman said the economic freedom of capitalism is a requisite for political freedom, a statement that has been continuously echoed by others, such as Andrew Brennan and Ronald Reagan. Friedman stated that centralized operations of economic activity are always accompanied by political repression. In his view, transactions in a market economy are voluntary, and the wide diversity that voluntary activity permits is a fundamental threat to repressive political leaders and greatly diminishes the power to coerce.

Here we believe is the *correct* historical dialectic of major economic stages, which we feel is in keeping with true progress for humankind. Rather than Marx's interpretation, capitalism *should evolve* into a decentralized "ownership society" rather than a centralized socialist/communist society.

Owning The Means Of Production
[did the Communists screw up a good idea?]

In practice, socialism didn't work. But socialism could never have worked because it is based on false premises about human psychology and society, and gross ignorance of human economy.
—David Horowitz, American conservative writer and public advocate[106]

Karl Marx talked about "workers owning the means of production." This is central to his philosophy. One can contend that Marx has been interpreted to devise a system whereby "ownership" would reside in the state rather than in a more modern approach via employee ownership programs, as proposed here.

In his famed *Communist Manifesto*, Marx lays out the separation of classes and gives them identifiable names. *Bourgeoisie* means the class of modern capitalists, owners of the means of social production, and employers of wage labor.[107] *Proletariat* means the class of modern wage laborers who, having no *means of production* of their own, are reduced to selling their labor in order to live.

Means of production refers to physical, nonhuman inputs used in production—in essence, the factories, machines, and tools used to produce wealth, along with both infrastructural capital and natural capital.[108] This consists of the input/resources minus financial capital and minus human capital, and includes two broad categories of objects: *instruments of labor* (tools, factories, infrastructure, etc.) and *subjects of labor* (natural resources and raw materials). People operate on the *subjects* of labor, using the *instruments* of labor, to create a product. Basically, labor acting on the means of production creates a product.

When used in the broad sense, *means of production* includes the means of distribution, which includes stores, banks, and railroads, for example.

The term can simply and quaintly be described, in an agrarian society, as the soil and the shovel. Then again, as it applies in an industrial society, it would be the mines and the factories.

The bottom line is that whether in an agrarian, industrial, or even today's information economic system, the reality is that a commoner has a difficult, though not impossible, task of building a business from scratch. The fact is, not everyone is equipped for such a venture. Nevertheless, that does not mean that in their role as employees, people cannot be a valuable element in a company's success. We contend that a way should exist for the masses of workers to access a portion of a business's equity as a fair exchange for their hard work.

Rising from meager means has always been the American Dream. Surely it is still possible. The point is not to deny its potential but to find a way to dramatically increase the odds that people can *participate* in the blessings of the capitalist system if they are not able or inclined to start a business themselves.

Marx understood the intrinsic unfairness of the capitalist system. In his momentous work, he very eloquently laid down the inherent problem in denying the means of production to the average person. It's important because we make the same point and agree with the social fairness of the concept. However, we propose that the mechanism for it to work best and most efficiently must be through *private industry*, not via the state. A key difference!

We understand the awesome power of Marx's social contract, which inspired the whole world. Yet, we now have the wisdom of history's lessons to know his way via state ownership was destined to fail. A new way—***THE 3rd WAY***—is the best way forward for *both* fairness *and* productivity!

Before moving forward to describe *THE 3rd WAY* in more detail, we need to understand people's deepest needs, using the concepts of the famous psychologist Abraham Maslow. Failing to understand Maslow's vitally important concepts has proven catastrophic in the annals of history, as we will soon come to learn.

Maslow
[ignore him at your peril]

> *True individual freedom cannot exist without economic security and independence.*
> —Franklin D. Roosevelt, thirty-second president of the United States[109]

Maslow's hierarchy of needs is a theory in psychology proposed by Abraham Maslow in his 1943 paper "A Theory of Human Motivation."[110] Maslow subsequently extended the idea to include his observations of humans' innate curiosity. His theories parallel many other theories of human developmental psychology, all of which focus on describing the stages of growth in humans. Maslow uses the terms physiological, safety, belongingness and love, esteem, and self-actualization needs to describe the pattern that human motivations generally move through.

Once a person's physical needs are relatively satisfied, the individual's safety needs take precedence and dominate behavior. In the absence of economic safety (due to economic crisis and lack of work opportunities) these safety needs manifest themselves in such things as a preference for job security, grievance procedures for protecting the individual from unilateral authority, savings accounts, insurance policies, reasonable disability accommodations, and the like.[111]

The overwhelming populist appeal of *THE 3rd WAY's* new capitalist paradigm must be based on Maslow's fundamental human understanding of our hierarchy of needs. Ignore the most basic level—physiological (food, water, etc.)—and you have the recipe for revolution. The French Revolution was a perfect example! There are countless other examples throughout history. The second level—safety (security)—is what we are facing at overwhelming levels in today's world. In this information age, we are all witnessing that people's incredible need for security is now becoming even more crucial and evident. It must be addressed! Whoever does so will be swept into power.

Everyone, from the highest-level white-collar employee to the masses of blue-collar workers, is silently crying out for the inner peace provided by gaining some measure of security and stability in their lives. If this silent inner turmoil by virtually everyone in society remains unaddressed, it could possibly eventually erupt into an outward expression of discontent we have not seen in our history!

Social Security gives us a window on the power of this need. In its time, Social Security paved a dramatic change in the way people viewed their relationships with both their employer and their government. Furthermore, its legacy as a central tenet in the social contract shows the validity of its fundamental fulfilling of a basic need—security. It has endured. However, in this new age, people's inner longing for security remains constant; it just needs to be addressed in a modern way.

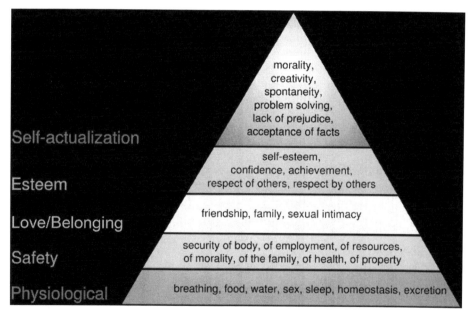

Figure 22. Maslow's hierarchy of needs pyramid (Source: J. Finkelstein)

In an excellent earlier book, *Own Your Own Job: Economic Democracy for Working Americans,* on the subject of economic democracy, author Jeremy Rifkin puts it best:
> Unmindful of the lessons of history, we have restruck an age-old bargain: rendering up the collective soul of a nation in hopes of buying a little more individual security. In Faustian style we have each sold our birthrights to the corporate temptress, and have purchased only our chains.[112]

Mao's Big Mistake
[millions died trying to reshape human nature]

> *Communism is in conflict with human nature.*
> —Ernest Renan, French philosopher,
> writer, political theorist, and historian[113]

Just as Maslow had a view of human nature that fits with *THE 3rd WAY's* perspective, Communist Mao had a failed view of human nature. The colossal failure of Mao Tse Tung's Cultural Revolution, with a death toll estimated as high as 40 million, demonstrated it is impossible to change natural human inclination to do what is in *one's own best interest.* Our concept and our nation's Constitution very wisely *work with these natural tendencies* for self-interest to bring forth the greatest good for the greatest number.

The Great Proletarian Cultural Revolution, commonly known as the Cultural Revolution, was a social-political movement that took place in the People's Republic of China from 1966 through 1976. Its stated goal was to enforce socialism in the country by removing capitalist, traditional, and cultural elements from Chinese society and to impose Maoist orthodoxy. After the failed "Great Leap Forward," the movement politically paralyzed the country and significantly affected the country economically and socially.[114]

The revolution was launched in May 1966. Mao alleged that bourgeois elements were infiltrating the government and society at large, aiming to restore capitalism. He insisted that these "revisionists" be removed through violent class struggle. This resulted in widespread factional struggles in all walks of life. Among the top leadership, it led to a mass purge of senior officials. During the same period, Mao's personality cult grew to immense proportions.[115]

Millions of people were persecuted in the violent factional struggles that ensued across the country, and suffered a wide range of abuses, including public humiliation, arbitrary imprisonment, torture, sustained harassment, and seizure of property. Historical relics and artifacts were destroyed. Cultural and religious sites were ransacked.

After Mao's death in 1976, reformers led by Deng Xiaoping gained prominence. Most of the Maoist reforms associated with the Cultural Revolution were abandoned by 1978. The Cultural Revolution has been treated officially as a negative phenomenon ever since.

Clearly the immense effort to alter human nature so people would work toward something other than their own self-interests was a colossal failure.

Contrast this with the clear-eyed understanding of human nature that America's founders had. The American political system (checks and balances, etc.) was built to *take advantage* of the realities of human nature rather than try to make it conform to some utopian vision.

Mao's system tried to wrench people's basic instinct of self-interest into some communist utopian fantasy. It was a tragic failure! History should have taught everyone that people will not subordinate and degrade their own self-interests into some groupthink scheme. Employee ownership and ESOPs consistently work because they take advantage of the natural human tendency to do what is in one's individual interests. The more directly a

WHAT IS THE ACADEMIC RATIONALE?

corporation can link workers' individual efforts with their own rewards, the more motivated the worker is. The consistent end result is a business that grows as a whole in both potential and profitability, generating wealth for everyone.

Working for their own self-interests has proven to be the solution for the political life of humans. Wise nations structure their political systems around that reality. ESOPs have already proven to have the same positive impact on *economic* life!

THE 3rd WAY presents a system of "economic empowerment" that moves away from the status quo to create a society that works *with* human nature instead of fighting it. It is based on a clear understanding of the great thinkers present and past. This book positions a new model—an ownership society versus old, strict models of capitalism and socialism.

What is the overall goal of *THE 3rd WAY*? Let's consider it in more detail.

The Exceptionalism Of The Few Meets The Self-Interest Of Us All
[human nature meets reality, and what to do about it]

Never underestimate the power of dreams and the influence of the human spirit. We are all the same in this notion: The potential for greatness lives within each of us.
—Wilma Rudolph, American Olympian, in the 1960s considered the fastest woman in the world, competing in two Olympic Games, in 1956 and in the 1960 Summer Olympics in Rome, where she became the first American woman to win three gold medals in track and field during a single Olympic Games[116]

In his writings, Adam Smith says that thankfully, human beings have a natural propensity to negotiate or, as he describes it, to trade, barter, and exchange. "Give me what I want, and you shall have what you want" is not only the manner in which we acquire most things in this world but is also the building block for an economically advanced society. Thus, as Smith declares in his most famous passage:

> It is not from the benevolence of the butcher, the brewer, or the baker that we expect our dinner, but from their regard to their own interest. We address ourselves, not to their humanity but to their self-love, and never talk to them of our own necessities but of their advantages.[117]

People who read this passage and nothing else of Smith's tend to regard it as an affirmation of selfishness over altruism. However, what he's saying is not just that we have selfish interests, but that only by understanding the interests of others are we able to fulfill our own. The commercial effect of this practice is that we individually learn how to make the kinds of products, services, and exchanges that, in the aggregate, lead to the wealth of a nation.

The contrast Smith makes is not only about our human nature. It also underscores his broader point about *who* makes capitalism work: not the all-powerful king, however wise and mighty, but the assistance and cooperation of many thousands. They are the base of the economic pyramid, and their individual actions ensure the bounty of Smith's famous "invisible hand" metaphor used to describe the self-regulating nature of the marketplace.

Writing a century after Smith's death, the steel magnate Andrew Carnegie, in his essay "The Gospel of Wealth," describes the decisive moment when human beings began to favor a model of free competition that saw the separation of "the drones from the bees," a process that allowed for the accumulation of wealth by those who have the ability and energy that produce it.[118] Carnegie says of such people that they are so essential to society's development, that those who object to the inequalities of a free-market system might as well "urge the destruction of the highest existing type of man." In the same spirit, roughly seventy-five years later, Ayn Rand, in her aptly titled "What Is Capitalism?" focuses on "the innovators" who promote a society's development. They are an "exceptional minority," she says, "who lift the whole of a free society to the level of their own achievements."[119]

This philosophy is a striking alternative to Smith's vision. Instead of the assistance and cooperation of many thousands, Carnegie and Rand describe an elite caste that provides the vision, brains, and organizational savvy that ensure a thriving economy. They are the "visible hand" of capitalism. For Carnegie, Rand, and others like them, if you want to know who makes capitalism work, simply stand at the base of the economic pyramid and look up—you'll find the "job creators" at the very top.

Because most innovation and wealth production happens in corporations, we need to figure a way for workers to get access to ownership in corporations. This is a fundamental link we must establish.

We think it right to accept both the truths embodied in Smith's reality of human nature and Rand's assertion as to the role of the best and brightest among us. The key, then, is how to best *harness them to produce the greatest good for the greatest number.*

Let's consider what role unions can play.

Cooperation Versus Confrontation
[end the zero-sum game]

Unions as they evolved in the United States became very adversarial, untrusting, and opposed to the success and prosperity of the business. This is my major objection to unions today—they harm the flourishing of the business for all the stakeholders. Instead of cooperation between stakeholders, they focus on competition between management and labor. Instead of embracing the notion of the "expanding pie" vision of capitalism (more for everyone, or win-win) they frequently embrace the zero-sum philosophy of win-lose.
  —John Mackey, co-CEO of Whole Foods Market[120]

THE 3RD WAY

The above quote is one person's viewpoint. We still think unions can be relevant. However, the state of working America as it relates to unionization in private industry is in nothing short of a crisis situation.

Declining Unionization

The percentage of the work force represented by unions was stable in the 1970s but fell rapidly in the 1980s and continued to fall in the 1990s and early 2000s (see fig. 22).[121] This falling rate of unionization has lowered wages, not only because some workers no longer receive the higher union wage but also because there is less pressure on nonunion employers to raise wages; the spillover or threat effect of unionism and the ability of unions to set labor standards have both declined. The possibility that union bargaining power has weakened adds a qualitative shift to the quantitative decline. This erosion of bargaining power is partially related to a harsher economic context for unions because of trade pressures, the shift to services, and ongoing technological change. However, analysts have also pointed to other factors, such as employers' militant stance against unions and changes in the application and administration of labor law that have helped to weaken unions and their ability to raise wages.

The history of unions includes a period in the 1920s where there was a debate about independent unions in contrast to company unions more dependent on management and business. Perhaps the principles in this book can help stabilize the overall situation for workers and unions that can have members who are owners. More importantly and most assuredly the Third Way creates a relatively safe place for workers of the present and future.

One thing is for sure. The status quo is unacceptable. Positive, significant change for the working class is a must.

WHAT IS THE ACADEMIC RATIONALE?

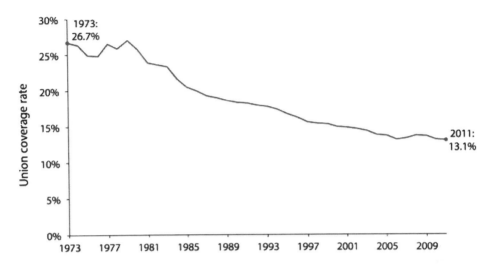

Figure 23. Union coverage rate in the United States, 1973–2011 (Source: Author's analysis of Hirsch and Macpherson (2003) and updates from the *Union Membership and Coverage Database*)

Confrontation

Death by Politics: When Teamwork Is Un-American
By John Case
Discussion of the negative effect of the Wagner Act on nonadversarial labor-management relations

At smart companies, labor and management don't fight anymore—but the law says that workers and managers are intractable enemies and fairness is possible only if the two "sides" wage a cockfight.

The story begins way back in the 1920s, when hundreds of American companies set up what were known as work councils or company unions—bodies designed to encourage shop-floor cooperation and to represent employee interests, but without any ties to organized labor. Some of those councils, such as Goodyear's so-called Industrial Assembly, had real power and did much to foster teamwork. Others were little more than employer-sponsored shams. Set up a docile house union, the theory ran, and you can persuade workers they don't need an independent one.

Organized labor, not surprisingly, hated them all. When the New Deal-era Congress was debating labor law in 1935, Senator Robert F. Wagner made sure his bill banned company unions. The Wagner Act thus institutionalized the idea that labor and management are intractable enemies. In effect, the new law said that cooperation was always a snare and a delusion. What the two adversaries needed was a level playing field where they could duke it out. That idea has defined labor relations ever since.

The Wagner Act's adversarial system worked fine for a while, mostly because big US companies dominated their markets. When companies and unions went to the mat, as they did regularly, the unions could win generous wage hikes and the companies could then raise prices. But starting in the mid-1970s, American businesses began learning harsh lessons about the new global economy they were competing in. They could no longer raise prices with impunity. They had to boost quality and service levels. Consumers now had more choices: if they didn't like Detroit's offerings, they could buy a Toyota.

In this new environment the adversarial approach to labor relations could be an albatross around business's neck. Union contracts fixed labor costs regardless of competitive conditions.

WHAT IS THE ACADEMIC RATIONALE?

Union work rules restricted management's ability to introduce new technology or reorganize production methods. Worst of all, the adversarial system engendered fear and loathing on the shop floor. Hard-nosed managers assumed employees were slugs. Wary workers figured managers were out to screw them. Quality? Hah. That's the company's problem.

That basic incompatibility (between new market conditions and the old adversarial system of labor relations) has spawned two unexpected developments in today's business world.

One is the near death of the labor movement. Union membership is shrinking. Contract negotiations are bitter and fruitless. Newly aggressive companies fight back rather than give in; unions cling desperately to old and ineffective strategies. The recent sorry dispute between Caterpillar and the United Auto Workers is the perfect example of a lose-lose battle. The union slunk back to work, defeated. The company earned the undying hostility of the very people it must depend on to ensure world-class quality.

The other big development: a startling proliferation of experiments in cooperative, nonadversarial labor-management relations.

Some companies have set up quality teams, self-directed work groups, or employee task forces. Others have established employee stock ownership plans or elaborate profit-sharing arrangements. The purpose of all those experiments: to get employees and managers working together, rather than at cross-purposes. Small companies such as Springfield Remanufacturing Corp. and Web Industries have been in the forefront of the movement. The results in many cases have been little short of spectacular.[122]

Here's the real scoop, folks: Many union members and their leaders may be concerned that ESOPs will make unions less necessary. We think that is absolutely not the case. ESOPs will make unions *more* necessary—especially in businesses where they are already in place. With ESOPs, unions will be doing twice as much for their members as they're doing now. In fact, they'll do even more than that because right now, unions mainly try to distribute through labor what is produced by capital rather than *also trying to make their members capital owners*. Once an ESOP is established, the job of the union is to make certain that year after year a reasonable amount of the company's growth is financed through the ESOP and that the wages of capital are paid fully and regularly to employees, just like the wages of labor.

Bottom line: a far better approach in any union's collective bargaining process is to *also ask for stock trusts instead of just wage increases.*

Cooperation

Management of a company requires knowledge of the interrelationships between all the components within the system and of the people that work in it. The secret is cooperation between components toward the aim of the organization.
—W. Edwards Deming, American statistician, professor, author, lecturer, and business consultant[123]

ESOP Association President J. Michael Keeling's remarks from the 2011 Las Vegas Conference and Trade Show emphasized that *ESOP companies are "more productive, more profitable, more sustainable, providing locally controlled jobs."* These are all very important attributes worthy of note.

Currently, many of the companies with significant ownership through their ESOPs are privately held and not publically traded, so very few are well known outside of their industry and/or region. Public companies that use company stock in a 401(k) often have

WHAT IS THE ACADEMIC RATIONALE?

an ESOP trust linked to the 401(k) plan trust. But these companies usually have only 5 percent or less of the company stock in trusts for the benefit of employees.

Having said this, Procter & Gamble is famous for compensating employees with P&G stock since the nineteenth century—currently about 8 percent of P&G stock is in its ESOP. Publix Supermarkets, which many people east of the Mississippi know about, has an ESOP. Several convenience-store chains have around 20 percent ownership through an ESOP. In the northeast, one might be aware of the Wawa chain. Hercules Chemical Company in New Jersey and Stewart's Shops in New York State are just two in a very long list of more local successful businesses with ESOPs.

Some large ESOP companies that are private but with many employees are: Houchens, which has in its family of subsidiaries Sonics fast food; Amsted, most famous for its company Baltimore Aircoil (BAC)—you can see BAC cooling and heating on top of buildings all over America; and Recology, a big waste-management company in California, primarily in San Francisco.

Several other high-profile US companies offer some form of broad-based employee stock option or stock plan to employees. Many of these companies have flourished, including Starbucks, Microsoft, Whole Foods Market, and Southwest Airlines.

Cogent data on how companies with ESOPs are outperforming the market in both *performance* and *stability of employment* in these changing times is powerful.

During the Great Recession, an analysis of the General Social Survey, conducted nationwide out of the University of Chicago, found that workers with employee ownership were laid off employees at a rate of less than 3 percent, whereas workers at conventionally owned companies laid off employees at a rate just above 12 percent.[124]

Research by the National Center for Employee Ownership (NCEO) shows employees of private companies with ESOPs are 2.5 times more likely to have two employer-sponsored retirement savings plans that those without; nearly half of all employees of private companies had zero retirement savings plans sponsored by their employer.

The book *Shared Capitalism at Work*, which reviewed over a hundred thousand data points, showed that companies with ESOPs had less turnover, more loyalty to the company by the employees, higher pay, more benefits, and greater employee wealth.

A survey of ESOP Association members indicated that average employee 401(k) account balances in 2010 were at nearly $200,000. However, the average account balances of employees in firms without ESOPs, based on national research bureaus such as Employee Benefit Research Institute, averaged around $70,000.

A dissertation by Dr. Bret Kramer of the City University of New York found an ESOP company's advantage over matched counterparts of, say, two hundred employees as an example was $9 million more per year in sales.

Research over an eleven-year period by Rutgers professors Dr. Joseph Blasi and Dr. Doug Kruse found that ESOP companies were still operating after the eleven-year period at a rate of 77.9 percent, compared with 64.3 percent for matched counterparts of the same size and industry but without ESOPs.

Additional research by NCEO lists top employee-owned companies and why they are great places to work.

NCEO The National Center for Employee Ownership

Table 2. The Employee Ownership 100: America's Largest Majority Employee-Owned Companies
(Source: http://www.nceo.org/articles/employee-ownership-100)

August 2013
Companies must be at least 50% owned by an ESOP or other qualified plan or by one or more other kinds of plans in which at least

WHAT IS THE ACADEMIC RATIONALE?

50% of full-time employees are eligible to participate. Employment includes all full- and part-time employees in the U.S. and worldwide. Data are from corporate Web sites, company responses to an email, or, if these are not available, the most recent public data, usually from 2013. Additions and corrections are welcome; contact us at research@nceo.org. Also see our list of Great Employee-Owned Workplaces.

Company	City	State	Plan	Start Date	Business	Employees
Publix Super Markets	Lakeland	FL	ESOP & Stock Purchase	1974	Supermarkets	159,000
Hy-Vee	West Des Moines	IA	Profit Sharing	1994	Supermarkets	56,000
CH2M Hill	Englewood	CO	Stock Incentive & Purchase Plan	2005	Engineering & construction	30,000
Price Chopper	Schenectady	NY	Profit Sharing	1996	Supermarkets	23,000
Lifetouch	Eden Prairie	MN	ESOP	1977	Photography	22,200
Daymon Worldwide	Stamford	CT	ESOP/ Others	2001	Food distribution	22,000
Penmac	Springfield	MO	ESOP	2010	Staffing	18,000
Houchens Industries	Bowling Green	KY	ESOP	1961	Supermarkets & other services	16,000
WinCo Foods	Boise	ID	ESOP	1985	Supermarkets	14,400
Alliance Holdings	Abington	PA	ESOP	1995	Holding company	13,000
Amsted Industries	Chicago	IL	ESOP	1984	Industrial components	12,000
Parsons	Pasadena	CA	ESOP	1974	Engineering & construction	11,500
Black & Veatch	Overland Park	KS	ESOP*	1998	Engineering	10,000
W.L. Gore & Associates	Newark	DE	ESOP	1974	Manufacturing	10,000
HDR	Omaha	NE	ESOP	1996	Architecture & engineering	8,000

Company	City	State	Plan	Start Date	Business	Employees
MWH Global	Broomfield	CO	ESOP*	N/A	Engineering & consulting	8,000
Herff Jones	Indianapolis	IN	ESOP	1989	Awards & gifts	7,800
Davey Tree Expert	Kent	OH	401KSOP & ESOP	1979	Tree services	7,400
Graybar Electric	St. Louis	MO	Stock purchase	1929	Electrical equipment wholesale	7,400
The Burnett Companies Consolidated, Inc.	Houston	TX	ESOP	2010	Staffing services	7,300
Schreiber Foods	Green Bay	WI	ESOP	1998	Dairy company	7,000
Brookshire Brothers	Lufkin	TX	ESOP	2001	Supermarkets	6,000
Austin Industries	Dallas	TX	ESOP	1986	Construction	5,600
Blue Tee Corp.	New York	NY	ESOP	1996	Industrial machinery distribution	5,000
CDM Smith	Cambridge	MA	Profit Sharing	1996	Engineering & construction	5,000
Piggly Wiggly Carolina Company	Charleston	SC	ESOP	1985	Supermarkets	5,000
Scheels All Sports	Fargo	ND	ESOP	1982	Retail sporting goods	5,000
PeopleCare Holdings.	New York City	NY	ESOP	1985	Engineering & Manufacturing	1,100
EmpRes Healthcare Management, LLC	Vancouver	WA	ESOP	2009	Health care staffing	4,350
Acadian Ambulance	Lafayette	LA	ESOP	1993	Ambulance services	4,000
Cianbro	Pittsfield	ME	ESOP*	1980	Construction	4,000
KeHE Distributors	Romeoville	IL	ESOP	2001	Food distribution	4,000
Sammons Enterprises	Dallas	TX	ESOP	1978	Diversified holding company	4,000
TMI Hospitality	Fargo	ND	ESOP	1998	Motel management	3,890

WHAT IS THE ACADEMIC RATIONALE?

Company	City	State	Plan	Start Date	Business	Employees
Schweitzer Engineering Laboratories	Pullman	WA	ESOP	1994	Engineering	3,690
Burns & McDonnell	Kansas City	MO	ESOP	1985	Architecture & engineering	3,600
Chemonics	Washington	DC	ESOP	2001	International development	3,600
Sterling Global Operations, Inc.	Lenoir City	TN	ESOP	2002	Security & munitions services	3,500
Gensler	San Francisco	CA	ESOP	1987	Architecture	3,500
Homeland Acquisition Corporation, Inc.	Oklahoma City	OK	ESOP	2011	Supermarkets	3,500
People Care Holdings, Inc.	New York	NY	ESOP	2007	Healthcare Services	3,500
HNTB	Kansas City	MO	ESOP	2000	Architecture & engineering	3,470
Lewis Tree Service	West Henrietta	NY	ESOP	1998	Tree services	3,470
Alion Science and Technology	McLean	VA	ESOP	2001	Technology services	3,400
Harps Food Stores	Springdale	AR	ESOP	1988	Supermarkets	3,400
RPCS, Inc.	Springfield	MO	ESOP	2004	Supermarkets	3,300
American Cast Iron Pipe	Birmingham	AL	Profit Sharing	1982	Manufacturing	3,000
Bi-Mart	Eugene	OR	ESOP	2003	Discount stores	3,000
CentiMark	Canonsburg	PA	ESOP	1988	Roof repair	3,000
KI	Green Bay	WI	Profit Sharing	1991	Furniture manufacturing	3,000
Miller's Health Systems	Warsaw	IN	ESOP	2006	Nursing homes	3,000
Reasor's	Tahlequah	OK	ESOP	2005	Supermarkets	3,000
Kinney Drugs	Gouverneur	NY	ESOP	1944	Drugstores	2,900
McCarthy Building Company	St. Louis	MO	ESOP	1996	Construction	2,800
Recology	San Francisco	CA	ESOP	1985	Waste management	2,800
Terracon	Olathe	KS	ESOP	1991	Engineering/consulting	2,800

Company	City	State	Plan	Start Date	Business	Employees
R.W. Baird	Milwaukee	WI	ESPP	1984	Brokerage	2,700
Rosendin Electric	San Jose	CA	ESOP	1992	Electrical Contracting	2,500
Abt Associates	Cambridge	MA	ESOP	1975	Consulting & research	2,400
Guckenheimer Enterprises	Redwood City	CA	ESOP	1987	Food distribution	2,400
Wright Tree Services	Des Moines	IA	ESOP	2002	Environmental Services	2,400
Kelly-Moore Paints	San Carlos	CA	ESOP	1998	Paint manufacturing/ retail	2,300
Cooperative Home Care Associates	Bronx	NY	Worker Cooperative	1995	Health care	2,200
Columbia Forest Products	Portland	OR	ESOP	1977	Plywood	2,000
Hensel Phelps Construction	Greeley	CO	Profit Sharing	1976	Construction	2,000
Kleinfelder	San Diego	CA	ESOP	1989	Engineering	2,000
Medicalodges	Coffeyville	KS	ESOP	1990	Nursing homes	2,000
The Saxton Group	New York	NY	ESOP	2013	Restaurants	2,000
TRAX International	Las Vegas	NV	ESOP	1997	Professional services	2,000
Westat	Rockville	MD	ESOP	1977	Research firm	2,000
Round Table Pizza	Concord	CA	ESOP	1984	Pizza Franchise	1,800
Appvion, Inc.	Appleton	WI	ESOP	1984	Paper products	1,700
Jasper Engines & Transmissions	Jasper	IN	ESOP	2010	Engine & transmission remanufacturing	1,700
S&C Electric	Chicago	IL	ESOP	1989	Electrical equipment	1,700
STV Group	Douglassville	PA	ESOP	1981	Engineering & architecture	1,670
Weston Solutions	West Chester	PA	ESOP	1984	Environmental engineering	1,650
Airborn Inc.	Addison	TX	ESOP	1996	Electronic Connectors	1,600

WHAT IS THE ACADEMIC RATIONALE?

Company	City	State	Plan	Start Date	Business	Employees
Ebby Halliday Realtors	Dallas	TX	ESOP	1991	Real estate	1,600
TDIndustries	Dallas	TX	ESOP	1989	HVAC supplies	1,600
American Systems	Chantilly	VA	ESOP	1990	Engineering	1,500
Brown and Caldwell	Walnut Creek	CA	ESOP	1962	Engineering	1,500
Dunn-Edwards Paints	Los Angeles	CA	ESOP	2000	Paint manufacturing	1,500
Martin & Bayley	Carmi	IL	ESOP	1984	Convenience stores	1,500
Sleep Train	Citrus Heights	CA	ESOP	2010	Mattress retailer	1,500
Barton Malow	Southfield	MI	Profit Sharing	1952	Construction	1,420
Applied Research Associates	Alburquerque	NM	ESOP	1993	Engineering research	1,400
Border States Industries	Fargo	ND	ESOP	1984	Electrical supplies	1,400
Bradford White	Ambler	PA	ESOP	1992	Water heaters	1,400
Dahl's Foods	Des Moines	IA	ESOP	1975	Supermarkets	1,400
Fred Weber	Maryland Heights	MO	ESOP	1986	Construction firm & materials supplier	1,400
Roberts Hawaii	Honolulu	HI	ESOP	2006	Tour bus operator	1,400
Sundt	Tempe	AZ	ESOP	1972	Construction	1,360
Swinerton	San Francisco	CA	ESOP	1962	Construction	1,330
Charles Machine Works	Perry	OK	ESOP	1985	Heavy equipment manufacturer	1,300
Dynetics	Huntsville	AL	ESOP	1988	Engineering, science, information technology services	1,300
FBG Service Corp.	Omaha	NE	ESOP	1992	Building services	1,300
Riesbeck Food Markets	St. Clairsville	OH	ESOP	1986	Supermarkets	1,300

Company	City	State	Plan	Start Date	Business	Employees
SRC Holdings	Springfield	MO	ESOP	1983	Equipment remanufacturing	1,300
Advent Software	San Francisco	CA	ESPP	2005	Software	1,200
Zandex Health Care	Zanesville	OH	ESOP	2003	Nursing homes	1,200

Plans similar to ESOPs, but not listed as ESOPs in Department of Labor data.

The following employee-owned companies have all been recognized as great workplaces by either <u>Winning Workplaces</u> or *Fortune* magazine's <u>100 Best Companies to Work For</u>. Employee-owned companies are consistently overrepresented on these lists, because in addition to an ownership interest, they often also provide an ownership culture of trust and respect between employees and company leadership.

Table 3. Great Employee-Owned Workplaces
(Source: http://www.nceo.org/great-employee)

Companies are listed by industry:
Jobs in Design, Production, and Manufacturing
<u>W.L. Gore & Associates</u>, Performance Wear, Electronics, Cables, and More.
<u>PCL Construction Enterprises,</u> Construction of Commercial Buildings and Civil Infrastructure.
<u>ATA Engineering</u>, Specializing in Complex Mechanical Structures.
<u>Restek,</u> Cromatography Products.
<u>David Evans & Associates</u>, Engineering, Architecture, and Consulting Firm.

Burns & McDonnell, Engineering, Architecture, and Consulting Firm.
Granite Construction, Infrastructure-Related Construction.
TDIndustries, Mechanical Construction and Facility Service.
Medtronic, Medical Technology.
Chroma Technology, Optical Filters.
Exactech, Orthopaedic Products and Solutions.
Hypertherm, Plasma Cutting Systems.
The Railroad Associates Corp., Railroad Design and Construction.
The Sky Factory, Residential and Commercial Skylights.
Skyline Construction Inc., Sustainable/Green Building Construction.
Barclay Water Management, Water Treatment Products and Solutions.

Jobs in Commercial Services
Paychex, Payroll and Human Resource Services.
Quad/Graphics, Print Media Services.
Biomarc, Sterilization of Commercial Environments.
Van Meter Industrial, Electrical and Mechanical Supplier.

Jobs in Finance
Phelps County Bank, General Banking and Investments.
Principal Financial Group, General Banking and Investments.
Bailard Inc., Investment Banking.

Jobs in the Food and Beverage Industry
New Belgium Brewery, Brewery based out of Fort Collins, CO.
King Arthur Flour, America's Oldest Flour Company.
Publix Supermarkets, Supermarkets throughout the Southeast.
QuikTrip, Convenience Stores in the Midwest and South.

Jobs in Software Design
Autodesk, 3D Design, Entertainment and Engineering Software.
Heavy Construction Systems Specialists Inc., Heavy Construction Software.

Analytical Graphics Inc., Space, Defense, and Intelligence Software.
Jobs in Consumer Goods Companies
Jackson's Hardware, Hardware Store in Northern California.
Men's Wearhouse, National Men's Clothing Store Chain.
Procter & Gamble, Nationally Distributed Household Products.

Common Sense
[should be common...]

All truth, in the long run, is only common sense clarified.
—Thomas Huxley, English biologist,
major advocate of Charles Darwin's theory of evolution[125]

In an ownership society, union officials in unionized companies should also *evolve* into being more like "captains of successful teams," rather than adversaries against the very organizations they and their members rely on for prosperity. All parties should strive for *cooperation versus confrontation*. Nevertheless, unions will always retain their core function of looking out for the rights of workers.

A rising tide of productivity lifts all boats. Shared capitalism does not just benefit a few, but everyone who plays a role in the creation of wealth.

If we can put a man on the moon, make heart transplants nearly routine, have in our pockets iPhones that can instantly access almost any information or contact almost any person on earth, we must have the intelligence, found in great political thinkers from Plato to the present, to devise a better political/economic system than the two flawed choices (capitalism and socialism) we are left with today.

WHAT IS THE ACADEMIC RATIONALE?

While other taxpayer measures, such as the "Flat Tax," the "Fair Tax," the "9-9-9 Plan," et cetera, may have real merit and include elements that perhaps should be considered for enactment, none of them has the political, social, psychological, and economic *transformative* quality of the measure we are proposing—to encourage widespread employee ownership. *THE 3rd WAY* is far more than just good tax reform. It is a substantial positive social and economic reform. It is a profound solution for the world—a solution where America can lead the way!

Each citizen needs to realize that corporate taxes are often passed on as a "cost of doing business" to the consumer in increased prices. What we are proposing is that corporate taxes serve a larger societal purpose to not only support the necessary activities of the government but also encourage widespread property ownership. It is axiomatic in some circles that what you tax you get less of. Our program of tax incentives is designed to increase economic growth and increase jobs by encouraging the creation of more entrepreneurial corporations of all sizes in the United States. With these tax incentives we propose, we hope to open a flood of capital formation, resulting in more growth and jobs. We also hope that by increasing the number of citizens who have real, significant capital stakes in the economy, we will increase, not decrease, the number of taxpayers and therefore broaden the tax base.

A great, simple analogy to explain *THE 3rd WAY* to every person is by showing the difference between a regular baseball game and Home Run Derby:

- In a regular game, the two sides (pitcher and batter) are pitted against each other.

- The umpire (government), though the ultimate authority, never gets involved in the actual game itself!

- In Home Run Derby, both the pitcher and the batter are on the *same side.* The pitcher (business) makes it as easy as possible for the batter (labor) to be successful. Everyone wins!

We are long overdue to institutionalize the productive alignment of both management and workers pulling together for the benefit of all. Clearly, we must institute a bold augmentation to our corporate taxing system to incentivize companies to establish opportunities for worker equity and ownership.

Everyone Wins—Even Uncle Sam
[no significant net loss of tax revenue to the government]

I think that Capitalism, wisely managed, can probably be made more efficient for attaining economic ends than any alternative system yet in sight.
—John Maynard Keynes, British economist, widely considered one of the founders of modern macroeconomics[126]

Under our proposal, instead of the government getting corporate taxes from employers, it gets, via the transfer of wealth, income taxes from the workers. Combine this with our call to cut some of the most egregious corporate tax loopholes (outlined later in the book) and the result can be crafted to result in a NO NET LOSS IN REVENUE TO THE US TREASURY.

Though the United States corporate tax rate is the highest in the world at 35%, the *effective* corporate tax rate is only HALF that for many corporations, with many paying zero taxes through a variety of methods.

Our proposal has many beneficial dimensions with no downside loss in overall tax revenue. Everyone wins.

Nevertheless, the overriding positive element is how economic democracy helps drive all the synergistic benefits to workers, their companies and the nation as a whole. For most of these workers,

WHAT IS THE ACADEMIC RATIONALE?

their income gain from ESOP equity is not the single factor in the positive effects on both worker and company. *Ownership* drives a much deeper core motivator.

Gaining some level of ownership in one's place of work brings with it a cascade of tangible benefits to all sides:
1. The better relationship between the workers and their employer
2. Enhanced employee loyalty to the company
3. A feeling of enhanced security by the employee
4. A sense by the employee of truly being involved in the company
5. A much more motivated work force
6. Improved performance of the firm

These positive elements not only redound to the company—they transfer to society as a whole:
1. A motivated employee is de facto a productive member of society.
2. Productive members of society need *dramatically fewer social services.*
3. They are positive role models for both their families and their community.
4. Inner-city youth involved in such programs tend not to be a drain on society via crime and negative behavior. They could become bright lights of hope to others all around them. A dramatic, positive social shift is at work!

The Foundation Of Binary Economics
[the economic underpinnings of this new way]

It sometimes takes decades, even centuries, for foundation-altering ideas to permeate the social hierarchies that prescribe and reward acceptable mainstream thought while ignoring and marginalizing the rest. Nevertheless, with the collapse of much state communism; with the growing recognition that the surviving capitalist economies are

facing worsening problems in achieving a just and efficient distribution; and with increasing calls for new alternatives beyond right, left and center, there is some reason to hope that people are sincerely ready to take a fresh look at economic assumptions. That look will come not a moment too soon.
—Robert Ashford and Rodney Shakespeare,
Binary Economics: The New Paradigm[127]

The term *binary* is derived from this approach's combined treatment of labor *and* capital. In binary economics, labor and capital are effectively "linked," thereby exerting the full power of both forces to drive the economy. In the current system, the two are increasingly disconnected, leading to inevitable grave inequities.

Binary economics is about enabling people to be productive through owning income-earning, productive capital assets through employment. What follows is an excellent excerpt on the entire subject.

Binary Economic Modes for the Privatization of Public Assets

By Jerry N. Gauche

Binary economics offers a new paradigm for economic growth in which the supply and demand sides of the economy are linked through broad-based capital ownership.

As technology advances, more and more income is earned by these assets compensating people for the decline in demand for traditional employment based methods of contributing to wealth creation. Everyone increasingly becomes a "capitalist."

"It takes money to make money," is an oft used phrase in the capitalist economies of the Western world. And while it is not entirely true…most of us actually exchange our labor for money… it has an intuitive logic that causes the hearer to nod in agreement.

WHAT IS THE ACADEMIC RATIONALE?

We all recognize that labor can produce only a limited amount of income and that "the real money" is made by those who invest their capital to produce income. This fact has become increasingly problematic in capitalist economies as the tools of technology produce an ever increasing portion of the wealth.

Binary economics, first expounded by Kelso and Adler in 1958, differs from classical economics in asserting that there are two factors of production, labor and capital. These factors of production command returns equal to the contribution each makes. With the application of technology capital is increasingly prevalent and productive and consequently commands an ever increasing portion of the total value produced in the economy. The contribution of labor, on the other hand, is relatively fixed. Even the most highly compensated laborers in our society, the doctors, lawyers and professional managers, are essentially hourly employees. They may earn very high hourly rates, but their income is limited by the number of hours they can, or are willing, to work.

Not so for the owner of capital. The income of the capital owner is limited only by the amount of capital that owner can productively invest. Classical economics presents the individual with a "Catch-22" which has serious implications for economic growth. If a member of the society does not have capital, he or she must develop that capital out of savings. The savings are produced from reduced consumption, thus, reducing the demand for goods and services in the economy as a whole.

Conventional methods of financing economic development and the creation of new capital rely heavily upon the use of credit. Borrowed money is used to purchase assets which produce income to amortize the financing. Once the financing is amortized the capital continues to produce income for its owner which may be used for consumption. This credit route to the creation of capital is common in corporate acquisitions, the purchase of real estate, and the development of new enterprises within existing organizations.

Unfortunately, the access to capital through credit is limited. Because lenders abhor undue risk, lending institutions look to existing capital as a form of guarantee for the credit. Thus, the financial strength (capital base) of the borrower is the source of comfort and reduced risk to the lender. This is true even in leveraged buyouts where the lender looks for security to the equity of the company, which admittedly may have been very small in the highly leveraged buyouts in the United States in the late 1980s. In some cases, the lender may look exclusively to the experience, expertise or energy of the buyer as security for the loan, but these situations are rare. More often existing capital is put "at risk" to assure the lender against the possibility that the new capital will not pay for itself. Thus, existing capital becomes the foundation upon which new capital is built. From the perspective of the individual, once he or she develops capital, whether from saving, inheritance, gifts or otherwise, that capital can guarantee access to additional capital.

This capital formation process forecloses the broad base of the population from participating in the income which capital can produce. They have no capital to serve as a guarantee and cannot easily reduce consumption to build capital from savings. At the same time, a few family units are already producing significantly more capital income than they can, or are willing to, consume. This excess income is reinvested in capital assets, producing ever more income that cannot be consumed and foreclosing other family units from participating in the growth of new capital to produce income for their consumption. The result is a significant concentration of capital in most economies in the hands of a very few family units (Kelso & Hetter, 1967a).

Binary economics holds out hope for those without access to capital. At the same time it offers the prospect of significant economic growth. It is unlike classical economics with its Supply Siders, who focus on capital formation, and its Keynesians, who focus on the creation of demand. Binary economics envisions the formation of capital in such a way that the income produced would be used for consumption rather than reinvestment. It is this connection between the formation of capital and the demand for goods and services that provides underperforming economies the prospect of significantly improved growth.

Binary economics invites us to reconsider the ways in which capital is formed and distributed in our economies. It suggests alternatives for capital formation in which the formerly disenfranchised may participate. Binary techniques involve providing access to credit for capital investment to those who have not, heretofore, had such access because they lacked existing capital. A range of options has been proposed by Louis Kelso, Patricia Hetter and others which would provide broad access to capital through credit guarantees (Kelso & Hetter, 1967b). It is important to note that binary economics does not demand the redistribution of existing capital. It does, however, imply that the ownership of existing capital should not provide the only route for access to new capital and proposes broader participation in the formation of capital in the economy through the use of credit.[128]

Concordian Economics
[further intellectual support for the ownership concept]

Concordian economics is the study of the organic and dynamic set of human relationships: How do people produce wealth? How do they divide the ownership of that wealth among themselves? How do they use money to buy and to sell goods? The attention is focused not on simplistic observations of markets but on the economic effects of the inner workings of economic justice.[129]

An Introduction to Concordian Economics
(an excerpt)
By Carmine Gorga,
author of *The Economic Process: An Instantaneous Non-Newtonian Picture* and founder of the website concordian-economics.org

To best understand Concordian economics, one has to relate it to the conditions of the modern world. The essentials of this condition can be put quite simply. While the followers of Don Quixote (artists and the literati) chase windmills, the followers of Galileo (scientists and technologists) build windmills; and a chosen few (the oligarchs) concentrate on *owning* the windmills.

The numbers are impressive. Summarizing the results of numerous studies and official government reports, [it was found] that, between 1972 and 2001, the wage and salary income of Americans at the 90th percentile of the income distribution rose only 34 percent, or about 1 percent per year. So being in the top 10 percent of the income distribution, like being a college graduate, wasn't a ticket to big income gains.

WHAT IS THE ACADEMIC RATIONALE?

But income at the 99th percentile rose 87 percent; income at the 99.9th percentile rose 181 percent; and income at the 99.99th percentile rose 497 percent. No, that's not a misprint.

Just to give you a sense of whom we're talking about: the nonpartisan Tax Policy Center estimates that this year the 99th percentile will correspond to an income of $402,306, and the 99.9th percentile to an income of $1,672,726. The center doesn't give a number for the 99.99th percentile, but it's probably well over $6 million a year.

Aren't you at least a little bit curious as to how the oligarchs do it?

Hint: They do it legally.

Double hint: They do not corrupt judges and legislators.

Triple hint: These results have nothing to do with the laws of supply and demand, but with the workings of the economic process as a whole.

I do not believe that "the state" will ever help us wrest the ownership of the windmills from the oligarchs. I do believe in the power of these four economic rights and responsibilities to set things right in the modern world:

1. We all have the right of access to land and natural resources. This is a natural right. It belongs to us just in virtue of our humanness. The oligarchs control an enormous portion of land and natural resources because they do not pay fair taxes on them.

2. We all have the right of access to national credit.

3. We all have the right to the fruits of our labor. This right should not be limited to the right to obtain only a wage. It

> should be extended to the right to the other major fruit of economic growth over time: capital appreciation—as well as being subject to capital loss, of course. While workers receive the pittance of a diminishing wage, the oligarchs receive the blessings of capital appreciation.
> 4. We all have the right to protect our wealth.
>
> I must say that there is not a stitch of originality in these principles. They all stem from the thought of Benjamin Franklin, Henry George, Louis D. Brandeis, and Louis O. Kelso. Read them in rapid succession, and you discover one picks up from where the other left off. Together they form a very sturdy compound; together they shape an unassailable, comprehensive, all-American economic policy concerning (1) land and natural resources; (2) money; (3) labor; and (4) physical capital.
>
> Do not fight the oligarchs; rather, join them. Ask them not for a wage, but for a share of the profits (a share of the ownership of the corporation in which you work) and assume the risks of doing so. Gradually transform the Labor Movement into an Ownership Movement.[130]

Stabilizing Employment
[employee ownership works on many levels!]

As legal slavery passed, we entered into a permanent period of unemployment and underemployment from which we have yet to emerge.
—Julian Bond, American social activist, civil rights leader, politician, professor, and writer[131]

WHAT IS THE ACADEMIC RATIONALE?

How Did Employee Ownership Firms Weather the Last Two Recessions? Employee Ownership and Employment Stability in the United States: 1999–2008

April 15, 2012

By:

Fidan Ana Kurtulus
University of Massachusetts Amherst
Department of Economics

Douglas Kruse
Rutgers
University School
of Management
Labor Relations

Do firms with employee ownership (EO) programs exhibit greater employment stability in the face of economic downturns? In particular, are firms with employee ownership programs less likely to lay off workers during negative shocks? The following examines the relationship between employee ownership programs and employment stability in the United States on a panel of publicly-traded companies during 1999–2008. We examine how firms with employee ownership programs weathered the recessions of 2001 and 2008 in terms of employment stability relative to firms without employee ownership programs, and also whether such firms were less likely to lay off workers when faced with negative shocks more broadly. In our econometric analyses, we use a rich array of measures of employee ownership at firms, including the presence of employee ownership stock in pension plans, the presence of Employee Stock Ownership Plans (ESOPs), the value of employee ownership stock per employee, the share of the firm owned by employees, the share of workers at the firm participating in employee ownership, and the share of workers at the firm participating in ESOPs. We also consider both economy-wide negative shock measures (increases in the unemployment rate, declines in the employment-to-population ratio) and firm-specific negative shock measures (declines in firm sales, declines in firm stock price). Our results indicate that employee ownership firms exhibit greater employment stability in the face of both economy-wide and firm-specific negative shocks. Here is a summary using several charts.

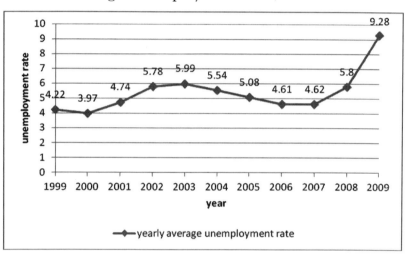

A. Average Unemployment Rate, 1999–2009

Employment is much more unstable in non Employee Ownership/ESOP (red line) companies. Conversely, Employee Ownership/ESOP (blue line) companies are far more stable.

WHAT IS THE ACADEMIC RATIONALE?

Average Yearly % Change in Employment (Comparing firms with and without Employee Ownership) '00–'08

B. Any Employee Ownership vs. No Employee Ownership

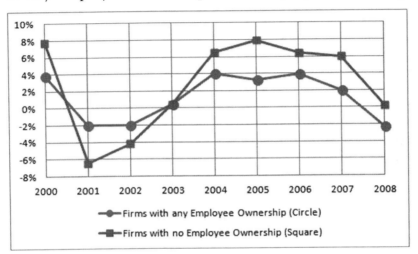

C. Firms with an ESOP vs. Firms without an ESOP

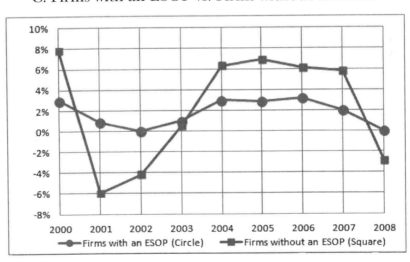

D. Firms more than 5 percent Employee-Owned vs. Firms less than 5 percent Employee Owned

Conclusion

Using data on all publicly-traded US companies during 1999–2008, this analysis has shown that firms with employee ownership exhibit greater employment stability in the face of economic downturn, both measured in terms of macroeconomic negative shocks (increases in the unemployment rate, decreases in the employment-to-population ratio) as well as firm-specific negative shocks (declines in firm sales, and to a lesser extent declines in firm stock price). These findings highlight the role employee ownership plays in stabilizing employment, particularly during recessions. They also underscore the importance of government policy that encourages employee ownership as a policy tool to curb unemployment during recessions.[132]

Optimal Inequality for Economic Growth, Stability, and Shared Prosperity: The Economics behind the Wall Street Occupiers Protest?

By Richard B. Freeman

The US economy performed well enough pre-2007 to convince many analysts that it was the best-performing major capitalist economy, but subsequent events proved this view illusory. Instead of reducing risk, Wall Street had enveloped the real economy in a highly leveraged financial house of cards—an estimated $22 of derivatives for every dollar of goods and services produced in 2009. Instead of creating a flexible labor market that could rebound quickly from a major economic shock, the US rapidly laid off workers in the recession but then increased employment slowly. Joblessness grew and many workers left the workforce because of the lack of demand for labor. Poverty increased and even fully employed workers came to rely on food stamps to keep their heads above water.[133]

Part II:

What Is An ESOP? What Other Steps Need To Be In Place?

Chapter 4:

HOW THE ESOP REALLY WORKS

The central purpose of this book is to make the case that *further enhancing* the tax incentives for corporations to share equity with their employees will redound to overall better performance by corporations, a more secure and motivated work force and countless benefits to society as a whole.

Introduction To ESOPs

The ESOP Association explains how the ESOP works as follows:
>An **employee stock ownership plan (ESOP)** is a defined contribution plan that provides a company's workers with an ownership interest in the company. Under the ESOP, companies provide their employees with stock ownership, typically at no cost to the employees. Shares are given to employees and are held in the ESOP trust until the employee retires or leaves the company, or earlier diversification opportunities, creating an opportunity for workers to amass long-term savings and benefit from their work.
>
>The growth of employee ownership since 1975 has been a significant development in the areas of business compensation, corporate finance and business continuation. Though there are several forms of employee ownership,

employee stock ownership plans, ESOPs have achieved the most widespread acceptance and support. The rapid and continuing growth in the number of ESOPs being established and the breadth of industries covered have important ramifications for employees, corporations, and the economy as a whole.[134]

Historical Background

The ESOP concept is based on the theories of capital ownership developed by Dr. Louis O. Kelso. Kelso reasoned that only through widespread capital ownership could modern economies provide for more equitable distribution of wealth. According to Kelso, the concentration of wealth in the US economy results from the fact that capital-producing assets are owned by a small minority of individuals. In an economy in which capital is inexorably replacing labor as the means by which wealth is produced, Kelso emphasized the importance of providing the majority, who do not presently own capital, with a means of achieving substantial stock ownership. Only by sharing in the ownership of productive capital would workers be able to obtain through the market the assets required to supplement the wages they earn through their labor, he said.

Since the average worker does not have the financial capability to buy that capital with his or her own earnings, Kelso conceived of the ESOP as a means of providing employees with access to capital credit. By giving employees a stake in corporate financial transactions, their capital ownership could be paid for out of the future earnings of the corporation. Widespread application of the ESOP concept would thus promote broadened ownership of wealth through free-enterprise initiatives, rather than resorting to government redistribution through taxation.

Kelso put his ideas into effect by helping install ESOPs in a number of companies during the 1950s, 1960s, and early 1970s.

But it was not until he attracted the support of US Senator Russell Long of Louisiana that ESOPs began to attract increasing attention. Senator Long was then chair of the Senate Committee on Finance, and he began to champion the ESOP cause on Capitol Hill.

The Employee Retirement Income Security Act of 1974 (ERISA) was the first major bill that facilitated the establishment of ESOPs. In the ensuing twelve years, Senator Long promoted the use of ESOPs in a number of additional legislative initiatives, culminating in the ESOP incentives included in the Tax Reform Act of 1986. Because of their unique character as a method of providing employees with an ownership stake in their companies, and because of the tax incentives used to promote their use as a technique for corporate finance, ESOPs have assumed a separate identity from other employee benefit plans. Since Senator Long's retirement in 1987, Congress has continued its support of laws promoting ESOPs. For example, in 1996–1997, Congress made it possible for S corporations to sponsor ESOPs with unique tax benefits. (An S corporation is one where the corporate entity pays no federal taxes because all its income is passed on to individual shareholders, who pay the taxes directly.) Now, more than three thousand S corporations are significantly owned by an ESOP for the benefit of employees.

Due primarily to vigorous legislative promotion by the US Congress, the number of ESOPs nationwide has increased from several hundred in 1974 to well over ten thousand by 2008, with continued growth expected.[135] Promoted as a means of broadening the ownership of capital and improving the productivity of the American work force, ESOPs have been at the forefront of the movement for employee ownership that is having profound effects on methods of employee compensation, techniques of corporate finance, and efforts to increase corporate performance and competitiveness.

The ESOP as an Employee Ownership and Benefit Plan

Unlike other employee benefit plans, which typically diversify their holdings by investing in a variety of assets, a company's ESOP, by law and design, invests primarily in the stock of the company, thereby making employees beneficial owners of the company where they work. Employees with an ownership stake in their company may be more motivated to improve corporate performance because they stand to benefit directly from company profitability and growth.

ESOPs as a Technique of Corporate Finance

In addition to the use of ESOPs as an employee benefit, Congress recognized that ESOPs may be an alternative vehicle for corporate financing. Because Congress identified the importance of making additional stock for a company's growth available, many tax incentives for ESOPs were intended to help promote the use of ESOPs as a technique of corporate finance. The tax benefits that ESOPs provide can indeed be an attractive incentive for corporations to share the benefits of corporate financial transactions with their employees.[136]

ESOPs and Corporate Finance

ESOPs provide an excellent means of encouraging workers to take a more active interest in company performance because they share in the equity growth created through productivity increases. As might be expected, employees tend to react to employee ownership in financial terms, and if contributions to an ESOP are small and account balances in the ESOP are negligible, the motivational effect may also be negligible.

A key factor determining positive employee attitudes toward an ESOP is the amount of stock and/or cash contributed to the plan on an annual basis. In other words, the greater the commitment a company makes to employee ownership by actually giving employees ownership (transferring a significant amount of stock to the employees) the greater the likelihood that employees will respond positively as owners.

What Is An ESOP?
[the legal framework]

An ESOP is a powerful, flexible vehicle for providing employers, shareholders, and employees with advantages not found in traditional tax-deferred benefit plans. Though ESOPs are unique in many respects, they do share some common characteristics with other employee benefit plans. As with all tax-qualified employees benefit plans, ESOPs must conform to the guidelines established by the IRS Code and ERISA (Employee Retirement Income Security Act of 1974).

General Plan Structure

Like all tax-qualified employee benefit plans, an ESOP must meet certain minimum requirements. It must be a defined-contribution plan that meets the qualification requirements of section 401(a) of the tax code in order for the contributions to be tax-deductible to the sponsoring employer.

Vesting

As with all tax-qualified benefit plans, employer-provided benefits under an ESOP must comply with at least one of two statutory minimum vesting schedules: three year "cliff" vesting, under which a participant is 100 percent vested after (but not before) three years of service, or six-year "graded" vesting, under which a participant is vested 20 percent after two years of service and is increasingly vested at an additional 20 percent per year until 100 percent vesting is reached after six years of service.

Voting Rights

ESOPs must meet the requirements of IRS Code section 409(c) with respect to voting rights on employer securities. This section sets out different rules depending, generally, on whether the plan sponsor is publically traded or closely held.

Diversification

ESOP participants must be given the opportunity to diversify their accounts as they approach retirement age. Participants who have attained at least age fifty-five and have completed at least ten years of participation in the ESOP are eligible to make annual elections over five years to diversify 25 percent of their ESOP stock account balance (on an aggregate basis) and at the end of the sixth year to make a final election to diversify up to 50 percent (again, on an aggregate basis). This does not apply, however, to certain "de minimis," or insignificant, amounts in participants' ESOP accounts.

To meet diversification requirements, the ESOP must offer at least three investment options other than employer securities. Alternatively, the ESOP may satisfy the diversification requirement by distributing to a participant the portion of the account balance the participant elected to diversify or allowing a transfer to another plan.[137]

Distribution of ESOP Benefits

Generally, unless the participant elects a later distribution, an ESOP must commence distribution of a participant's account balance not later than one year after the close of the plan year in which the participant separates from service due to normal retirement age, disability, or death, or one year after the close of the fifth plan year after the plan year the participant separated from service for other reasons.

ESOP Incentives
[legislative history]

To broaden ownership of capital and provide employees with access to capital credit, Congress has created a number of specific incentives meant to promote the increased use of the ESOP concept—particularly leveraged ESOPs, which provide for a more accelerated transfer of stock to employees. These ESOP incentives provide numerous advantages to the sponsoring employer, lenders, and selling shareholders. Since 1998, when a new law permitted S corporations to sponsor ESOPs, there have been differences between C and S corporations in the incentives provided, except for the deductibility of ESOP contributions.

Following is a summary of the major federal laws that have been passed to promote the use of ESOPs:

1. **Employee Retirement Income Securities Act of 1974 (ERISA)**

This law provided the first specific statutory framework for ESOPs and for the first time included a definition of "employee stock ownership plan" as a qualified plan under the Internal Revenue Code.

2. **Tax Reform Act of 1976**

The act contained a strong statement of congressional intent supporting ESOPs and directing the IRS to rewrite proposed ESOP regulations that Congress considered burdensome to ESOPs.

3. **Revenue Act of 1978**

This act required all ESOPs to offer employees put options in cases where the employer stock was not publically traded. It also permitted a cash distribution option.

4. **Economic Recovery Act of 1981**

This act revised the tax-deductible limits for leveraged ESOPs by excluding contributions used to pay loan interest from the 25 percent of covered payroll limit.

5. **Tax Reform Act of 1984**

This act provided significant new tax incentives for ESOPs sponsored by C corporations.

6. **Tax Reform Act of 1986**

This act revised rules for all qualified employee-retirement plans on a variety of provisions, including vesting, coverage requirements, minimum participant requirements, contribution limits, and the distribution of benefits. This act also contained significant additional tax incentives for ESOPs.

7. **Omnibus Budget Reconciliation Act of 1989**

This act limited the ESOPs lender's exclusion to situations in which the ESOP owns more than 50 percent of the company's common equity and required pass-through of voting rights on stock acquitted with a qualifying loan.

8. **Small Business Job Protection Act of 1996**

This act repealed the ESOP lender's interest exclusion effective for loans made after August 20, 1996. This act also permits an ESOP, as well as other tax-exempt trusts, to hold the stock of a subchapter S corporation.

9. **Taxpayer Relief Act of 1997**

This act amended the 1996 law mentioned above, permitting S corporations to have ESOPs, in very important ways.

10. **Economic Growth and Tax Relief Act of 2001**

This act amended the S corporation ESOP laws of 1996 and 1997 and expanded the 1984 DEFRA law permitting a C corporation to deduct dividends paid on ESOP stock under certain circumstances.

11. **Pension Protection Act (PPA) of 2006**

This act recruits S corporations with a securities acquisition loan as of September 25, 2005, to use pre-PPA vesting schedule of a five-year cliff or a seven-year graded schedule until the loan is paid.

The PPA of 2006 modified the vesting requirements applicable to all employer contributions to defined-contribution plans. It provides that any contributions made in plan years beginning after December 31, 2006, must vest under either the three-year cliff or six-year graded schedule. Thus, all employer contributions, not just matching contributions, must vest under these schedules:

Three-Year Cliff

Years of Service	Vested Percentage
Less than 3	0 percent
3 or more	100 percent

Six-Year Graded

Years of Service	Vested Percentage
Less than 2	0 percent
2	20 percent
3	40 percent
4	60 percent
5	80 percent
6 or more	100 percent

Pre-2007 vesting schedules were the five-year cliff and seven-year graded vesting schedules. For benefits accrued related to the years 1998 to 2006, benefits must generally vest at least as quickly as one of the two schedules above.

Employees receive the vested portion of their accounts at either termination, disability, death, or retirement. These distributions may be made in a lump sum or in installments over a period of years. If employees become disabled or die, they or their beneficiaries receive the vested portion of their ESOP accounts immediately.

Managing Risk
[even the most risk-averse workers prefer shared capitalism]

> *Risk comes from not knowing what you're doing.*
> —Warren Buffett, American business magnate, widely considered the most successful investor of the twentieth century, ranked the world's wealthiest person in 2008[138]

A major concern from the labor side is the matter of risk. There is no such thing as a completely risk-free method for gaining the measure of ownership advocated. Yet the upside of ownership to the employee is too significant to let the opportunity pass. Thus, companies and workers must manage this risk responsibly.

The first way to manage the risk is for workers to take advantage of the fact that ESOPs are not financed with worker savings or wages. Companies buy stock and grant the stock to workers, using private credit with federal tax incentives. The loan is to the corporation. Individual workers do not mortgage away any of their personal assets with an ESOP. Workers should be very wary of any ESOPs that ask for personal workers' investments (most do not).

The second way to manage the risk is to make sure the ESOP is in *addition* to a properly diversified retirement plan.

The third way to manage risk is for workers to be sure that their overall portfolio is properly diversified so that their general risk exposure is reduced.

The fourth way to manage risk is to be sure the companies whose stock is purchased by workers and managers with ESOPs have sound business plans approved by objective lenders, have an objective board of directors with some nonexecutive worker members, and have a program to involve all workers in solving key company problems.

The key points to realize are the various ways to ameliorate such risk. With the understanding that ownership stock supplemented to an employee's ESOP accounts is almost always contributed by the employer, it should relieve some concerns.

In addition, the classic method to modify risk in general is through proper diversification. It is advisable for workers to maintain other forms of investments thus insuring their total portfolios and retirement are diversified.

> **Excerpt from *Shared Capitalism at Work*:**
> Employee-owners bear two distinct types of risk. First, employees who have their own "skin in the game," having purchased company stock with their own funds, bear the risk of potential loss. The risk is minimized in ESOPs because the company stock allocated to workers' ESOP accounts is almost always contributed by the employer with no out-of-pocket cost to the employee. At the other extreme, company stock acquired through employee purchase plans is financed primarily by employee savings.
>
> Second, employees who have concentrations of assets invested in a single company bear risk associated with inadequate diversification. This problem is exacerbated by a firm-specific risk for employee owners whose jobs (and incomes), as well as a substantial portion of their savings, depend on the fortunes of the company they work for. This is an inevitable feature of any form of employee ownership, but it is likely to be greatest for ESOP employees who accumulate company shares in retirement accounts with limited opportunities for diversification.

Federal law now allows workers close to retirement to diversify holdings in their ESOP accounts. The risk, however, appears generally to be manageable: portfolio theory suggests that a moderate amount of employee ownership can be part of a prudent portfolio depending on how other assets are diversified.

The higher compensation associated with shared capitalism helps address financial risk concerns. Risk is obviously an important issue when variable pay (of any sort) is substituted for fixed pay, and risk-averse people will require a risk premium (higher average pay) to compensate for the added risk. We find that the shared capitalism package generally included more than enough compensation for the added risk associated with variable pay—it provides gravy even after taking the extra risk into account, as shown by the reduced turnover intentions. Some firms combine lower risk forms of shared capitalism (such as profit sharing and gain sharing and stock options) with higher risk forms of shared capitalism—such as those based on buying company stock with worker savings. Even when shared capitalism and not gravy, portfolio theory suggests that shared capitalism can be part of a prudently-diversified portfolio if properly managed. Having a separate diversified retirement plan in addition to an employee ownership plan, being paid above market wages, and not funding employee stock ownership using worker savings, can all play a role in minimizing risk. So concerns over financial risk can be overcome: it is striking that even the most risk-averse workers are likely to prefer some shared capitalism in their pay.[139]

So, through wise diversification and proper management of their complete investment portfolios, workers are more than able to take advantage of the opportunity for employee ownership if the risk is properly managed.

With the substantial addition of an *ownership* component in his or her assets, any worker should see the incredible value it represents.

Open-Book Management
[some of what it takes to be a successful company in this new age]

To many, if not most, owners, this idea sounds insane. But to a growing movement of companies, it's the only way to do business. I've been doing it for almost 30 years.
—Jack Stack, founder and CEO of SRC Holdings (comprising more than thirty-five separate companies), dubbed by Inc. magazine "The Father of Open-Book Management," recipient of the Business Enterprise Trust Award[140]

While it's great to want a powerful transformation to occur in the workplace, it has to be implemented properly to succeed. Two of the more well-known books on the subject are *The Great Game of Business* by Jack Stack and *Open-Book Management* by John Case.

We can create a society that's continually getting better, a society in which people can do more to help each other. As it is, we're becoming a society of haves and have-nots. What's happening is the rich know how to play the Game [of Business] and they're playing it well. Meanwhile, the society as a whole has a declining standard of living.
—Jack Stack

THE 3RD WAY

In the early 1980s, Springfield Remanufacturing Corporation (SRC) in Springfield, Missouri, was a near-bankrupt division of International Harvester. That's when a green young manager, Jack Stack, took over and turned it around. He didn't know how to "manage" a company, but he did know the principles of athletic competition and democracy: keeping score, having fun, playing fair, providing choice, and having a voice. With these principals he created his own style of management: open-book management. As he writes in *The Great Game of Business*:

> We went from a loss of $60,488 in our first year to pretax earnings of $2.7 in our fourth year. We never laid off a single person. By 1991, we had annual sales of more than $70 million and our work force had increased to about 650 people from the original 119. But the most impressive number is the value of our stock, worth 10 cents a share at the time of the buyout [from International Harvester] and now worth $18.30, an increase of 18,200 percent in nine years. As a result, hourly workers who had been with the Springfield Manufacturing Corp. (SMC) from the beginning had holdings in the Employee Stock Ownership Plan (ESOP) worth as much as $35,000 per person. That's almost the price of a house in Springfield.[141]

The key is to let everyone in on financial decisions. At SRC, everyone learns how to read a P&L—even those without a high school education know how much the toilet paper they use cuts into profits. SRC employees have a piece of the action and a vote in company matters. Imagine having a vote on your bonus and on what businesses the company should be in. SRC restored the dignity of economic freedom to its people. Stack's "open-book management" is the key—a system that, as he describes it, is literally a *game*, and one so simple anyone can use it.[142]

HOW THE ESOP REALLY WORKS

Don't use information to intimidate, control or manipulate people. Use it to teach people how to work together to achieve common goals and thereby gain control over their lives.
—Jack Stack[143]

The Great Game of Business has become the most celebrated approach to open-book management, a unique and well-proven approach to running a company, based on a simple, yet powerful belief: when employees think, act, and feel like owners, everybody wins.

The Great Game of Business Inc., a company founded to help companies implement open-book management practices, has hosted more than four thousand companies from around the world (including Southwest Airlines, Harley-Davidson, and Whole Foods Market) prompting *BusinessWeek* to label SRC Holdings a "Management Mecca." In 2009 alone, *The Great Game of Business* and open-book management was profiled in the *Wall Street Journal* and the *New York Times*, featured on MSNBC, selected as one of the 100 Best Business Books of All Time, and chosen as the "#1 Most Innovative Business Practice" by *Inc.* magazine.[144]

Management has to have credibility. *Without it, people won't listen to you and they won't believe the numbers you give them. If you set up a bonus program or some other game, they'll think it's a gimmick, a trick, a scheme to get them to work harder for less money, so that you can get richer and they can get screwed.*
—Jack Stack[145]

John Case is a veteran observer and interpreter of the business world. A senior writer at *Inc.* magazine, he authored the popular syndicated newspaper column "The Inc. Report," as well as numerous feature articles for the magazine itself. As an editor of *Inc.*, he explains the powerful management tool that is revolutionizing American business—describing how and why it works and illustrating how all companies can utilize it to realize higher profits.[146]

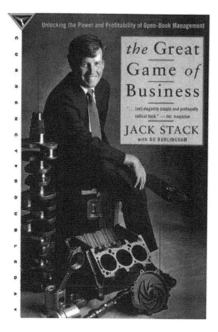

Figure 24. (Source: The Great Game of Business; Crown Business Publisher, July 16, 2013) (Source: Open Book Management; HarperBusiness Publisher; Reprint edition, April 12, 1996)

His book is about a new idea—a new way of running a business.[147] It's called open-book management. We hope that after you read the book, you think the idea is a good one. But the real test of a new idea, in business as in any other endeavor, isn't how it looks on paper. It's whether the idea works in practice. To change the culture and operations of a company, you must both think and act anew. Open-book management works.

Here are some cogent ideas from these important works on how to implementing open-book management:

> **First Principle: Information, Please!**
> *Everyone has to know what's going on in the business.*
> Get the information out there! Tell employees not only what they need to know to do their jobs effectively but how the company as a whole is doing.
>
> **Second Principle: Business Literacy**
> *Everyone has to understand the information they get.*
> Most people don't understand financial statements—the fundamental data that show how a company is doing. They all need to learn it!
>
> **Third Principle: Empowerment**
> *Does empowerment make sense? Sure—but only when people understand the financials.*
> Empowered employees must be willing (indeed, should be required) to assume responsibility for their decisions and hence for their numbers.
>
> **Fourth Principle: A Stake in Success**
> *Make sure people share directly in the company's success—and the risk of failure.*
> Open-book management teaches employees to think of themselves as businesspeople rather than hired hands. To make that real, they need a stake. Part of what they earn must be tied to the company's performance.[148]

Corporate Corruption
[we have a problem...]

Corruption has its own motivations, and one has to thoroughly study that phenomenon and eliminate the foundations that allow corruption to exist.
—Eduard Shevardnadze, former Soviet minister of foreign affairs, later Georgian statesman from the height to the end of the Cold War[149]

We all need to face the current reality of the markedly dwindling trust in many institutions, business entities, and organizations at all levels of society. Leading that trend is the perception that the business community may be of most concern in the ever-eroding level of ethical standards we all require. These standards are essential for the confidence so needed for a properly functioning capitalist economy. Even a significant level of corrosive skepticism about business not acting above reproach is undoubtedly not a healthy inclination. We need to admit it exists.

Clearly, a level of rock-solid trust is indispensable for the investment community to be able to operate with any degree of certainty. Without it, critical investment dollars based fundamentally on trust become scarce.

What hurts confidence in the business community hurts all of us, whether direct investors or not.

Conversely, what strengthens confidence can only have a tangible positive effect on Wall Street and the capital markets so vital to our and the world's economy. Let us therefore endeavor to seek ways the ESOP concept can play a pivotal part in bringing the kind of welcome change that is needed.

Some say that you cannot legislate morality. However, to take a blind eye to it and not propose real solutions is both foolish and irresponsible. An astonishing article recently appeared in the *New*

HOW THE ESOP REALLY WORKS

York Times on just this subject and the degree to which the problem has festered. Following is an excerpt from that major story.

The New York Times

The Spreading Scourge of Corporate Corruption
By Eduardo Porter
Published July 10, 2012

The misconduct of the financial industry no longer surprises most Americans. Only about one in five has much trust in banks, according to Gallup polls, about half the level in 2007. And it's not just banks that are frowned upon. Trust in big business overall is declining. Sixty-two percent of Americans believe corruption is widespread across corporate America. According to Transparency International, an anticorruption watchdog, nearly three in four Americans believe that corruption has increased over the last three years.

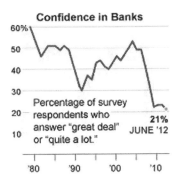

We should be alarmed that corporate wrongdoing has come to be seen as such a routine occurrence. Capitalism cannot function without trust. As the Nobel laureate Kenneth Arrow observed, "Virtually every commercial transaction has within itself an element of trust."

And waves of mistrust can spread broadly. After years of dismal employment prospects, Americans are losing trust in a broad range of institutions, including Congress, the Supreme Court, the presidency, public schools, labor unions and the church.

Company executives are paid to maximize profits, not to behave ethically. Evidence suggests that they behave as corruptly as they can, within whatever constraints are imposed by law and reputation.

Extrapolating from frauds that were uncovered during and after the dot-com bubble, the economists Luigi Zingales and Adair Morse of the University of Chicago and Alexander Dyck of the University of Toronto estimated conservatively that in any given year a fraud was being committed by 11 to 13 percent of the large companies in the country.

The inexorable rise of income inequality is also likely to encourage fraud, fostering resentment and undermining trust in capitalism's institutions and rules. Economic research shows that participants in contests in which the winner takes all are much more likely to cheat. And the United States is becoming a winner-takes-all economy.

It's hard to fathom the broader social implications of corporate wrongdoing. But its most long-lasting impact may be on Americans' trust in the institutions that underpin the nation's liberal market democracy.[150]

Optimal Inequality for Economic Growth, Stability, and Shared Prosperity: The Economics behind the Wall Street Occupiers Protest?
By Richard B. Freeman

The greater the concentration of income in a society, the more the wealthy will act collectively to advance their interests against that of other citizens. "Crony capitalism" describes economic systems where wealthy insiders work in concert with politicians to enrich themselves. Many blame the economic problems of developing countries, such as the late-1990s Asian financial crisis, on this phenomenon. Until the latest financial crisis, most economists viewed the US and other advanced capitalist countries as largely immune to "crony capitalism." "Regulatory capture"—the process by which regulators become so entwined with the group they regulate that they worry more about the interests of that group than the interests of the public—was supposed to be a problem limited to specific industries, regulations and agencies rather than a systemic disease that afflicted the entire economy. The Wall Street crisis and its aftermath changed this view.[151]

The first step in solving any difficult situation is to admit you have a problem. The next step is to devise the proper type and proper degree of reform that could make a real difference. We contend there is no better place to begin this much needed healthy, measured reform than through the ESOP vehicle and with the workers who have the closest stake in the health and integrity of the business organizations they are involved with.

THE 3RD WAY

Regulations are needed to better understand and prevent the breakdown of businesses and financial instruments and their abuse by the few. They need not be burdensome, just rooted in common sense. Some of the possible solutions include, but are not limited to:

- Transparency (undoubtedly the overriding element required to bring more accountability; sunlight is always the best disinfectant)

- Independent board members on the board of directors

- Enhanced shareholder empowerment

- An annual audit by an independent entity reporting to the shareholder employees

- The ability of shareholders to designate their proxy votes to independent board members

- A representative of the ESOP group on the board of directors

By whatever means chosen, to the extent that more workers know how the firm is truly doing, management will have less incentive to cook the books on its behalf since it is sharing ownership with workers as well as with nonemployee shareholders.

Checks And Balances
[it works in politics/it can work in economics too]

The attempt to combine wisdom and power has only rarely been successful and then only for a short while.
—Albert Einstein, German-born Nobel Prize–winning theoretical physicist, regarded as the father of modern physics[152]

Via the Third Way model, where employees have a stake in the company through an enhanced ESOP system, *a natural check and balance is exerted on the corporation.* However, while the track record of employee-owned companies as successful companies is impressive compared with competitors, especially among privately held companies, there is no law and no *current* intangible aspect of employee stock ownership that automatically ensures employees can police management from flimflamming employee owners or the trustee of the ESOP trust-owned stock. Some people are just dishonest, and current employee ownership rights will not de facto ensure honest management.

Nevertheless, the fact that employees own a portion of the company does give them a measure of input not available to others. Shareholders are granted special privileges based on the class of stock, including the rights to vote on matters such as elections to the board of directors, to share in distributions of the company's income, to purchase new shares issued by the company, and to claim a company's assets during a liquidation of the company.[153]

Directors and officers of a company are bound by fiduciary duties to act in the best interest of the shareholders. What is needed is further legal *employee empowerment* to ensure this is always the case.

ERISA law requires the ESOP's sponsor to provide an annual statement to employees on what their shares are worth. But just as management can lie to top minds on Wall Street, and government regulators, they can lie to employees.

Employees further empowered (via legislation) could potentially take action and turn a publically traded or private company around by checking or getting bad management out of the picture. While we have already seen private ESOP companies turn around after workers and managers bought them, it would be wrong to claim it was because employees were part of making management changes. Typically, managers and lenders came to decisions about the management needed.

This is another potential area of opportunity where requiring further transparency and sunlight by management to their employees could have a salutary effect. Legislative action in this area could be a boon to all parties, including the stock market and overall shareholder confidence. For how often have we seen in the news executives at the top abusing their positions to swindle either their clients and/or the workers and ultimately destroy the corporation? While companies like Enron are prime examples of such avarice, one could list other examples as long as your arm.

It's critical to note that although Enron had some employee ownership, the publicity was actually about stock in the company's 401(k) plan. Moreover, Enron's demise was primarily during the transition from former CEO Kenneth Lay to Jeffrey Skilling, who ruined the company. This was hidden from the shareholders and the employees.

Enron employees owned quite a lot of company stock. It didn't work out too well for them. The chief potential problem with that employee ownership was insufficient diversification and the fact that workers bought stock with their savings. Therefore, employees need to be encouraged, even compelled, to diversify.

HOW THE ESOP REALLY WORKS

> The **Enron scandal**, revealed in October 2001, eventually led to the bankruptcy of the Enron Corporation, an American energy company based in Houston, Texas, and the dissolution of Arthur Andersen, which was one of the five largest audit and accountancy partnerships in the world. In addition to being the largest bankruptcy reorganization in American history at that time, Enron was attributed as the biggest audit failure.
>
> Enron was formed in 1985 by Kenneth Lay after merging Houston Natural Gas and InterNorth. Several years later, when Jeffrey Skilling was hired, he developed a staff of executives that, through the use of accounting loopholes, special purpose entities, and poor financial reporting, were able to hide billions in debt from failed deals and projects. Chief Financial Officer Andrew Fastow and other executives not only misled Enron's board of directors and audit committee on high-risk accounting practices, but also pressured Andersen to ignore the issues.
>
> Shareholders lost nearly $11 billion when Enron's stock price, which hit a high of US$90 per share in mid-2000, plummeted to less than $1 by the end of November 2001. The US Securities and Exchange Commission (SEC) began an investigation, and rival Houston competitor Dynegy offered to purchase the company at a fire sale price. The deal fell through, and on December 2, 2001, Enron filed for bankruptcy under Chapter 11 of the United States Bankruptcy Code. Enron's $63.4 billion in assets made it the largest corporate bankruptcy in US history.[154]

Sadly, these executives who abuse their power often have an escape plan reserved just for themselves in the form of a "golden parachute" that allows them to get away with piles of cash while shareholders and loyal employees are left holding the bag. Legislation is needed to empower employees and other shareholders to be more involved at the front of the process.

How often have we seen the locked gate of an abandoned factory whose executives got out with whatever wealth was remaining in the company while the employees were left out in the cold with no jobs and a bankrupt company! A vibrant ESOP program, while not a panacea, would offer a marked level of disclosure and involvement by the workers in the financial activities of the company. It would be much harder for unscrupulous executives to either defraud the public or set themselves up with a methodology that insulated *just them* from any catastrophic event.

The hope is that, with transparency and more responsible governance, many of these catastrophic collapses built out of greed and mismanagement could be headed off, thus sparing employees, customers, and shareholders such pain.

What Our Founders Knew
[heed the wisdom of the great thinkers in history]

> *Power tends to corrupt and absolute power corrupts absolutely.*
> —Lord Acton, English Catholic historian, politician, and writer, in 1887 letter to Bishop Mandell Creighton

We have only to look at the majesty of our own US Constitution to see how our founders embedded a system of checks and balances in our *political* life, in the structure and running of our government, which very wisely took into account the natural tendencies of human beings. At its most obvious level, the creation of the three branches of government (executive, legislative, and judicial) made sure to not concentrate all power in the hands of one person or one level of ruler, as the monarchies of the past did.

We can learn and apply a version of these principles to business. Through employee ownership and ESOPs, absolute power can be checked in a variety of innovative ways.

The introduction and use of checks and balances was a major step forward for human society. Human society in Europe progressed during the seventeenth and eighteenth centuries because of the new use of checks and balances in government.[155] Before the use of checks and balances, the monarch possessed the sole ability to make laws and collect money, and was above the law.

Before checks and balances came to be used, the monarchy enjoyed far too much control. King James of England is a prime example of a monarch possessing too much power. He was conducting government matters not for the good of the country but for the good of himself. While some monarchs enjoyed taking their authority to the limit, it turned out to be their downfall. Had they not abused the power they possessed, they may not have lost it. We are coming to that same conclusion in corporate life.

Thomas Jefferson, when writing the US Constitution, followed the philosophy of Hobbes, Locke, and Rousseau. In practice, checks and balances were applied to the appointing of officials, government dealings, and the introducing and changing of laws.

The great trio of Hobbes, Locke, and Rousseau saw that the current form of monarchical government was flawed—as is the case at times in business. They had suggestions for how to make it better. Hobbes, believing humans were by nature power hungry, knew there was a need to put a check on the use of power. Locke thought law was based on consent, an idea that would keep a ruler from becoming dictatorial. Rousseau thought the strong would dominate the weak and so the weak needed to be protected. Each of the three had different views, and none had systems of law based solely on his own ideas, but they did recognize a problem, as well as a way to solve it. Some of their ideas were adopted and applied. The result was the progression of human society.

THE 3RD WAY

France's revolutionary Declaration of the Rights of Man gave citizens power over their government. If the government wanted monetary support, it would have to do right by the people. With these checks in place, the government would receive only the money that was needed, and frivolous spending would be eliminated and accountability instilled.

The use of checks and balances in government produced a huge gain in human society and had an impact not just on France and England in the seventeenth and eighteenth centuries, but also on many other subsequent governments (most notably the United States) and it will continue to have an effect in the future as governments are reformed all over the world.

If *political* systems can be introduced by people to limit the power of the few and their ability to abuse it, these same common-sense principles can and should be build into *economic* life through enhanced employee ownership and *THE 3rd WAY* system.

USA—We're No. 1
[our corporate tax system is a burdensome mess]

The only difference between a tax man and a taxidermist is that the taxidermist leaves the skin.
—Mark Twain, American author and humorist[156]

How can the United States, or any country, continue to remain competitive in a world market with a corporate tax system designed to discourage the very growth essential for a healthy economy? It is often considered axiomatic that whatever you tax

HOW THE ESOP REALLY WORKS

more, you get less of. Why then would we ever want to cripple the growth of our companies and the wealth they produce by laying on the highest taxes in the world?

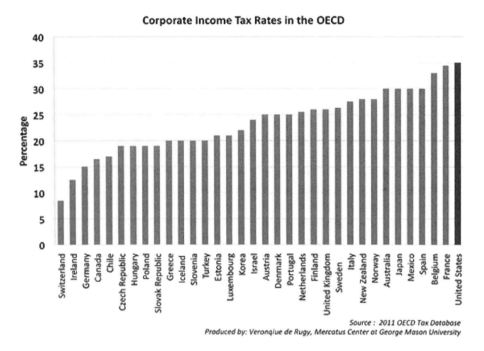

Figure 25. Corporate income tax rates in the OECD (Source: Veronique de Rugy, the Mercatus Center at George Mason University)

Naturally, some see it as a way of getting even with the "evil" rich. Of course, it's understandable how some could come to that conclusion. But this misguided retribution only serves to undermine the very engine that produces the wealth every country and person in it depends on. It hurts the very prosperity needed to lift all of us toward a better standard of living. *So, why not use the desperately needed reduction in corporate taxation to fuel our populist plan to grant these tax reductions—though only if they are done in conjunction with measures to pass those tax dollars on to workers in the form of corporate owner's equity?*

Clearly, in a misguided effort to ameliorate this onerous level of taxation, Congress has piled on layer upon layer of loopholes. While some of these deductions have merit, a good portion of them could be phased out.

Also, all these loopholes in the tax law are a literal goldmine for the dreaded lobbyists we hear so much about. The American people do not want their tax system muddled by this plethora of loopholes. The current system is designed to benefit mainly the *insiders* in the system—politicians and lobbyists and very narrow interests.

Once the people are *educated* on what is going on behind the scenes in Congress, as it relates to corporate tax law, they will be outraged. Ironically, the towering level of both corporate taxes and corporate loopholes *hurts everyone.*

Yes, we propose dramatically cutting corporate taxes, but if and only if those cuts are matched by employees gaining equity. Anyone concerned about any appreciable loss of revenue must realize that despite the high tax rate, the corporate tax percentage of the total tax collected is relatively insignificant. Corporate taxes fell from 26.4 percent of total tax revenue in 1950 to just 7.4 percent in 2010.[157] And remember, those employees acquiring equity in the form of stock will be paying taxes on it themselves.

Moreover, the effective tax rate has also plummeted, as the following chart dramatically demonstrates. We need to cut out the loopholes that allow this to happen and principally limit the deduction on corporate taxes to those who share equity with their employees.

HOW THE ESOP REALLY WORKS

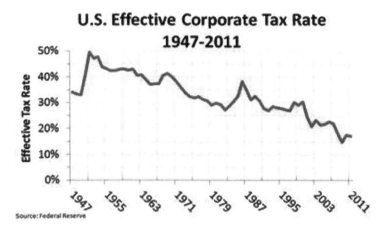

Figure 26. US effective corporate tax rates 1947–2011 (Source: US Federal Reserve)

With the attention the inordinately high level of corporate taxation is getting in the media these days, we all know the rate must come down for our nation to remain competitive in the global economy. *It's how it's done that matters.*

In a perfect world we would bring corporate tax rates down to 25 percent or less so we can get competitive in the world economy.
—Eric Cantor, Republican House Majority Leader[158]

Yet, any thought of simply reducing this rate will be met with entrenched opposition *if* it does not have something to offer the ideological interests of both political parties. Thankfully, the concept of employee ownership and ESOPS are uniquely positioned to appeal to everyone.

Unless you have a veto-proof majority in both Houses of Congress (very rare), it is extremely difficult to get a measure through when either the Democrats or Republicans are steadfast *against* a particular piece of legislation. For everyone not schooled in the art of politics, this is called "realpolitik." We average folks need to know how, in fact, most law gets enacted. It's hardball. And it is often said by some that it's like watching sausage being made.

Realpolitik is related to the philosophy of political realism, and both suggest working from the hypothesis chiefly based on the pursuit, possession, and application of power.[159] Realpolitik is a prescriptive guideline limited to policy-making, such as domestic or foreign policy. The bottom line is that we should not be deluded about getting a policy in the form of legislation through the system. *A degree of compelling force must be exerted on both sides of the political aisle.* That is the job of an educated, motivated citizenry! Such is the purpose of this book—to bring such positive force to bear.

Party's Over!
[cut corporate deductions, and establish a fair, effective tax rate]

The difference between tax avoidance and tax evasion is the thickness of a prison wall.
—Denis Healey, British Labour politician[160]

While US corporations pay the highest corporate tax rate in the world, given the plethora of deductions they enjoy, their *effective rate* is, of course, reduced. Nevertheless that effective rate is still higher than desired. What we have is a grossly burdensome tax rate matched with a slew of deductions. The entire system is out of whack.

The US economy's 35 percent corporate tax rate is among the highest in the industrial world, reducing the ability of our nation's businesses to compete in the global economy and to invest and create jobs at home.[161] By limiting investment and growth, the high rate of corporate tax also hurts US wages.

HOW THE ESOP REALLY WORKS

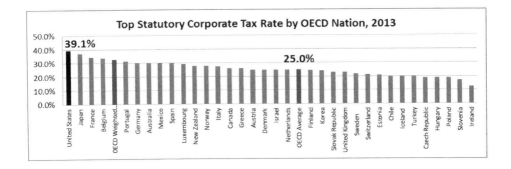

Figure 27. Top statutory corporate tax rate by OECD nation, 2013 (Source: Kyle Pomerleau, "Another Study Confirms: US Has One of the Highest Effective Corporate Tax Rates in the World," May 31, 2013)

We need to shift corporate incentives toward including the proper empowerment of their employees through employee ownership as *the primary means for corporations to receive tax deductions*. Lowering the corporate tax rate to one competitive in the world market is a splendid idea. However, it must be done in a way that leaves a significant incentive for those same companies to allow their employees to build equity in the very companies they are helping to build!

Citizens for Tax Justice is one of the several watchdog organizations keeping an eye on the kind of tax avoidance going on in corporate America today. Following is the organization's report on corporate tax dodging.

The Sorry State of Corporate Taxes
What Fortune 500 Firms Pay (or Don't Pay) in the USA — 2008 to 2012

EXECUTIVE SUMMARY

Profitable corporations are supposed to pay a 35 percent federal income tax rate on their U.S. profits. But many corporations pay far less, or nothing at all, because of the many tax loopholes and special breaks they enjoy. This report documents just how successful many Fortune 500 corporations have been at using these loopholes and special breaks over the past five years.

The report looks at the profits and U.S. federal income taxes of the 288 Fortune 500 companies that have been consistently profitable in each of the five years between 2008 and 2012, excluding companies that experienced even one unprofitable year during this period. Most of these companies were included in our November 2011 report, *Corporate Taxpayers and Corporate Tax Dodgers*, which looked at the years 2008 through 2010. Our new report is broader, in that it includes companies, such as Facebook, that have entered the Fortune 500 since 2011, and narrower, in that it excludes some companies that were profitable during 2008 to 2010 but lost money in 2011 or 2012.

Some Key Findings:

- As a group, the 288 corporations examined paid an effective federal income tax rate of just 19.4 percent over the five-year period — far less than the statutory 35 percent tax rate.

26 Corporations Paying No Total Income Tax in 2008-12

Company ($-millions)	08-12 Profit	08-12 Tax	08-12 Rate
Pepco Holdings	$ 1,743	$ −575	−33.0%
PG&E Corp.	7,035	−1,178	−16.7%
NiSource	2,473	−336	−13.6%
Wisconsin Energy	3,228	−436	−13.5%
General Electric	27,518	−3,054	−11.1%
CenterPoint Energy	4,078	−347	−8.5%
Integrys Energy Group	1,623	−133	−8.2%
Atmos Energy	1,486	−114	−7.7%
Tenet Healthcare	854	−51	−6.0%
American Electric Power	10,016	−577	−5.8%
Ryder System	1,073	−51	−4.7%
Con-way	587	−21	−3.5%
Duke Energy	9,026	−299	−3.3%
Priceline.com	557	−17	−3.0%
FirstEnergy	7,236	−216	−3.0%
Apache	7,580	−184	−2.4%
Interpublic Group	1,305	−28	−2.1%
Verizon Communications	30,203	−535	−1.8%
NextEra Energy	11,433	−178	−1.6%
Consolidated Edison	7,581	−87	−1.1%
CMS Energy	2,471	−26	−1.1%
Boeing	20,473	−202	−1.0%
Northeast Utilities	2,820	−19	−0.7%
Corning	3,438	−10	−0.3%
Paccar	1,711	−1	−0.1%
MetroPCS Communications	1,956	−1	−0.1%
TOTAL	**$ 169,504**	**$ −8,676**	**−5.1%**

Two fine articles outline some of the numerous tax-avoidance strategies employed by corporate America, allowing corporations to work the system to their advantage. They are summarized in the following two excerpts.

Top 10 Corporate Tax Deductions
By Sherrie Scott, Demand Media

Businesses may deduct ordinary operating expenses.

The IRS allows business deductions for ordinary and necessary business expenses. Current expenses are expenses needed to keep the corporation running and are fully tax deductible. Capital expenses such as investments and real estate also qualify for deductions if purchased to generate income for the business. IRS tax codes determine which deductions a business qualifies for and which expenses do not qualify for deductions.

Operating Expenses

Operating expenses are customary tax deductions. Operating expenses include the expenses businesses rely on to run day to day operations such as payroll, rent and office supplies.

Employee Expenses

Businesses can deduct employee-related expenses such as health benefits and employee salaries. Pay distributed for bonuses, awards, sick leave, vacations and tuition reimbursement are also tax deductible. Employers that reimburse employees for work-related expenses such as travel or business use of a personal vehicle receive tax deductions as well.

Insurance

Insurance premiums qualify for corporate tax deductions. Insurance premiums for fire and theft insurance are deductible. Liability and worker's compensation insurance premiums also qualify for tax deductions. Business owners who operate a professional trade such as an accountant, attorney or doctor can deduct malpractice or errors and omissions insurance premiums from their taxes as well.

Travel

Expenses related to local and long distance travel qualify for corporate tax deductions. These expenses include air travel as well as travel by train or bus. Entertainment expenses while traveling for business are fully tax deductible, including meals and gratuities.

Bad Debts

Bad debts owed to an organization qualify for tax deductions. Corporations have the option to write off bad debts and losses related to credit sales from customers.

Interest

Interest payments from business loans and other forms of credit acquired to fund business expenses are ordinary tax deductions. Interest paid or accrued during the tax year are fully tax deductible.

Equipment

Various forms of business equipment and property are tax deductible. The IRS typically requires businesses to spread the deductible cost of business property out over time. To achieve this, businesses may only deduct the depreciated amount of the property in most cases.

Taxes

Companies pay taxes to operate and these taxes qualify for tax deductions. Corporations can deduct sales taxes, excise and fuel taxes, federal income taxes and real estate taxes paid on business property.

Professional Services

Fees paid for professional services such as tax preparation, legal services and bookkeeping and accounting qualify for tax deductions.
Fees paid for professional services must be ordinary and necessary expenses related to operating the business.

Advertising

Business advertising costs are tax deductible. Costs associated with business cards, yellow pages ads and other materials that promote the business qualify for deductions.[163]

┼┼┼ THE FiscalTIMES

10 Big Corporate Tax Breaks, and Who Benefits
By Sarah Stodola

US corporations (like many Americans) exploit every available rule in the tax code to minimize the taxes they pay. The United States has one of the highest corporate tax rates in the world, at 35 percent (not including any state levies), yet the actual amount in corporate taxes that the government collects ("the effective tax rate") is lower than those of Germany, Canada, Japan and China, among others. The reason is confusingly called "tax expenditures," a doublespeak term designed to legitimize special interest tax breaks and loopholes.

Those "expenditures" will cost the US government $628.6 billion over the next five years, according to a 2010 report from the Tax Foundation. With advice from the Urban Institute's Eric Toder, one of the country's foremost authorities on corporate tax policy, we assembled the 10 most costly corporate tax loopholes and who benefits from them.

10) Graduated Corporate Income

This policy places the first $50,000 of a corporation's profit at a 15 percent tax rate, with higher profit levels garnering higher tax rates, until it tops out at 35 percent for taxable corporate income exceeding $335,000. The result is that an owner of a small corporation pays only 15 percent in taxes on the first $50,000 of profit, leaving more left over potentially for reinvestment and growth.

5-yr Cost to Government (2011–2015): $16.4 billion
Who benefits: Individuals that own small corporations.

THE 3RD WAY

9) Inventory Property Sales

Foreign income of American companies is taxed in the country in which it is generated, and the US gives a tax credit for that amount in order to avoid double taxation. Some companies have accumulated a glut of such tax credits (the "inventory"), and in order to use them up, they artificially boost foreign income through a "title passage rule" that allows companies to allocate 50 percent of income from US production sold in another country as income generated by that foreign country (the "property sales").

5-yr Cost to Government: $16.7 billion

Who benefits: Multinationals with operations in high-tax foreign countries.

8) Research and Experimentation Tax Credit

Intended to spur research and development within companies, in its simplest form this break allows for a 20 percent tax credit for "qualified research expenses." There are more complex applications, as well. Detractors complain that it is paying corporations to do research they would have done anyway.

5-yr Cost to Government: $29.8 billion

Who benefits: Pharmaceutical companies, high tech companies, engineers, agriculture conglomerates.

7) Deferred Taxes for Financial Firms on Certain Income Earned Overseas

Because most financial firms conduct their foreign operations as branches rather than as subsidiaries, as most companies in other industries do, they do not benefit from the tax breaks afforded to foreign subsidiaries. To compensate, this loophole enables financial firms to treat income from their foreign branches as if they were subsidiaries, along with all of the attendant tax benefits.

HOW THE ESOP REALLY WORKS

5-yr Cost to Government: $29.9 billion

Who benefits: Any financial firm with foreign operations.

6) Alcohol Fuel Credit

This is a tax credit for the production of alcohol-based fuel, most commonly ethanol, which is made from corn. The credit ranges from $0.39 to $0.60 per gallon. In theory, the credit is meant to encourage alternative forms of energy to imported oil. It is largely responsible for propping up the price of corn, and is extremely popular in corn-producing states like Iowa and Illinois.

5-yr Cost to Government: $32 billion

Who benefits: Food and agricultural conglomerates in the Midwest.

5) Credit for Low-Income Housing Investments

As you might expect, this one gives tax breaks to companies that develop low-income housing. It's the rule that's responsible for so many larger new developments setting aside 20 percent or 40 percent of their units for people whose income is well below the area's median gross income.

5-yr Cost to Government: $34.5 billion

Who benefits: Real estate developers.

4) Accelerated Depreciation of Machinery and Equipment

This one allows companies to deduct for all of the depreciation of a piece of equipment at once (as opposed to over the, say, 20 years it actually takes the item to depreciate). This is the equivalent of the US government giving the company an up-front, interest free loan. Congress recently made this expenditure temporarily even larger for 2011, to encourage investment in equipment.

5-yr Cost to Government: $51.7 billion

Who benefits: Airlines and manufacturers using large equipment that lasts many years.

3) Deduction for Domestic Manufacturing

This loophole enables a tax deduction for manufacturing activities conducted by American companies within the United States. It covers conventional manufacturers, but also extends to industries like software development and film production. The intent is to keep manufacturing from being outsourced.

5-yr Cost to Government: $58 billion

Who benefits: Any US company that produces a product within US borders.

2) Exclusion of Interest on State and Local Bonds

Companies (and individuals) do not pay federal income tax on interest from their investments in state and municipal bonds. What's more, private companies can in some cases issue tax-free bonds of their own for projects that benefit the public, such as construction of an airport, stadium or hospital.

5-yr Cost to Government: $59.8 billion

Who benefits: High-income investors and corporations.

1) Deferral of Income from Controlled Foreign Corporations

Multinational companies can defer paying US income taxes until they transfer overseas profits back to the United States, under this law. In practice, many companies leave much of their profits overseas indefinitely, thus paying only the tax in the relevant foreign country, which is likely far lower than the US rate, and avoiding US taxes permanently. The list of corporations enlisting this loophole is seemingly endless.

5-yr Cost to Government: $172.1 billion

Who benefits: Every multinational company.[164]

Chapter 5:

HOW THE THIRD WAY FOSTERS MAJOR SOLUTIONS FOR SOCIETY

An End To Alienation!
[are we all just insignificant cogs in a wheel?]

> *Alienation, which is growing rampant in our society and in all other countries of the globe, begins with economic alienation. Economic alienation begins with the erosion of productive power, which each man who has only his labor to sell, must necessarily suffer in an industrial society.*
> —Louis O. Kelso, political economist, lawyer, author, and merchant banker[165]

Perhaps the most salient aspect to this movement is the realization that we don't have to live like this any longer. *There **is** a better way forward!* It is time to speak truth to power in a new and very special way.

We *can* transform society into a better place for all. We *can* have businesses be both productive and fair. We *can* build harmony across the classes with a rising tide of productivity lifting all boats.

In the outstanding treatise *Shared Capitalism at Work,* irrefutable hard data points the way. The authors' conclusions indicate that shared ownership builds wealth for employees, while the businesses they are involved with consistently thrive. In their sample data set, the average value of company stock held by each ESOP employee owner is almost $86,000 and the average value of stock options held by each employee is almost $283,000.

We *can* move away from this unending futile debate between capitalism and socialism; between taxing and spending, between individual liberty and the state, between Republicans and Democrats—all of which leads us to the same *frustration* and failed answers.

Our proposals for this transformation involve a 50% or 100% tax credit for corporations on the value of employer stock contributed to employees' compensation. In Enterprise Zones where the impact on poverty can be greatest, the tax credit would be 100%, while the tax credit would be 50% in all other areas.

Finally, in order to incentivize banks to make "Employee Friendly" loans to corporations that want to set up Employee Stock Ownership Plans, a bank or other financial institution could be allowed to exclude 50% of its interest income on a loan to help set up and ESOP from its taxable income.

These common sense, straightforward proposals will have a massive positive impact on expanding capital ownership and begin to dramatically reverse the seriously troubling, ever expanding wage inequality conundrum.

Yet, let us have no illusions. This proposal in itself is not a panacea. It is not claiming to usher in some miraculous utopia. When some demigod promises such, we suggest you run as fast as you can the other way!

What *THE 3rd WAY* does unmistakably represent are real solutions to modern challenges. Yet, the current socialist/capitalist straitjacket leads us forever back and forth around to the same tired debates on class and redistribution of wealth. Today the malaise and feeling of estrangement are palpable in society at every demographic level and economic strata.

Are we witnessing some parallels to the inexorable decline of the Roman Empire? Have many of our economic and political conceptions become outdated and eclipsed? Are well-meaning but fatally flawed economic policies to blame? Is innovation, whether through entrepreneurship and/or technological advancement, being wrongly disconnected from the vast majority of our labor force? Is our outmoded pattern of tax collection one that disincentivizes both free enterprise and a healthy broad-based ownership stake by the populace? Is an element of our decline attributable to a general malaise, fostered by suppression of "A New American Dream" of capital ownership championed in this book? Is the theory of moral decay involved—the greed of a few to not share the blessings of capitalism with the many? Surely all this points unmistakably toward the urgency for incentives to be put in place for business leaders to take the just and appropriate action now.

Today the top 1% owns more than 50% of all wealth, all capital income and all income growth for the last 20 years. And the top 10% is between 80% and 90% of all three of those. Frightening.

Presently, we are marching *backward* toward Feudalism – when the top 5% own more than 80% of everything. That will de facto result in a society of masters and servants. We need truly intelligent public policy immediately to halt and reverse this menacing trend.

For a comprehensive understanding of the solution, look no further than the recent excellent book, "The Citizens Share" that chronics the precise thoughts of our brilliant Founding Fathers on this matter. If you look at the conservative ideology of our Founding Fathers they had three pillars to their conservative ideology - small government, low taxes and broad property ownership. And they believe that the third one *caused* the first two.

Unfortunately that's missing in the mind and speeches of many Conservatives today. They need to go back and re-read *all* of what the Founding Fathers instructed them, and we the citizenry that want to live in a universally prosperous and free society to do.

Somehow they think small government and low taxes come from some ether out of the air. It doesn't. It comes from people having enough economic independence so they don't *need* the government as much. Then if everyone has property, reasonable modest taxes on that property will give you enough to support charitable and general government functions for all.

Here's the bottom line: Dramatically accelerate broad based properly/capital ownership. Do that by requiring every corporate tax incentive conditioned on having some form of a broad based ownership share plan for their workers. Period.

Can we make the vital systemic corrections the Roman Empire failed to do? If not, are the barbarians soon to be at the gate? If so, the decay and corrosive unrest (just as with the Romans) will have come from within!

We are in trouble. Surely, in the overall scheme of economics, there is no doubt that government spending as a percentage of GDP must be significantly reduced. In 2011, US debt reached 100 percent of our country's GDP. Our debt is quickly about to surpass more than $20 trillion (over $175,000 per taxpayer). We are on the same alarming path to insolvency that is now happening all over Europe. In addition, there is no doubt we need to expand both free and fair trade, especially as it relates to China. There is also no doubt we must greatly expand all our domestic energy resources in as clean and safe a manner as possible. And there is no doubt the education establishment is failing our students and is crying out for reform. These are all grave matters indeed.

However, the *most important* and effective step we need taken immediately is to incentivize the corporate tax system in exchange for a transformation in the measure of employees' equity in their place of work. This is fundamental. And it will fundamentally correct the economic system we operate under for the better. Yes, we need to cut corporate taxation, but *only* if it is

HOW THE THIRD WAY FOSTERS MAJOR SOLUTIONS...

offset with *equivalent* employee ownership. Only then can we obtain the greatest good for the greatest number. Only then can we unleash the *full* power of our nation's people!

From a global perspective, some stark, plain talk is also in order. More than in order, it's required. Gross inequality without any hope is a potential component for serious trouble. A permanent underclass anywhere in the world *without any real hope* to share in any measure of the blessings of prosperity is, frankly, a caldron for radicalization. We see this both *within* countries with large and growing disparities of incomes and *between* countries.

Senseless violence can be a way an uninformed element of the population knows how to vent their boiling frustration. Wisdom can stop it! Great leaders such as Martin Luther King Jr., Mahatma Gandhi, Nelson Mandela, and others like them were successful in bringing about positive change through peaceful means, once the populace was informed and mobilized. The same is called for here if the required diffusion of economic power is to occur in our postindustrial world. To avert much more serious trouble, it *must* happen. We already know that technological progress linked to capitalism has an enormously powerful capability for creating massive wealth. Yet, it does not have to be a zero-sum game, where the prosperity of a few is gained at the expense of the many.

There is a mechanism to deal with the realities of the modern economic world we live in today. That mechanism is before you: *involving employees in the ownership of the capital and wealth they are instrumental in producing.* It's one hell of a big idea. A movement so powerful and a path so significant it is worthy of claiming its own broad title—***THE 3rd WAY.***

Of all the concepts presented in this book, the most critically preeminent is the pressing relationship between labor and technology. Addressed more fully at the beginning of our work, it is the single concept deserving reprise. We must understand this decisive relationship and how we must deal with it effectively in the modern age.

While men and women have natural limits to the labor they can produce, technology, and more importantly its fundamental connection to capital and by extension capitalism, must be reconciled. Who *owns* the capital is the point. Technology continues relentlessly and at an infinite degree to march on—ever expanding its capabilities. A person's labor is finite. Unless we reconcile a bold new system to address this intensifying inequity in the modern world, we are on an inescapable collision course toward a social, economic, and political calamity of epic scale.

It is imperative that our elected officials, the media, and most importantly the general public realize what must be done.

The ever-widening gap between technology and labor is a cold reality. The central question for our age is how we resolve the two as it relates to public policy. The decisions we make have massive social, economic, and political implications. We must get this right. And the time to act is now.

Dire consequences await us all if we do not act appropriately and expeditiously! An understanding of a bold new paradigm is before you. The employee ownership movement is already successfully underway. We must nurture and build on it in geometric proportions.

Economic democracy and employee ownership represent the only new and real way forward. Built out of decades of helpful legislation and countless examples of its remarkable successes, it is time to blow the doors off what we already know works! Decades of real wealth creation have been established. Decades of real cooperation have also followed between labor and management at all levels.

Meanwhile, anyone who doubts the gravely high levels of authentic anxiety coursing through the populace is either disinterested, uninformed, or a fool. A perpetual proliferation of chain stores, restaurants, retail outlets, and big business in general clearly serves to exacerbate levels of alienation. Moreover, the displacement of independent businesses by chains just adds to the feelings of disaffection. These are immutable realities neither political party is presently equipped to answer effectively.

Now we have a mechanism we know can move economic life to truly higher ground. We can move to a society evolving into one that promotes honest and secure feelings of belonging to something of value, rather than one of organizations that see its workers as merely dispensable units.

Most men lead lives of quiet desperation and go to the grave with the song still in them.
—Henry David Thoreau, American author, poet, philosopher, abolitionist, naturalist, tax resister, development critic, historian, and leading transcendentalist[166]

Behold a new paradigm! It is a solid alternative modification to the two, poor rigid choices of pure capitalism or hard socialism we have been stuck with.

A bold new form of economic empowerment embodied in "democratic capitalism" awaits. A new world of optimism grounded in the proven successes of the people and companies already engaged assures us to confidently move ahead at Godspeed.

So let us forever mark this day as apart from all others. Let us commit to take the action necessary to bring forth the desperately needed change longed for in the hearts and minds of all.

Nature has planted in our minds an insatiable longing to see the truth.
—Cicero, Roman philosopher, statesman, lawyer, orator, and political theorist[167]

Ownership is the key! Let us strive forever forward, focused on what is best for our own interests. Yet, in so doing, as *employee owners,* we together move both levels of prosperity and righteousness ever upward.

Let us endeavor to create a just *and* prosperous society allowing people to pursue lives of fulfillment, actualization, and shared universal harmony that shall endure.

HOW THE THIRD WAY FOSTERS MAJOR SOLUTIONS...

Action Steps
[each of us can be a one-person army!]

For real change to occur, it will take more than just reading this book. Here are some suggestions for actions you can take that will make a real difference:

- Go to our Website: http://THE3rdWAYbook.com/

- "Like" us on Facebook:
  http://facebook.com/THE3rdWAYbook

- Follow us on Twitter:
  http://twitter.com/THE3rdWAYbook

- Watch us on YouTube:
  http://youtube.com/THE3rdWAYbook

- Follow us on GooglePlus:
  http://google.com/+THE3rdWAYbook

- Endorse us on LinkedIn:
  http://linkedin.com/in/THE3rdWAYbook

- Visit our Blog:
  http://THE3rdWAYbook.com/blog

- Sign our Petition at Change.org
  http://www.change.org/p/THE3rdWAYbook

*** SHARE OUR LINKS WITH ALL YOUR FRIENDS ***

THE 3RD WAY

- Call your two US Senators
  http://www.senate.gov/index.htm

- Call your House representative
  (http://www.house.gov/representatives/find/).

- Contact any national, state, or local elected official
  (http://www.usa.gov/Contact/Elected.shtml).

- Insist your library carry several copies of this book.

- Contact local and national media and ask that they devote more attention to this movement:
  - Associated Press (AP), http://www.ap.org/, phone 212-621-1500
  - United Press International (UPI), http://www.upi.com/, executive editor phone number: 202-898-8000
  - Reuters, http://www.reuters.com/, phone 646-223-4000

- For a current list of companies offering ESOP opportunities, contact:

The ESOP Association
1726 M Street NW, Suite 501
Washington, DC 20036
Phone: 202-293-2971; toll-free: 866-366-3832; fax: 202-293-7568
E-mail: esop@esopassociation.org
Web: www.esopassociation.org

HOW THE THIRD WAY FOSTERS MAJOR SOLUTIONS...

The National Center for Employee Ownership (NCEO)
1736 Franklin St., 8th Floor
Oakland, CA 94612
Phone: 510-208-1300: Fax: 510-272-9510
Email: customerservice@nceo.org

- Encourage your state and federal legislators to buy and read the book.

- Encourage your friends and associates to buy and read the book.

- Ask your clubs and associations to buy the books in quantities.

- Ask your business, association and club to inquire about buying the books in quantities.

- Call #(908) 580-0302 to contact us.

NOTES

[1] Richard A. Lovett, "Supercontinent Pangaea Pushed, Not Sucked, into Place," *National Geographic News* (September 5, 2008).

[2] John Menke, Menke Group blog, http://www.menke.com/blog/the-origin-and-history-of-the-esop-and-its-future-role-as-a-business-succession-tool/.

[3] Norberto Bobbio and Allan Cameron, *Left and Right: The Significance of a Political Distinction* (Chicago: University of Chicago Press, 1997), 8. ISBN 0-226-06245-7, ISBN 978-0-226-06245-7.

[4] Michael Freeden, *Liberal Languages: Ideological Imaginations and Twentieth-Century Progressive Thought* (Princeton, NJ: Princeton University Press, 2004), 198.

[5] Louis O. Kelso, "Democratic Capitalism - Our Time! For Economic Justice" (December 6, 2012).

[6] Joseph A. Schumpeter, *Capitalism, Socialism and Democracy*, 2nd ed. (Eastford, CT: Martino Fine Books, 2010), 146.

[7] Ralph Nader, "Remarks by Ralph Nader on Raising Minimum Wage," *Nader Page*, June 6, 2012.

[8] Pope John Paul II, *Centesimus Annus*, 1991.

[9] For more information please see: http://www.investopedia.com/terms/k/ksop.asp.

[10] For more information please see: http://en.wikipedia.org/wiki/Employee_stock_option.

[11] For more information please see: http://en.wikipedia.org/wiki/Profit_sharing.

[12] Arindrajit Dube and Richard Freeman, "Complementarity of Shared Compensation and Decision-Making Systems:

Evidence from the American Labor Market" (September 26, 2006), http://users.nber.org/~confer/2006/SCf06/dube.pdf.

[13] Douglas Kruse, Richard Freeman, and Joseph Blasi, eds., *Shared Capitalism at Work: Employee Ownership, Profit and Gain Sharing, and Broad-based Stock Options,* National Bureau of Economic Research (Chicago: University of Chicago Press, 2010), ISBN: 0-226-05695-3, http://www.nber.org/chapters/c8090.pdf.

[14] Louis O. Kelso and Mortimer J. Adler, *The Capitalist Manifesto* (Literary Licensing, 2011), 189–190.

[15] President Ronald Reagan, "Remarks on Receiving the Report of the Presidential Task Force on Project Economic Justice," August 3, 1987, http://www.youtube.com/watch?v=06vP84SqnS4.

[16] US Senator Bernard Sanders, "Address to Attendees of 2012 ESOP Association Conference and Trade Show," Las Vegas, NV, http://www.youtube.com/watch?v=aTiPCsxf_qg.

[17] Benjamin Franklin, Remarks by Mr. Lieberman, US Senate (April 25, 2006).

[18] Louis O. Kelso (1964), http://www.kelsoinstitute.org/.

[19] Norman G. Kurland and Dawn K. Brohawn, "Louis Kelso's Economic Vision for the 21st Century," Center for Economic and Social Justice.

[20] Abraham Lincoln, "State of the Union Address" (December 3, 1861).

[21] For more information please see http://en.wikipedia.org/wiki/Capital_(economics).

[22] Louis O. Kelso, *San Francisco Examiner & Chronicle* (1978).

[23] Friedrich A. von Hayek, *Law, Legislation, and Liberty,* vol. 2, *The Mirage of Social Justice* (Chicago: University of Chicago Press, 1978).

[24] Definition from http://www.merriam-webster.com/dictionary/ideology.

[25] Richard B. Freeman, "Optimal Inequality for Economic Growth, Stability, and Shared Prosperity: The Economics behind the Wall Street Occupiers Protest?" *Insights: Melbourne Business*

and Economics 11 (April 2012), http://insights.unimelb.edu.au/vol11/01_Freeman.html.

[26] As quoted in Raymond Lonergan, *Mr. Justice Brandeis - Great American* (St. Louis: Modern View Press, 1941), 42.

[27] Fed Chair Unsure If Capitalism or Oligarchy Describes the U.S. May 8, 2014 By Susan Jones (CNSNews.com) http://cnsnews.com/news/article/susan-jones/fed-chair-unsure-if-capitalism-or-oligarchy-describes-us

[28] http://www.dol.gov/whd/minwage/chart.htm

[29] Card, David and Krueger, Alan B. "Minimum Wages and Employment: A Case Study of the Fast-Food Industry in New Jersey and Pennsylvania." *American Economic Review*, September 1994, 84(4), pp. 772–93.

[30] Fuller, Dan and Doris Geide-Stevenson (2003): *Consensus Among Economists: Revisited*, in: Journal of Economic Review, Vol. 34, No. 4, Seite 369-387

[31] Solman, Paul. "The Alternative American Dream: Inclusive Capitalism." PBS Newshour. Qtd by Christopher Mackin as qtd in "The Asset Price Meltdown and the Wealth of the Middle Class" by Edward Wolff, pg. 45. (August 23, 2013).

[32] From Louis O. Kelso and Patricia Hetter Kelso, "Binary Economics in Eight Easy Lessons," 1989.

[33] "The Citizens Share" p38

[34] "The Citizens Share" p42

[35] Kruse, Freeman, and Blasi, *Shared Capitalism at Work*, 351.

[36] Josh Bivens, Elise Gould, Lawrence Mishel, and Heidi Shierholz, *The State of Working America 2012/2013*, an Economic Policy Institute Book (Ithaca, NY: Cornell University Press, forthcoming in 2012).

[37] Freeman, "Optimal Inequality for Economic Growth, Stability, and Shared Prosperity."

[38] Ibid.

[39] Bertrand Russell, *Sceptical Essays* (London: George Allen & Unwin Ltd., 1928), chapter 13.

[40] Louis O. Kelso and Walter A. Lawrence, *The Second Income Plan* (1965), 8.

[41] Winston Churchill, "Demobilisation," speech in the House of Commons (October 22, 1945).

[42] For more information please see: http://en.wikipedia.org/wiki/Russell_B._Long#cite_note-Mann_2003-3.

[43] John H. Cushman Jr., "Russell B. Long, 84, Senator Who Influenced Tax Laws," *New York Times* (May 11, 2003).

[44] George Bernard Shaw, *The Intelligent Woman's Guide to Socialism and Capitalism* (1928), 214.

[45] For more information consult *Blackwell Encyclopedia of Political Thought* (Blackwell Publishing, 1991), 91.

[46] For more information from *Wikipedia*: http://en.wikipedia.org/wiki/Velocity_of_money.

[47] Martin Wolf, Why Globalization works, p. 43–45

[48] Dennis Prager, "Socialism Kills" (September 2, 2003).

[49] For more information from *Wikipedia*: http://en.wikipedia.org/wiki/Communist_state#cite_note-1.

[50] From *Wikipedia*, http://en.wikipedia.org/wiki/Cuba.

[51] Human Rights Watch, New York, NY (2005), http://www.hrw.org/world-report-2006/cuba.

[52] For more information from *Wikipedia*, http://en.wikipedia.org/wiki/Soviet.

[53] "World Report 2009: China," Human Rights Watch (retrieved July 14, 2009).

[54] Andrew Chack, John V. Farr, and James H. Schreiner, "A Systems Perspective of Foreign Intervention with Regards to Democratic People's Republic of Korea," Center for Nation Reconstruction and Capacity Development, Department of Systems Engineering, United States Military Academy, West Point,

NJ (2012), http://www.usma.edu/cnrcd/CNRCD_Library/White%20Paper%20Korea%202012.pdf.

[55] For more information from *Wikipedia*: http://en.wikipedia.org/wiki/North_Korea.

[56] "The Pilgrims' Failed Experiment with Socialism," *Freedom Post* (November 25, 2009).

[57] For more information please see: http://www.creationworldview.org/articles_view.asp?id=18.

[58] Thomas Sowell, "Civil Rights: Rhetoric or Reality?" (December 17, 1985).

[59] Arthur Laffer, "The Four Pillars of Reaganomics" (January 16, 2007).

[60] For more information from *Wikipedia*: http://en.wikipedia.org/wiki/Athenian_democracy.

[61] For more information from *Wikipedia*: http://en.wikipedia.org/wiki/Civil_Rights_Act_of_1964.

[62] Alexis de Tocqueville, "Discours prononcé à l'assemblée constituante le 12 Septembre 1848 sur la question du droit au travail," *Oeuvres complètes*, vol. IX, 546.

[63] Preface to Kelso and Adler, *The Capitalist Manifesto*.

[64] Paul M. Johnson, Auburn University, Department of Political Science (2005).

[65] Monty G. Marshall and Benjamin R. Cole, "Global Report 2011: Conflict, Governance, and State Fragility" (Vienna: Center for Systemic Peace, December 1, 2011), retrieved August 15, 2012. For more information from *Wikipedia*: http://en.wikipedia.org/wiki/Anocracy.

[66] For more information from *Wikipedia*: http://en.wikipedia.org/wiki/Democratization.

[67] Kruse, Freeman, and Blasi, *Shared Capitalism at Work*.

[68] http://www.brainyquote.com/quotes/quotes/d/dantealigh381206.html.

[69] Constantine Von Hoffman, "Why Greece Will and Should Default on Its Debts" (May 16, 2012), http://www.cbsnews.com/8301-505123_162-57434749/why-greece-will-and-should-default-on-its-debts/.

[70] For more information from *Wikipedia*: http://en.wikipedia.org/wiki/Economy_of_Greece.

[71] David Charter, "Storm over Bailout of Greece, EU's Most Ailing Economy," *Time* online, 2010.

[72] Hellenic Statistical Authority, "Annual National Accounts: Year 2011 (2nd Estimation)" (October 5, 2012).

[73] For more information see: http://en.wikiquote.org/wiki/Alexander_Fraser_Tytler.

[74] Louis O. Kelso and Patricia Hetter Kelso, "Why I Invented the ESOP LBO," *Leaders* 12, no. 4 (December 1989).

[75] Mahatma Gandhi, *The Way to God: Selected Writings from Mahatma Gandhi*, 36.

[76] Shannon Allen, "Paul Ryan, in His Own Words," *Examiner.com*, (August 16, 2012).

[77] http://usdailyreview.com/tag/james-gilmore.

[78] "The Growth Code," Free Congress Foundation Inc., Alexandria, VA.

[79] Thomas Jefferson, "First Inaugural Address," Washington, DC (March 4, 1801).

[80] "Get Society Rich Quick: The Ideal Level of Government Spending," http://thinkbynumbers.org/economics/gdp/ideal-level-of-government-spending/.

[81] *The Rahn Curve and the Growth-Maximizing Level of Government*, video by Center for Freedom and Prosperity, freedomandprosperity.org; June 29, 2010, with subtitles, dotsub.com.

[82] H. G. Wells, *The New World Order*, 46.

[83] Louis O. Kelso and Walter A. Lawrence, *The Second Income Plan* (1965), 2.

[84] Tim Dickinson. "Meet Gary Johnson, the GOPs Invisible Candidate," *Rolling Stone* (June 15, 2013).

[85] Arthur Sullivan and Steven M. Sheffrin, *Economics: Principles in Action* (Upper Saddle River, NJ: Pearson Prentice Hall, 2003), 350. ISBN 0-13-063085-3.

[86] Frederick Douglass, *The Life and Times of Frederick Douglass: From 1817–1882.*

[87] Adam Smith, *The Wealth of Nations* (1776).

[88] "A Conversation with Arthur C. Brooks, Part 1," *National Review Online* (June 23, 2010).

[89] David A. Spitzley, "Louis Kelso Made Simple." More Information and additional sources can be found at: http://cog.kent.edu/lib/spitzley2.html.

[90] Kelso and Adler, *The Capitalist Manifesto,* http://www.amazon.com/dp/1258153602/, accessed October 15, 2011.

[91] Stephen Moore and John Silvia, "The ABCs of the Capital Gains Tax" (October 4, 1995).

[92] Douglas Holtz-Eakin, "The Need for Pro-Growth Corporate Tax Reform," New America Foundation (August 2011).

[93] Mieko Nakabayashi and James Carter, "America Goes It Alone on High Corporate Taxes," *Wall Street Journal* (July 19, 2013).

[94] Bruce Stokes, "The Progressive Case for Corporate Tax Reform" (January 26, 2012).

[95] Ron Paul, "Ron Paul 2012: In Defense of Liberty!"

[96] "Yes, There Is an Alternative to Capitalism: Mondragon Shows the Way." Richard Wolff. *theguardian.com,* June 24, 2012, http://www.theguardian.com/commentisfree/2012/jun/24/alternative-capitalism-mondragon.

[97] Robert Kiyosaki and Sharon L. Lechter. *Rich Dad Poor Dad* (2001).

[98] For more information from *Wikipedia*: http://en.wikipedia.org/wiki/Robert_Kiyosaki.

[99] From *The Concise Columbia Dictionary of Quotations*. Columbia University Press, 1989.

[100] Joseph Blasi, Douglas Kruse, and Aaron Bernstein, *In the Company of Owners* (Basic Books, 2003), 3, 79.

[101] Milton Friedman, quoted in "Free to Chose" PBS TV series (1980).

[102] Louis O. Kelso, "Labor's Untapped Wealth," address delivered at Air Line Pilots Association Retirement and Insurance Seminar, Washington, DC (March 1984).

[103] From Larry Johnson, *Politics: An Introduction to the Modern Democratic State*, 55.

[104] For more information from *Wikipedia*: http://en.wikipedia.org/wiki/Karl_Marx.

[105] Karl Marx and Friedrich Engels, *The Communist Manifesto*, chapter 1, "Bourgeois and Proletarians."

[106] 99 David Horowitz, *Left Illusions: An Intellectual Odyssey*, 431.

[107] Samuel Moore, trans., *Manifesto of the Communist Party* (Zodiac, 1888), available online at: http://www.marxists.org/archive/marx.

[108] For more information from *Wikipedia*: http://en.wikipedia.org/wiki/Means_of_production.

[109] Franklin D. Roosevelt, "State of the Union Message to Congress" (January 11, 1944). Text from the speech can be found online at http://www.presidency.ucsb.edu/ws/?pid=16518, Gerhard Peters and John T. Woolley, the American Presidency Project.

[110] For more information from *Wikipedia*: http://en.wikipedia.org/wiki/Maslow's_hierarchy_of_needs, as cited from: A. H. Maslow, "A Theory of Human Motivation," *Psychological Review* 50, no. 4, (1943) 370–96. Retrieved from http://psychclassics.yorku.ca/Maslow/motivation.htm.

[111] Uday Hiwarale, Ramavatar Meena, and Jayant Kumar Mohanta, "Role of Employee Motivation in Quality Improvement Programs" (unknown year).

[112] Jeremy Rifkin, *Own Your Own Job: Economic Democracy for Working Americans* (New York: Bantam Books, 1977).

[113] From: Henry Louis Mencken, *The American Mercury*, vol. 45, 51.

[114] For more information from *Wikipedia*: http://en.wikipedia.org/wiki/List_of_campaigns_of_the_Communist_Party_of_China.

[115] For more information from *Wikipedia*: http://en.wikipedia.org/wiki/Cultural_Revolution. Additional information can be found in: Malcolm MacDonald, Malcolm, *Inside China* (Boston: Little, Brown, 1980), 82.

[116] Corinne J. Naden and Rose J. Blue, *Wilma Rudolph*, 7.

[117] John Paul Rollert, "Who Makes Capitalism Work? Adam Smith Would Disagree with Today's Conservatives," *Next New Deal: The Blog of the Roosevelt Institute* (August 8, 2011), http://www.nextnewdeal.net/who-makes-capitalism-work-adam-smith-would-disagree-todays-conservatives.

[118] Andrew Carnegie, *The Gospel of Wealth Essays and Other Writings*.

[119] Quote found online at: http://www.aynrand.org/site/PageServer?pagename=reg_ar_capitalism.

[120] Sunni Maravillosa, "Interview with John Mackey" (October 20, 2005).

[121] Lawrence Mishel, "Unions, Inequality, and Faltering Middle-Class Wages," Economic Policy Institute (August 29, 2012).

[122] John Case, "Death by Politics: When Teamwork Is Un-American," *Inc.*

[123] W. Edwards Deming, *The New Economics for Industry, Government, Education, and Government* (Massachusetts Institute of Technology, Center for Advanced Educational Services, 1993).

[124] "Questions for the Record," from Senator Bernard Sanders for Treasury Secretary Jacob J. Lew (April 2013). For a transcript please see: http://www.esopassociation.org/docs/default-source/advocacy/here.pdf.

[125] Thomas Huxley, *Select Works of Thomas H. Huxley*, 649.

NOTES

[126] George G. Brenkert and Tom L. Beauchamp, eds., "John Maynard Keynes," *The Oxford Handbook of Business Ethics*, 74.

[127] Robert Ashford and Rodney Shakespeare, "Activist Alert: Sins of Omission," *Binary Economics: The New Paradigm*, 49.

[128] Jerry N. Gauche, "Binary Economic Modes for the Privatization of Public Assets," The Kelso Institute (2000).

[129] Carmine Gorga, "Concordian Economics" (September 2, 2008).

[130] Ibid.

[131] Julian Bond, *A Time to Speak, a Time to Act: The Movement in Politics*.

[132] Fidan Ana Kurtulus and Douglas Kruse, "How Did Employee Ownership Firms Weather the Last Two Recessions? Employee Ownership and Employment Stability in the US: 1999–2008," April 15, 2012.

[133] Freeman, "Optimal Inequality for Economic Growth, Stability, and Shared Prosperity."

[134] ESOP Association, 1726 M Street NW, Suite 501, Washington, DC 20036.

[135] Commonwealth Competition Council. *Competition Watch* (2000). Please see: http://state.vipnet.org/ccc/june99.htm.

[136] Michael Golden and Matthew Wright, "Lending to ESOPs: Of a Different Color, This Horse Still Races," *Journal of Lending & Credit Risk Management* (May 1999).

[137] Tara Silver-Malyska and Elizabeth Jenkins, "The Pension Protection Act of 2006: An Overview of the Defined Benefit and Defined Contribution Provisions of the Act," *Benefits Law Journal* (Winter 2006).

[138] Robert G. Hagstrom, *The Warren Buffett Way: Investment Strategies of the World's Greatest Investor*, 95.

[139] Kruse, Freeman, and Blasi, *Shared Capitalism at Work*.

[140] Jack Stack, "Introducing 'Open the Books': Why Would Anyone Do This?" *New York Times* (December 15, 2009).

[141] Jack Stack with Bo Burlington, *The Great Game of Business: Unlocking the Power and Profitability of Open-Book Management* (New York: Crown Publishing). ISBN-13: 9780385475259. For purchasing information, please see: http://www.barnesandnoble.com/w/great-game-of-business-jack-stack/1100985823?ean=9780385475259&itm=1&usri=9780385475259.

[142] Ibid.

[143] Dan Crim and Gerard Seijtsm "Jack Stack: The Ten C's of Employee Engagement," *Ivey Business Journal* (March/April 2006).

[144] For more information please see: http://greatgame.com/about/.

[145] Jack Stack, "Springfield Remanufacturing Bought the Company and Learned to Play the Game of Open-Book Management," *National Productivity Review* (Winter 1993).

[146] John Case, *Open-Book Management: The Coming Business Revolution,* reprint ed. (New York: Harper Business, 1996), 95. Purchasing information available at: http://www.amazon.com/dp/0887308023.

[147] Ibid.

[148] Ibid.

[149] José Edgardo L. Campos and Sanjay Pradhan, *The Many Faces of Corruption,* 267, http://books.google.com/books?id=Wy-oNmjqq-QC&pg=PA267&dq=%E2%80%9CCorruption+has+its+own+motivations,+and+one+has+to+thoroughly+study+that+phenomenon+and+eliminate+the+foundations+that+allow+corruption+to+exist.%E2%80%9D++Eduard+Shevardnadze&hl=en&sa=X&ei=XjqAUaTiB_fj4APG5ICgAg&ved=0CDMQ6wEwAA.

[150] Eduardo Porter, "The Spreading Scourge of Corporate Corruption," *New York Times* (July 10, 2012).

[151] Freeman, "Optimal Inequality for Economic Growth, Stability, and Shared Prosperity."

[152] Carl Seelig, *Ideas and Opinions,* 27.

[153] For more information from *Wikipedia*: http://en.wikipedia.org/wiki/Stock#Shareholder, Additional references can be found in: Jones v. H. F. Ahmanson & Co., 1 Cal. 3d (1969).

[154] Winston Overton, *Wall Street Scandals: Greed and Trading on Wall Street the American Way*, (Xlibris Corporation, 2013), 1919.

[155] Additional information is available at: http://www.historians.org/teaching/aahe/kelly/pew/Portfolio/Student%20Work/F99-1-6.html.

[156] Alex Ayres, ed., *The Wit and Wisdom of Mark Twain: A Book of Quotations* (1987).

[157] AFL-CIO, "Taxpayers & Tax Dodgers, 2008–2010," Citizens for Tax Justice and the Institute on Taxation and Economic Policy (November 3, 2011).

[158] Steve Moore, 'Things Could Get Pretty Messy," *Wall Street Journal* (October 2, 2010).

[159] For more information from *Wikipedia* http://en.wikipedia.org/wiki/Realpolitik. See also for additional information.

[160] Denis Healey, *The Economist* 354, 186.

[161] Alex Mills, "Mills: Romney banks on oil industry for economic recovery." *(Wichita Falls, TX) Times Record News* (September 2, 2012), http://www.timesrecordnews.com/news/2012/sep/02/romney-banks-on-oil-industry-for-economic-/?print=1.

[162] Robert S. McIntyre, "The Sorry State of Corporate Taxes What Fortune 500 Firms Pay (or Don't Pay) in the USA And What they Pay Abroad - 2008 to 2012, Citizens for Tax Justice (February 2014), http://www.ctj.org/corporatetaxdodgers/sorrystateofcorptaxes.pdf

[163] Robert S. McIntyre, "Big No-Tax Corps Just Keep on Dodging," Citizens for Tax Justice (April 9, 2012), http://www.ctj.org/pdf/notax2012.pdf.

[164] Sherrie Scott, "Top 10 Corporate Tax Deductions," Demand Media, *Houston Chronicle* (2012).

[165] Stevenson, Guy. "Louis Kelso: Saving the Economy." Online Video Clip. Youtube.com. Posted on June 9 2011. (August 13, 2013).

[166] Henry David Thoreau, *Civil Disobedience and Other Essays*. Purchasing information can be found at: http://www.amazon.com/dp/0486275639.

[167] Cicero, *Tusculanae Disputationes*.

BIBLIOGRAPHY

Alighieri, Dante. *The Divine Comedy.* Translated by John Ciardi. New York: Penguin, 1954.

Allen, Sharon. "Paul Ryan in His Own Words." *Examiner.com.* August 16, 2012.

Ashford, Robert, and Rodney Shakespeare. *Binary Economics: The New Paradigm.* University Press of America, 1999. ISBN: 9780761813200.

Ayres, Alex, ed. Twain, Mark. *The Wit and Wisdom of Mark Twain: A Book of Quotations.* New York: Harper &Row, 1987.

Bianchi, Giuliano. "Pay at Top Related to Incentive Pay via Capital Income." Image from "Essays on CEO Compensation: New Evidence on the Managerial-Power vs. Optimal Contracting Debate." Universita di Bologna, 2013.

Blasi, Joseph R., Richard B. Freeman, and Douglas L. Kruse. *The Citizen's Share: Putting Ownership Back into Democracy.* New Haven: Yale University Press, 2013.

Blasi, Joseph R., and Douglas L. Kruse. *The New Owners: The Mass Emergence of Employee Ownership in Public Companies and What It Means to American Business.* New York: Harper Collins, 1991.

Blasi, Joseph, Douglas Kruse, and Aaron Bernstein. *In the Company of Owners.* Basic Books. New York: Basic Books, 1987.

Bobbio, Norberto, and Allan Cameron. *Left and Right: The Significance of a Political Distinction.* Chicago: University of Chicago Press, 1997. ISBN 0-226-06245-7, ISBN 978-0-226-06245-7.

Bond, Julian. *A Time to Speak, a Time to Act: The Movement in Politics.* New York: Simon & Schuster, 1972.

Boughton, George Henry. "Puritans Going to Church," 1885. Image. Library of Congress.

Brenkert, George, and Tom L. Beauchamp. Quote from John Maynard Keynes. *The Oxford Handbook of Business Ethics.* New York: Oxford University Press, 2010.

Brimelow, Peter. "Why the Deficit Is the Wrong Number." *Forbes*, March 5, 1993.

Brooks, Arthur C. "A Conversation with Arthur C. Brooks, Part 1." *National Review Online*, June 23, 2010.

Campos, Jose Edgardo, and Sanjay Pradhan. *The Many Faces of Corruption*. Washington, D.C.: World Bank, 2007.

Carnegie, Andrew. *The Gospel of Wealth Essays and Other Timely Essays.* New York: Forgotten Books, 2012. Originally published 1886 by Forum Publishing Company.

Case, John. "Death by Politics: When Teamwork Is Un-American." *Inc.*, November 1, 1993.

Case, John. *Open-Book Management: The Coming Business Revolution*. Reprint, New York: Harper Business, 1996.

Center for Freedom and Prosperity. "The Rahn Curve and the Growth-Maximizing Level of Government," vol. IV, video V. Video. June 29, 2010. http://freedomandprosperity.org/2010/videos/the-rahn-curve-and-the-growth-maximizing-level-of-government/.

Chack, Andrew, John V. Farr, and James H. Schreiner. "A Systems Perspective of Foreign Intervention with Regards to Democratic People's Republic of Korea." Center for Nation Reconstruction and Capacity Development, Department of Systems Engineering, United States Military Academy, West Point, NJ. 2012. http://www.usma.edu/cnrcd/CNRCD_Library/White 20Paper%20Korea%202012.pdf.

Charter, David. "Storm over Bailout of Greece, EU's Most Ailing Economy." *Time* online: Brussels, 2010.

BIBLIOGRAPHY

Churchill, Winston. "Demobilisation," speech in the House of Commons (October 22, 1945). Text from this speech can be found at http://hansard.millbanksystems.com/commons/1945/oct/22/demobilisation#column_1703.

Cicero, Marcus Tullius. *Tusculanae Disputationes.* London: Bell, 1900.

Citizens for Tax Justice and the Institute on Taxation and Economic Policy. "Corporate Taxpayers & Tax Dodgers, 2008–2010." November 3, 2011.

CNBC. "Untold Wealth: The Rise of the Super Rich." Video. July 28, 2011.

Commonwealth Competition Council. "An Eventful Year for Employee Ownership Research." *Competition Watch* 4, no. 2 (June 1999). http://state.vipnet.org/ccc/june99.htm.

Creation Worldview Ministries. "Pilgrims and Their Experiments with Communism." http://www.creationworldview.org/articles_view.asp?id=18.

Crim, Dan, and Gerard Seljts. "What Engages Employees Most or, the Ten C's of Employee Engagement." *Ivey Business Journal*, March/April 2006.

Cushman, John H. Jr. "Russell B. Long, 84, Senator Who Influenced Tax Laws." *New York Times*, May 11, 2003.

De Rugy, Veronique. "The Corporate Income Tax Rates in the OECD." Mercatus Center at George Mason University, May 9, 2011.

De Tocqueville, Alexis. "Discours prononcé à l'assemblée constituante le 12 Septembre 1848 sur la question du droit au travail," *Oeuvres complètes*, vol. IX. Paris: Editions Gallimard, 1998.

Demine, W. Edwards. *The New Economics for Industry, Government, Education, and Government.* Cambridge, MA: Massachusetts Institute of Technology, 1993.

Dickinson, Tim. "Meet Gary Johnson, the GOPs Invisible Candidate." *Rolling Stone*, June 15, 2013.

Dilliard, Irving. *Mr. Justice Brandeis, Great American.* Saint Louis: Modern View Press, 1941.

Douglass, Frederick. *The Life and Times of Frederick Douglass: From 1817–1882*. Mineola, NY: Dover Publications, 2003. Originally published by De Wolfe & Fiske Co., 1892.

Dube, Arindrajit, and Richard Freeman. "Complementarity of Shared Compensation and Decision-Making Systems: Evidence from the American Labor Market," September 26, 2006. http://users.nber.org/~confer/2006/SCf06/dube.pdf.

Einstein, Albert, and Carl Seelig, *Ideas and Opinions*. New York: Crown Publishing Group, 1956.

ESOP Association. "How Do ESOPs Work?" http://www.esopassociation.org/explore/how-esops-work/what-is.

Ferris, Jean Leon Gerome. "The First Thanksgiving," 1912. Image. US Library of Congress.

Forbes "The World's Billionaires 2013" Kroll, Luisa. (2013, March), Vol. 191, Issue 4. Pp. 85-90.

Franklin, Benjamin. As quoted by Senator Joe Lieberman. US Senate, April 25, 2006.

Free Congress Research and Education Foundation Inc. "The Growth Code." Alexandria, VA, November 4, 2011.

Freeden, Michael. *Liberal Languages: Ideological Imaginations and Twentieth-Century Progressive Thought*. Princeton, NJ: Princeton University Press, 2004.

Freedom Post. "The Pilgrims Failed Experiment with Socialism." November 25 2009.

Freeman, Richard. "Optimal Inequality for Economic Growth, Stability, and Shared Prosperity: The Economics Behind the Wall Street Occupiers Protest?" *Insights: Melbourne Business and Economics* 11, April 2012. http://insights.unimelb.edu.au/vol11/01_Freeman.html.

Friedman, Milton. In "Free to Choose," PBS TV Series, 1980.

Gandhi, Mahatma, edited by M. S. Deshpande. *The Way to God: Selected Writings from Mahatma Gandhi*. Berkeley, CA: North Atlantic Books, 2009.

BIBLIOGRAPHY

Gauche, Jerry N. "Binary Economic Modes for the Privatization of Public Assets." The Kelso Institute, 2000. http://www.kelsoinstitute.org/pdf/binaryeconomicmodes.pdf.

Gilmore, James. "The 'Growth Code' to Economic Recovery." Interview by Kevin Price. *US Daily Review*, June 27 2012. http://usdailyreview.com/tag/james-gilmore.

Golden, Michael, and Matthew Wright. "Lending to ESOPs: Of a Different Color, This Horse Still Races." *Journal of Lending & Credit Risk Management*, May 1999.

Gorga, Carmine. "An Introduction to Concordian Economics." September 02, 2008. http://www.concordian-economics.org/.

Hagstrom, Robert G. *The Warren Buffett Way: Investment Strategies of the World's Greatest Investor.* Wiley & Sons. Edison, NJ. April 7, 1997.

Harpers Collins Publishers. "John Case." http://www.harpercollins.com/authors/1569/John_Case/index.aspx.

Healey, Denis. *The Economist*, vol. 354.

Hellenic Statistical Authority. "Annual National Accounts: Year 2011 (2nd Estimation)," October 5, 2012. PDF file retrieved October 7, 2012.

Historians.org. "Checking on the Changing Balance of Power." Student paper. Fall 1999. http://www.historians.org/teaching/aahe/kelly/pew/Portfolio/Student percent20Work/F99-1-6.html.

Hiwarale, Uday, et al. "Role of Employee Motivation in Quality Improvement Programs (Study of Human Emotions, Motivation, and Psychology." Unknown year.

Holtz-Eakin, Douglas. "The Need for Pro-Growth Corporate Tax Reform." New America Foundation, August 2011.

Horowitz, David. *Left Illusions: An Intellectual Odyssey*. Spence Publishing Company. Dallas, TX. October 2003.

Human Rights Watch. "World Report 2006: Cuba." 2006. http://www.hrw.org/world-report-2006/cuba.

Human Rights Watch. "World Report 2009: China." 2009. http://www.hrw.org/world-report-2009/china.

Huxley, Thomas Henry. *Select Works of Thomas H. Huxley.* John B. Alden Publisher, 1886.

Investopedia. "KSOP Definition." http://www.investopedia.com/terms/k/ksop.

Jefferson, Thomas. "First Inaugural Address." Washington, DC, March 4, 1801.

Johnson, Paul M. "Autocracy." In "A Glossary of Political Economy Terms." Auburn University, Department of Political Science, 2005.

Johnston, Larry. *Politics: An Introduction to the Modern Democratic State.* Toronto: University of Toronto Press, 2007.

Kelso, Louis O. "Labor's Untapped Wealth, an Address Delivered by Louis O. Kelso at the Air Line Pilots Association Retirement and Insurance Seminar," Washington, DC, March 1984.

Kelso, Louis O. Quote from *San Francisco Examiner & Chronicle*, 1978.

Kelso, Louis O. and Mortimer J. Adler. *The Capitalist Manifesto.* Literary Licensing. Whitefish, MT, 2011.

Kelso, Louis O., and Mortimer J. Adler. *The New Capitalists: A Proposal to Free Economic Growth from the Slavery of Savings.* New York: Random House, 1961.

Kelso, Louis O. and Patricia Hetter Kelso. *Democracy and Economic Power.* Ballinger Publishing. Pensacola, FL.1986.

Kelso, Louis O., and Patricia Hetter Kelso. "The Concentration of the Ownership of Capital over the Period of the Industrial Revolution." *Binary Economics in Eight Easy Lessons*, 1989.

Kelso, Louis O., and Patricia Hetter Kelso. "Why I Invented the ESOP LBO." *Leaders* 12, no. 4 (December 1989). http://www.kelsoinstitute.org/esoplbo.html.

Kelso, Louis O., and Walter A. Lawrence. *The Second Income Plan*. Center for Economic and Social Justice (CESJ). Washington, DC. 1965.

Kelso, Louis O. and Patricia Hetter Kelso. Two-factor Theory: the Economics of Reality, Vintage Books, 1967

Kiyosaki, Robert, and Sharon L. Lechter. *Rich Dad Poor Dad*. New York: Warner Books, 1998.

Kiyosaki, Robert, and Sharon L. Lechter. *Rich Dad's Cashflow Quadrant: Rich Dad's Guide to Financial Freedom*. New York: Warner Books, 1998.

Kiyosaki, Robert, and Sharon Lechter. *Why We Want You to Be Rich: Two Men One Message*. Rich Press. Sacramento, CA. 2007.

Kruse, Douglas, and Joseph Blasi. "Public Opinion Polls on Employee Ownership and Profit Sharing." *Journal of Employee Ownership Law and Finance* 11, no. 3 (Summer 1999).

Kruse, Douglas, Richard Freeman, and Joseph Blasi, eds. *Shared Capitalism at Work: Employee Ownership, Profit and Gain Sharing, and Broad-Based Stock Options* (National Bureau of Economic Research). Chicago: University of Chicago Press, 2010. ISBN: 0-226-05695-3. http://www.nber.org/chapters/c8090.pdf.

Kurland, Norman G., and Dawn K. Brohawn. "Louis Kelso's Economic Vision for the 21st Century." Center for Economic and Social Justice, 2004.

Kurtulus, Fidan Ana, and Douglas Kruse. "How Did Employee Ownership Firms Weather the Last Two Recessions? Employee Ownership and Employment Stability in the US: 1999–2008." April 15, 2012.

Laffer, Arthur. "The Four Pillars of Reaganomics." Address to the Heritage Foundation's President's Club, 2006. http://www.heritage.org/research/reports/2007/01/the-four-pillars-of-reaganomics, January 16, 2007.

Leonhardt, David. "The Paradox of Corporate Taxes." *New York Times,* February 1, 2011. http://www.nytimes.com/2011/02/02/business/economy.

Lincoln, Abraham. "State of the Union Address." December 3, 1861.

Lord Acton. "Letter to Bishop Mandell Creighton, April 5, 1887." In *Historical Essays and Studies,* edited by J. N. Figgis and R. V. Laurence. London: Macmillan, 1907.

Lovett, Richard A. "Supercontinent Pangaea Pushed, Not Sucked, Into Place." *National Geographic News,* September 5, 2008.

MacDonald, Malcolm, and William MacQuitty. *Inside China.* Boston, MA: Little, Brown, 1980.

Maravillosa, Sunni. "Interview with John Mackey." October 20, 2005. http://www.endervidualism.com/salon/intvw/mackey.htm.

Marshall, Monty G. "Polity IV Project: Political Regime Characteristics and Transitions, 1800–2012." Societal-Systems Research Inc., 2005.

Marshall, Monty G., and Benjamin R. Cole. "Global Report 2011: Conflict, Governance, and State Fragility." Vienna: Center for Systemic Peace, December 1, 2011. PDF file retrieved August 15, 2012.

Marx, Karl, and Friedrich Engels. *The Communist Manifesto.* International Publishers. New York, NY. June 1948.

McIntyre, Bob. "Big No-Tax Corps Just Keep on Dodging." Citizens for Tax Justice, April 9, 2012.

Menke, John. Menke Group Blog, 2012. http://www.menke.com/blog/the-origin-and-history-of-the-esop-and-its-future-role-as-a-business-succession-tool/.

Miller, David, et al. *Blackwell Encyclopedia of Political Thought.* Wiley-Blackwell Publishing. Hoboken, NJ. 1991.

Mills, Alex. "Mills: Romney Banks on Oil Industry for Economic Recovery." (*Wichita Falls, TX*) *Times Record News,* September 2, 2012.

BIBLIOGRAPHY

Mishel, Lawrence, et al. *The State of Working America 2012/2013*. An Economic Policy Institute Book. Ithaca, NY: ILR Press, 2012.

Mishel, Lawrence. "Unions, Inequality, and Faltering Middle-Class Wages." Economic Policy Institute, August 29, 2012.

Moore, Samuel, trans. *Manifesto of the Communist Party*. Zodiac, 1888. http://www.marxists.org/archive/marx/works/1848/communist-manifesto/index.htm.

Moore, Stephen, and John Silvia. "The ABCs of the Capital Gains Tax." Heartland Institute, October 4, 1995.

Moore, Steve. "Things Could Get Pretty Messy." *Wall Street Journal*, October 2, 2010.

Naden, Corinne, and Rose J. Blue. *Wilma Rudolph*. Heinemann-Raintree Library. Chicago, IL. 2003.

Nader, Ralph. "Remarks by Ralph Nader on Raising Minimum Wage." *Nader Page*, June 6, 2012.

Nakabayashi, Mieko, and James Carter. "America Goes It Alone on High Corporate Taxes." *Wall Street Journal*, July 19, 2013.

NCEO (National Center for Employee Ownership). "The Employee Ownership 100: America's Largest Majority Employee-Owned Companies." June 2012.

NCEO (National Center for Employee Ownership). "Great Employee-Owned Places to Work." NCEO. Oakland, CA, August 2013.

Organization for Economic Cooperation and Development (OECD). *OECD Economic Outlook*.

Overton, Winston. *Wall Street Scandals: Greed and Trading on Wall Street the American Way*. Xlibris Corporation. Bloomington, IN. 2013.

Paul, Ron. *"Ron Paul 2012: In Defense of Liberty!"* For Liberty: How the Ron Paul Revolution Watered the Withered Tree of Liberty. Video. Edit Lab Films. 2009.

Pomerleau, Kyle. "Another Study Confirms: US Has One of the Highest Effective Corporate Tax Rates in the World." Tax Foundation. May 31, 2013.

Pope John Paul II. *Centesimus Annus*. 1991.

Porter, Eduardo. "The Spreading Scourge of Corporate Corruption." *New York Times*, July 10, 2012.

Prager, Dennis. "Socialism Kills." *WND Commentary*, September 2, 2003.

Rand, Ayn. *"What Is Capitalism?"* Capitalism: The Unknown Ideal. 2nd Edition. New American Library. New York, NY. 1967.

Reagan, Ronald. "Remarks on Receiving the Report of the Presidential Task Force on Project Economic Justice." Video speech. August 3, 1987. http://www.youtube.com/watch?v=06vP84SqnS4.

Reber, Gary. "Democratic Capitalism and Binary Economics: Solutions for a Troubled Nation and Economy." *For Economic Justice*, February 2012. http://foreconomicjustice.org/11/economic-justice/

Renan, Ernest. *American Mercury*, vol. 45.

Rifkin, Jeremy. *Own Your Own Job: Economic Democracy for Working Americans.* New York: Bantam Books, 1977.

Rollert, John Paul. "Who Makes Capitalism Work? Adam Smith Would Disagree with Today's Conservatives." *Next New Deal: The Blog of the Roosevelt Institute*, August 2011.

Roosevelt, Franklin D. "State of the Union Message to Congress," January 11, 1944. Online by Gerhard Peters and John T. Woolley, American Presidency Project. http://www.presidency.ucsb.edu/ws/?pid=16518.

Russell, Bertrand. *Sceptical Essays.* London: George Allen & Unwin Ltd., 1928.

Saez, Eric. "Average Income per Family, Distributed by Income Group." Image. University of California, 2010.

Sanders, Senator Bernard. "Address to Attendees of 2012 ESOP Association Conference and Trade Show, Las Vegas, NV." Video, November 12, 2012. http://www.youtube.com/watch?v=aTiPCsxf_qg&feature=youtu.be.

Sanders, Senator Bernard. "Questions for the Record: The President's Fiscal Year 2014 Budget and Revenue Proposals." For

Treasury Secretary Jacob J. Lew, April 17 2013. Transcript at http://www.esopassociation.org/docs/default-source/advocacy/here.pdf.

Schumpeter, Joseph A. *Capitalism, Socialism, and Democracy.* Eastford, CT: Martino Fine Books, 2010.

Scott, Sherrie. "Top 10 Corporate Tax Deductions." *Houston Chronicle.* Demand Media, 2012.

Shaw, George Bernard. *The Intelligent Woman's Guide to Socialism and Capitalism.* Transaction Publishers. Piscataway, NJ. 1928.

Silver-Malyska, Tara, and Elizabeth Jenkins. "The Pension Protection Act of 2006: An Overview of the Defined Benefit and Defined Contribution Provisions of the Act." *Benefits Law Journal,* December 22, 2006.

Smith, Adam. *The Wealth of Nations.* 1776. Thrifty Books. Auburn, WA. October 27, 2009.

Sowell, Thomas. *Civil Rights: Rhetoric or Reality?* New York: William Morrow Paperbacks, 1985.

Spitzley, David A. "Louis Kelso Made Simple." http://cog.kent.edu/lib/spitzley2.html.

Stack, Jack. "Introducing 'Open the Books': Why Would Anyone Do This?" *New York Times,* December 15, 2009.

Stack, Jack. "Springfield Remanufacturing Bought the Company and Learned to Play the Game of Open-Book Management." *National Productivity Review* 13, no. 1 (Winter 1993).

Stack, Jack, and Bo Burlington. *The Great Game of Business: Unlocking the Power and Profitability of Open-Book Management.* New York: Crown Publishing Group, 1994. ISBN-13: 9780385475259.

Stodola, Sarah. "10 Big Corporate Tax Breaks, and Who Benefits." *Fiscal Times,* February 9, 2011. http://www.thefiscaltimes.com/Articles/2011/02/09/10-Big-Corporate-Tax-Breaks.aspx#TJtCfMb0MWdmP7pj.99.

Stokes, Bruce. "The Progressive Case for Corporate Tax Reform." New America Foundation, January 26, 2012.

Sullivan, Arthur, and Steven M. Sheffrin. *Economics: Principles in Action.* Upper Saddle River, NJ: Pearson Prentice Hall, 2003. ISBN 0-13-063085-3.

Thinkbynumbers.org. "Get Society Rich Quick: The Ideal Level of Government Spending." http://thinkbynumbers.org/economics/gdp/ideal-level-of-government-spending/.

Thoreau, Henry David. *Civil Disobedience and Other Essays.* Dover Publications. Mineola, NY. 1993.

Traynor, C. J. "Jones v. H. F. Ahmanson & Co. (1969) 1 C3d 93." California Supreme Court, November 7, 1969. http://online.ceb.com/calcases/C3/1C3d93.htm.

United States Department of Defense. "North Korea by Night." Image. 2003.

United States Federal Reserve. "US Effective Corporate Tax Rates 1947–2011." 2012.

Von Hayek, Friedrich A. Law. *Legislation and Liberty,* vol. 2, *The Mirage of Social Justice.* Chicago: University of Chicago Press, 1978.

Von Hoffman, Constantine. "Why Greece Will and Should Default on Its Debts." *Moneywatch,* May 16, 2012. http://www.cbsnews.com/8301-505123_162-57434749/why-greece-will-and-should-default-on-its-debts/.

Wells, H. G. *The New World Order.* Filiquarian Publishing, Minneapolis, MN. 2007.

Wolff, Edward. "The Asset Price Meltdown and the Wealth of the Middle Class." National Bureau of Economic Research. Volume 18859. Issued November 2012. Print.

Wolff, Richard. "Yes, There Is an Alternative to Capitalism: Mondragon Shows the Way." *The Guardian,* June 24, 2012.

Worstall, Tim. "The Rahn Curve." Adam Smith Institute, July 16, 2011.

Wikipedia, the Free Encyclopedia:
http://en.wikiquote.org/wiki/Alexander_Fraser_Tytler
http://en.wikipedia.org/wiki/Athenian_democracy
http://en.wikipedia.org/wiki/Capital_(economics)
http://en.wikipedia.org/wiki/Capitalism
http://en.wikipedia.org/wiki/Civil_Rights_Act_of_1964
http://en.wikipedia.org/wiki/Communist_state#cite_note-1
http://en.wikipedia.org/wiki/Cuba
http://en.wikipedia.org/wiki/Cultural_Revolution
http://en.wikipedia.org/wiki/Democratization
http://en.wikipedia.org/wiki/Economy_of_Greece
http://en.wikipedia.org/wiki/Employee_stock_option
http://en.wikipedia.org/wiki/Karl_Marx
http://en.wikipedia.org/wiki/List_of_campaigns_of_the_Communist_Party_of_China
http://en.wikipedia.org/wiki/Maslow's_hierarchy_of_needs
http://en.wikipedia.org/wiki/Means_of_production
http://en.wikipedia.org/wiki/North_Korea
http://en.wikipedia.org/wiki/Profit_sharing
http://en.wikipedia.org/wiki/Realpolitik
http://en.wikipedia.org/wiki/Robert_Kiyosaki
http://en.wikipedia.org/wiki/Russell_B._Long#cite_note-Mann_2003-3
http://en.wikipedia.org/wiki/Soviet
http://en.wikipedia.org/wiki/Stock#Shareholder
http://en.wikipedia.org/wiki/Velocity_of_money

INDEX

401 (k) Plan, xx, 6, 7, 24, 133, 184

A

Adler, Mortimer J., 10, 63, 147
African Americans, xxi, 42, 59, 60, 61–62
Alaska Permanent Fund, 9
Alighieri, Dante, 67
American Revolution, 11
Anarchy, 64
Andersen, Arthur, 185
Applebaum, Binyamin, 101
Armey, Richard K. (House Majority Leader - Republican), 80, 81
Arrow, Kenneth (Nobel Laureate), 180
Ashford, Robert, 146
Athens, 61
Australia, 45
Austria, 18
Autocracy, 63–64

B

Bianchi, Giuliano, 31
Binary Economics, 145, 146, 147, 149

INDEX

Blair, Tony (UK Prime Minister), xxvi, 116
Blasi, Joseph R., xiv, xv, xx, xxi, xxii, xxvii, 134, 205
Bolsheviks, 49, 50
Bond, Julian, 152
Bradford, William, 55, 56, 57
Brandeis, Louis D. (Justice), 21, 152
Brennan, Andrew, 118
Broad-Based Property Ownership, 66, 68, 133, 205
Brohawn, Dawn K., 12
Brooks, Arthur C., 98
Buffett, Warren, 170
Bush, George H. (US President), xx, 93
Bush, George W. (US President), xviii

C

California, 8, 23, 30, 75, 133
Cantor, Eric, 191
Capitalist Manifesto, 10
Capone, Al, 6
Card, David, 23
Carnegie, Andrew, 126, 127
Case, John, 129, 173, 175
Castro, Fidel (Cuban President), 48
Chhibber, Parag, xvi
China, People's Republic of, 44, 47, 48, 50–51, 53, 79, 123, 199, 206
Chivukula, Upendra (NJ BPU Commissioner), xiv, xv, xxi, 23
Churchill, Winston (UK Prime Minister), 37
Cicero, Marcus T., 209
Civil Rights Act, 62
Clinton, William (US President), xvii–xviii, xx, 93
Cohn, Michael, 101

Common Sense (pamphlet), 142
Concordian Economics, 150
Connecticut, 57
Creighton, Mandell (Bishop), 186
CSOP (Consumer Stock Ownership Plan), 8
Cuba, 47, 48
Cushman, John H. Jr, 39

D

Dahlberg-Acton, John E. (Lord), 186
Darwin, Charles, 142
Deming, Edwards, 132
Democratic Capitalism, 3, 209
Democrats, xvii, xx, xxii, xxiv, xxxi, 37, 38, 39, 41, 191, 204
Douglass, Frederick, 94
Dyck, Alexander, 180

E

Economic Democracy:
    Bipartisan Idea, xxi, xxii
    Broad-based Property Ownership, 80, 94, 144
    Diffuse Economic Power, 15, 71
    Failed Alternatives, 123
    Proven, Best Idea, xxiv, 5, 6, 58
    Social/Political/Economic Movement, xxiii, xxiv, xxvi, xxviii, xxxi, 18, 20, 46, 61, 66
Economic Recovery Act, 168
Employee-Owned Workplaces, 135, 140
Employee Ownership (EO):
    Aligns with Natural Law, 124
    Bad Forms, xx, 184

INDEX

    Bipartisan Idea, 38, 75
    Broad-based Property Ownership, 6, 10, 92-94, 112, 119, 143
    Corporate Tax Reform, 100, 191, 193, 207
    Economic Check and Balance, 188
    Essential Structure, 161, 163-65
    Employee Ownership List, 134
    Effective Economic System, xxi–xxiv
    Historical Perspective, 187
    Powerful Idea, 9, 110
    Proven, Best Idea, xxvi, 66, 113, 133, 152-56
    Risk Amelioration, 171-73, 183
    Social/Political/Economic Movement, xxxi, 18, 20, 80
    System for the Modern Age, 208
    Worker Empowerment, 45, 46
Employee Retirement Income Security Act (ERISA), 163, 165, 167
Employee Stock Ownership Plan (ESOP):
    Aligns with Natural Law, 124, 125
    Ameliorate Corporate Corruption, 178, 182, 183, 186
    Association, 11
    Bank Incentives, xx, 92-94, 204
    Bipartisan Idea, 74, 75, 191
    Definition, 6, 7, 9, 159, 161-72
    Core Worker Motivation, 145
    Corporate Tax Reform, 76, 91, 100, 114
    Current and Historical Position, xxiv
    Economic Check and Balance, 187
    Employee Ownership List, 140
    Employee Stability, 153-55
    Federal Legislation, xix
    Kelso Vision, 71, 99
    Incentives Needed, 38
    Income Inequality, 27
    New Model for Unions, 131-134

Our Plan, 90
   Reagan (President), 39-41
   Real Life Examples, 174
   Wages vs Capital's Productive Power, 24
   Worker Empowerment, 37, 80, 181
Employee Stock Purchasing Plan (ESPP), 7
Employment Act, 36, 72
Enron (ENE), 185
ERISA (Employee Retirement Income Act), 90, 163, 165, 167, 183
Evans, David, 140

F

Fastow, Andrew, 185
Federal Reserve, 22
Feudalism, 21, 37, 117–18, 205
Founding Fathers, 75, 205
France, 188
Freeman, Richard B., xv, xxi, xxvii, 21, 31, 66, 157, 181
Friedman, Milton, 114, 118

G

Galileo, Galilei, 150
Gandhi, Mohandas K. (Mahatma), 11, 59, 74, 207
Gauche, Jerry N., 146
Gelber, Alex, 31
George, Henry, 152
Germany, 103, 116, 182, 199
Gilmore, James (VA Governor), 76
Gilpin, Stephen, 41
Gingrich, Newt (Speaker of the House - Republican), 103
Gorbachev, Mikhail S. (USSR President), 49
Gorga, Carmine, 150

INDEX

Great Game of Business, 173, 174, 175, 176
Greece, 61, 68–69, 71
Grow, Galusha A. (Speaker of the House - Republican), 25, 26
Growth Code, the, 76, 78, 79

H

Hayek, Friedrich A., 18
Healey, Denis, 192
Hegel, George W. F., 116–18
Hetter, Patricia, 149
Hobbes, Thomas, 187
Holland, 55
Holtz-Eakin, Douglas, 100
Homestead Act, xxi, xxvii, 24, 25–26, 89
Hooker, Thomas, 57
Horowitz, David, 119
Huxley, Thomas H., 142

I

Illinois, 201
Inclusive Capitalism. See Economic Democracy
Income Inequality, 5, 15, 21, 22–23, 26, 27, 31–33, 46, 53, 58, 93, 95, 126, 146, 180, 204, 207
India, 11, 56, 57, 59, 74
Internal Revenue Service (IRS), 6, 78, 93, 100, 101, 103, 165, 166, 167, 196, 198, 199
Iowa, 201

J

James I and VI (King of England and Scotland), 187
Japan, 79, 199

Jefferson, Thomas (US President), xxviii, 16, 80, 187
Johnson, Gary, 91
Johnson, Lyndon B. (US President), 62

K

Keeling, Michael, 24, 132
Kelso, Louis O., 12, 39, 98
Kelso, Patricia H., xxix, 16, 71
Kennedy, John F. (US President), 79, 87, 100
Kenya, 64
Keynes, John M., 6, 144, 149
King, Martin Luther, Jr., 58, 207
Kiyosaki, Robert, 109, 110, 111
Korea, 51–52
Kruse, Douglas L., xv, xx, xxi, xxii, xxvii, 66, 134
KSOP (Combining 401K and ESOP), 7, 9
Kurland, Norman G., xxiii

L

Labor Unions, 24, 36, 180
Labor Workers, xxviii–xxix, 15, 16
Laffer, Arthur, 59
Lay, Kenneth, 184
Lechter, Sharon L., 111
Lenin, Vladimir (Soviet Union Premier), 49–50
Lincoln, Abraham (US President), xxi, xxvii, 13, 14, 25, 114
Locke, John, 187
Long, Russell B. (US Senator - Democrat), 39, 163
Louisiana, 39, 163

INDEX

M

Mackey, John, 127
Mandela, Nelson (South African President), 207
Marx, Karl, 6, 46, 47, 55, 116–20
Maslow, Abraham, 120–23
Massachusetts, 55, 57
Mayflower Compact, 55
Microsoft (MSFT), 133
Minimum Wage, 23, 24, 59
Mississippi, 133
Missouri, 174
Mondragon Corporation (MC), 105–8
Morse, Adair, 180
Musum, Veny W., xiv, xv, xvii, xxi, 20, 23, 24
Musum Company & Sons, 97
Musumeci, Venerando, 97

N

Nader, Ralph, 5
National Bureau of Economic Research (NBER), 66
National Center for Employee Ownership (NCEO), 133, 134
New Deal, 86, 130
New York, 133, 134
New Zealand, 45
North Korea, 51, 52

O

Obama, Barack H. (US President), xviii, 100, 101, 103
Occupy Wall Street, xxvi, 4, 12, 21, 31, 157, 181

Open Book Management, 173, 174–77
Optimal Inequality, 21, 31, 157, 181
Organization for Economic Cooperation and Development (OECD), 69, 83, 104, 189, 193

P

Paul, Ron (Congressman), 105
Pension Protection Act (PPA), 168–69
Pilgrims, 54, 55, 56, 57
Plato, 142
Plutocracy, xxx, 3, 15, 17
Polity IV Project, 63–65
Pomerleau, Kyle, 193
Pope John Paul II, 6
Porter, Eduardo, 179
Prager, Dennis, 46
Puritans, 79

R

Rahn, Richard, 85–86
Rand, Ayn, 127
Randolph, William C., 101
Reagan, Ronald (US President), 11, 39–40, 59, 75, 79, 118
Renan, Ernest, 123
Republicans, xv, xvii, xx, xxii, xxiv, xxxi, 25, 37, 38–39, 41, 75, 76, 94, 191, 204
Research and Experimentation Tax Credit, 200
Ricardo, David, 44
Richard III (King of England), 4
Rifkin, Jeremy, 123

INDEX

Rohrabacher, Dana (US Congressman - Republican), 39, 75
Roman Empire, 125, 205, 206, 209
Romney, Mitt (MA Governor - Republican), 103
Roosevelt, Franklin D. (US President), 87, 121
Rousseau, Jean-Jacque, 187
Rudolph, Wilma, 125
Russell, Bertrand, 34
Rutgers University, xiv, xv, xxii, xxvii, 134
Ryan, Paul (US Congressman - Republican), 76

S

Saez, Emmanuel, 30
Sanders, Bernard (US Senator - Democrat), 11, 75
S Corporations, 163, 167, 168
Scott, Sherrie, 196
Shakespeare, Rodney, 146
Shakespeare, William, 4
Shared Capitalism, 27, 66–67, 134, 142, 170, 171, 172, 203
Shaw, George B., 41
Shevardnadze, Eduard, 178
Silicon Valley, 112
Skilling, Jeffrey, 184, 185
Smith, Adam, xxix, 6, 13, 17, 44, 45, 60, 71, 72, 85, 95, 125–27
Somalia, 64
South Korea, 51, 52
Soviet Union, 48–50, 52
Sowell, Thomas, 58
Spain, 105, 107
Stack, Jack, 173–75
Stalin, Joseph (USSR General Secretary), 49
Stodola, Sarah, 199
Stokes, Bruce, 103

T

Taft, William H. (US President), 112
Tax Reform Act, 163, 167, 168
Tax Relief Act, 168
Tea Party, xxvi, 4, 11
Thoreau, Henry D., 209
Tiananmen Square, 50, 51
Tianyong, Zhou, 51
Tocqueville, Alexis de, 62
Trump, Donald, 109, 110, 111
Twain, Mark, 188
Tytler, Alexander, 70

U

United Auto Workers, 131
United Kingdom (Great Britain), 54, 116
Urban Enterprize Zones (UEZs), 92
US Constitution, 62

V

Vermont, 11, 75
Vietnam, 47
Voting Rights Act, 62

W

Wagner, Robert F. (US Senator - Democrat), 129, 130
Wolff, Edward, 24
Wolff, Richard, 105
Worstall, Tim, 85

INDEX

Y

Yellen, Janet (Chairwoman of US Federal Reserve), 22

Z

Zedung, Mao (Chinese Communist Party Chairman), xxvi, 123, 124

ABOUT THE AUTHORS:

Upendra Chivukula and Veny W. Musum in front of the stature of Thomas Paine in Morristown New Jersey, "the military capital of the American Revolution."

Paine was an English-American political activist, philosopher, author, political theorist and revolutionary. His principal contribution was the powerful, widely read pamphlet *Common Sense* (1776). He inspired the American Revolution and his ideas reflected Enlightenment-era rhetoric of transnational human rights.

Upendra Joge Chivukula (born October 8, 1950) of Franklin Township holds the distinction as the first and only South Asian representative in the history of the New Jersey Legislature. He won election to the legislature in 2001, becoming the first Franklin resident to serve in the Assembly since the 1820s. Chivukula has served Franklin Township as a councilman from 1997 to 2005, deputy mayor from 1998 to 2000, and mayor of Franklin from 2000 to 2001.

Chivukula was nominated by Governor Chris Christie as a Commissioner to the N.J. Board of Public Utilities on September 18, 2014 and confirmed by the Senate on September 22, 2014.

He was a Presidential Electoral College member in 2004 and has been a delegate to the Democratic National Convention five times.

An information-technology company executive and former mayor of Franklin Township, Chivukula completed serving his sixth consecutive two-year term in the New Jersey General Assembly where he was also the Assembly Deputy Speaker. He represented the 17th Legislative District, which contains the Middlesex County communities of Milltown, New Brunswick, North Brunswick, and Piscataway, and the Somerset County community of Franklin Township.

ABOUT THE AUTHORS:

Chivukula, has a professional background in electrical engineering and is considered one of the legislature's leading experts on telecommunications, science, and technology issues. He has authored nearly fifty laws. Currently, he serves as chair of the Telecommunications and Utilities Committee, vice-chair of the Homeland Security Committee, and member of the Transportation Committee and of the Health Information Technology Commission.

He was a leading force behind the creation of the bipartisan, bicameral Legislative Caucus on Science and Technology in 2004, a panel charged with enhancing the state's position as a leader in research, technological development, and innovation.

Chivukula served at the National Conference of State Legislatures (NCSL) as a member of the Executive Committee; past chair of Communications, Interstate Commerce, and Technology Committee; member of the Energy and Utilities Committee; and member of the Homeland Security Task Force, Immigration Task Force, and Military Sustainability Task Force. He is co-chair of the Energy Task Force at the Council of State Governments (CSG).

Born in Nellore, India, Chivukula came to the United States in 1974 to attend college. He worked for CBS Television from 1977 to 1978. He served as senior management consultant and systems engineer with AT&T Bell Labs and many divisions of AT&T from 1981 to 1998.

Chivukula currently serves as consultant at Web Team Corporation, a Somerset-based information technology firm. Chivukula holds a master's degree in electrical engineering from the City College of the University of New York. He is the co-author of a six-book engineer series, Best Manufacturing Practices, and a three-book series, Supplier Management.

He and his wife, Dayci, have a son, Suraj, and a daughter, Damianty, and two grandchildren.

Veny William Musum (born January 4, 1955) began work in corporate America as district manager for Clairol Inc. (January 1981–November, 1984) where he broke numerous sales records. He managed the number one district in the number one region in the country. He moved on to John Paul Mitchell Systems in Beverly Hills, CA, and quickly rose to become Senior Vice President. He was the longest-serving executive since the company's inception and has since retired. He is credited with developing many of the company's most innovative sales and marketing programs and successful strategies responsible for the corporation's current position as a worldwide leader in the professional hair-care market.

He began his career at Musum Company & Sons, Inc., Newark, NJ (January 1977–January 1981) in an entry-level position and rose to become the COO of the company. Musum Company was the oldest and one of the largest beauty and barber supply businesses in the state, originally founded by his grandfather.

Also a successful real estate and equity investor, Musum has learned firsthand the importance of cash-flow producing assets.

Presently a Guest Lecturer at Rutgers University, Musum enjoys imparting to their students his firsthand expertise and the significance of acquiring income producing capital.

ABOUT THE AUTHORS:

Musum's other passion is helping wipe the scourge of chronic illness (currently 80% of our healthcare costs) from the face of the earth. He is currently assisting the top metagenomic scientists in the world, including Dr. Trevor Marshall, with this important effort.

Veny has also been involved in local and state government. In 1998 he was selected by New Jersey Governor Whitman to serve on the state's Property Tax Commission to find effective methods of reducing the tax burden while maintaining proper levels of quality service. He co-chaired the subcommittee on regionalization and efficiency. Later, Governor Whitman appointed Veny as a founding member of newly formed New Jersey Council on Physical Fitness, Sports, Nutrition, and Wellness. Currently he is serving his eighth term on the Bernards Townships Republican County Committee.

Musum received a BA in 1983 from Rutgers College, Rutgers University. He is a Phi Alpha Theta Life Member Honoree—Rutgers Historical Honors Society; a member of the Colonel Henry Rutgers Society, a foundation for substantial donors to the University; and a member of Who's Who in Finance and Industry. Musum also studied with world-renowned American statistician and quality-enhancement consultant Dr. Edwards Deming.

THE 3RD WAY

Capitalism works, but is not fair.
Socialism is fair in theory, but does not work.
HERE IS THE SOLUTION.

DO YOU HEAR THE PEOPLE SING
Les Misérables Lyrics ... based on the novel by Victor Hugo [backdrop: the French Revolution]

"Do you hear the people sing? Singing a song of angry men? It is the music of a people who will not be slaves again! When the beating of your heart echoes the beating of the drums, there is a life about to start when tomorrow comes!"

ONE DAY MORE…
"One day to a new beginning. Raise the flag of freedom high! Every man will be a king.

There's a new world for the winning. There's a new world to be won!"

ABOUT THE AUTHORS:

Franklin D. Roosevelt
Fourth and Final Inaugural Address
Saturday, January 20, 1945

We shall strive for perfection. We shall not achieve it immediately—but we still shall strive. We may make mistakes—but they must never be mistakes which result from faintness of heart or abandonment of moral principle.

I remember that my old schoolmaster, Dr. Peabody, said, in days that seemed to us then to be secure and untroubled: "Things in life will not always run smoothly. Sometimes we will be rising toward the heights—then all will seem to reverse itself and start downward. The great fact to remember is that the trend of civilization itself is forever upward; that a line drawn through the middle of the peaks and the valleys of the centuries always has an upward trend."

THE3rdWAYbook.com

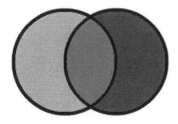

Republicans EOs Democrats

A Better Idea!

Made in the USA
Middletown, DE
17 October 2015